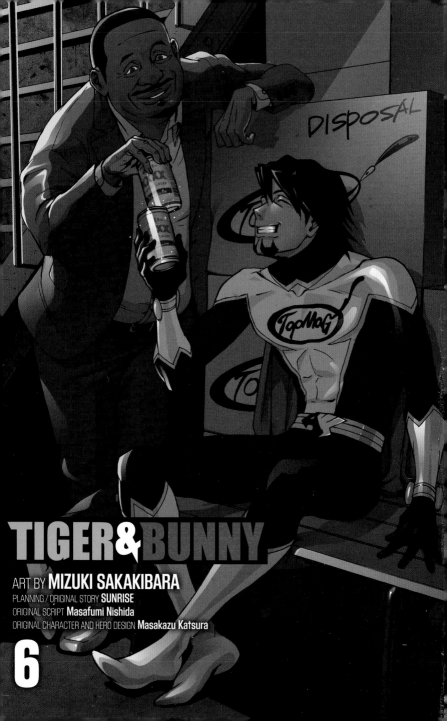

# TIGER & BUNNY

ART BY **MIZUKI SAKAKIBARA**

PLANNING / ORIGINAL STORY **SUNRISE**

ORIGINAL SCRIPT **Masafumi Nishida**

ORIGINAL CHARACTER AND HERO DESIGN **Masakazu Katsura**

**6**

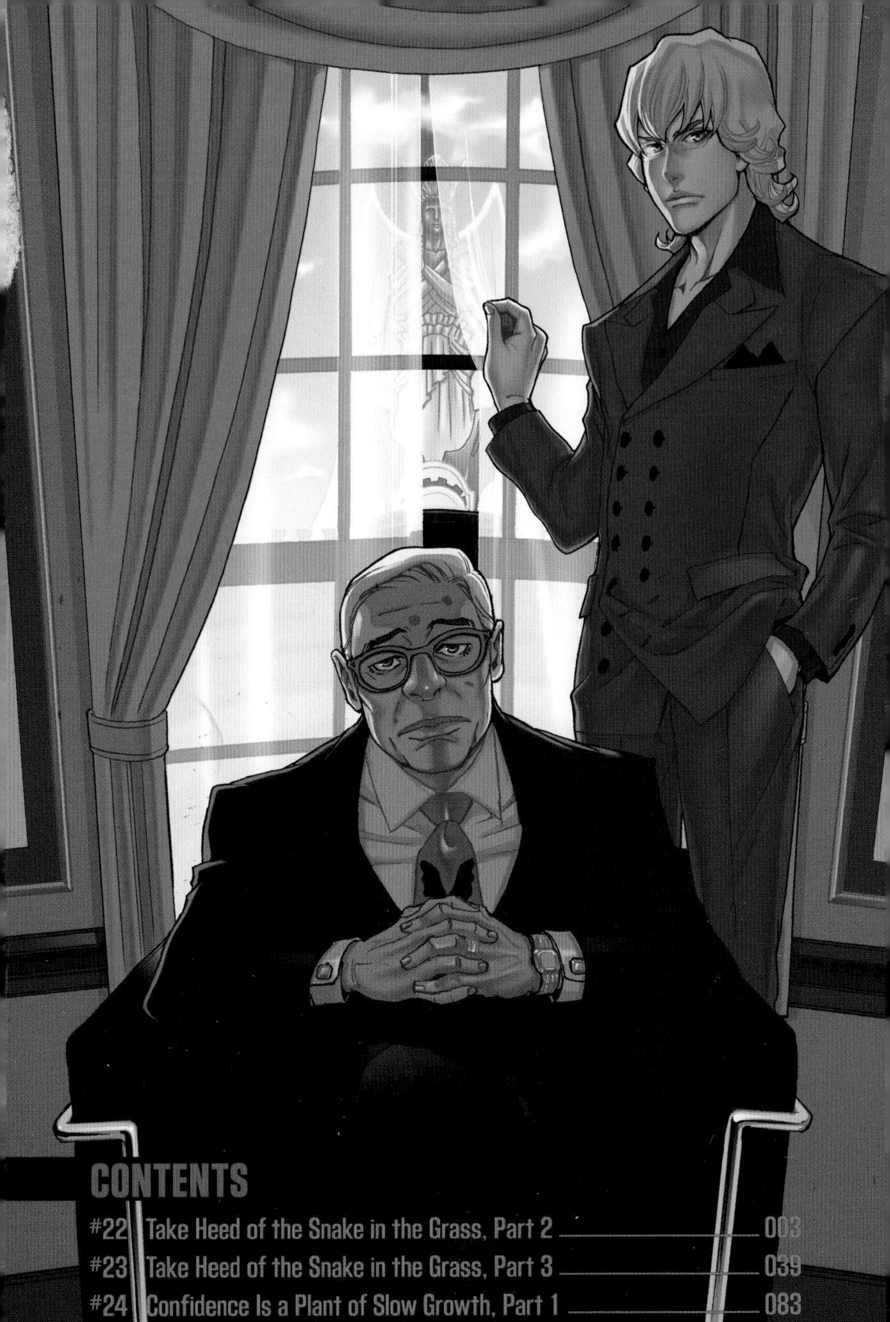

# CONTENTS

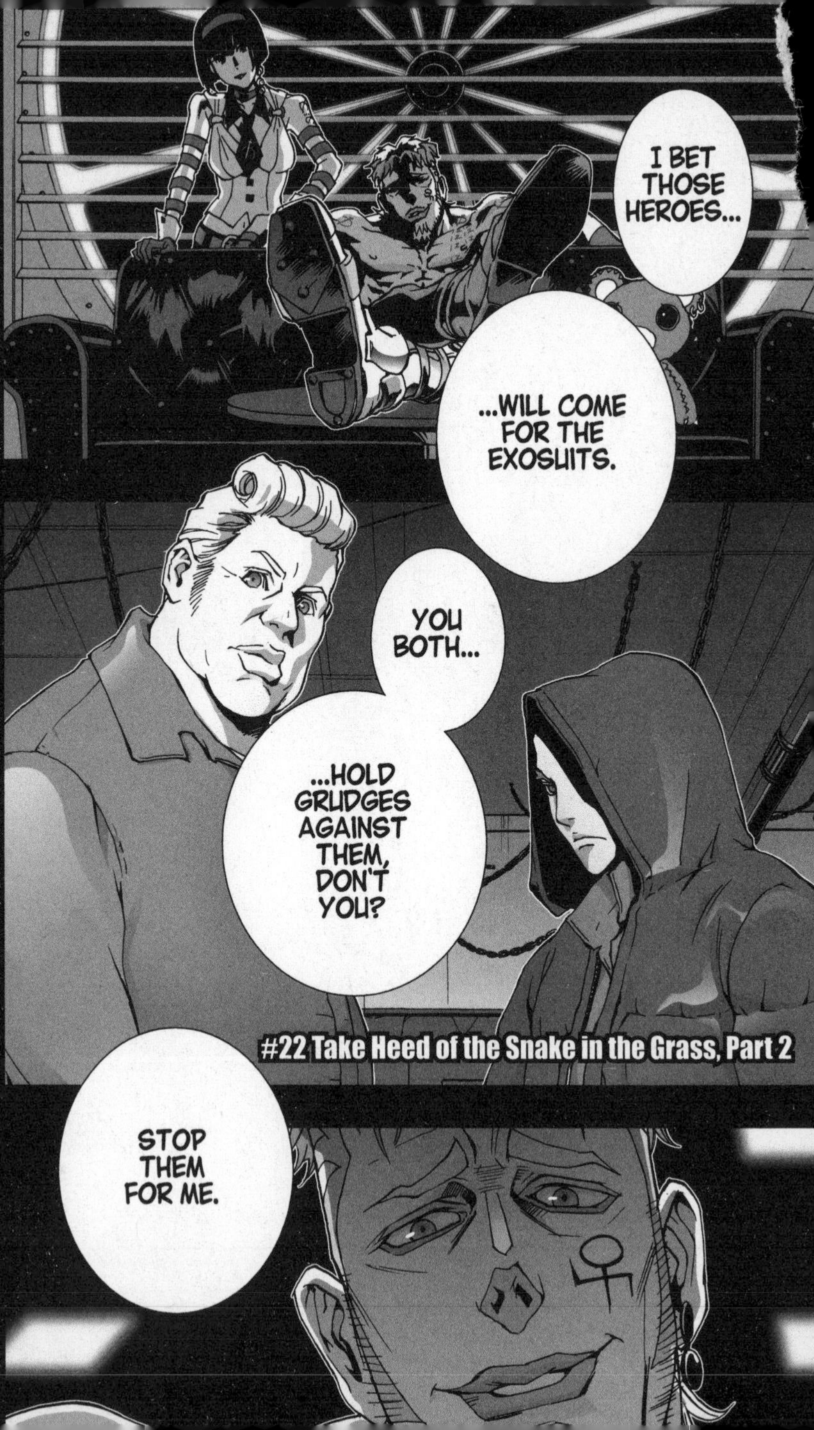
I BET THOSE HEROES...
...WILL COME FOR THE EXOSUITS.
YOU BOTH...
...HOLD GRUDGES AGAINST THEM, DON'T YOU?
#22 Take Heed of the Snake in the Grass, Part 2
STOP THEM FOR ME.

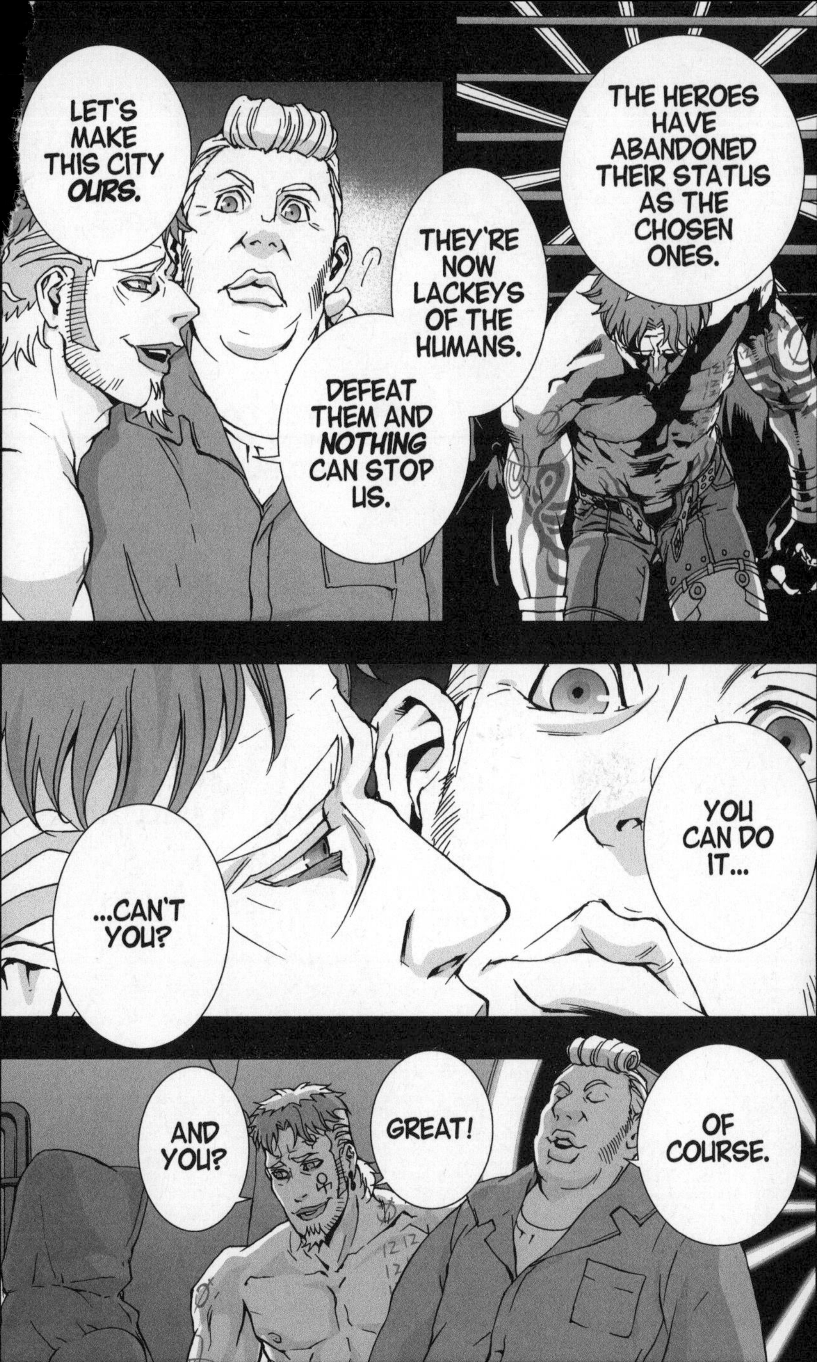
THE HEROES HAVE ABANDONED THEIR STATUS AS THE CHOSEN ONES.
THEY'RE NOW LACKEYS OF THE HUMANS.
DEFEAT THEM AND *NOTHING* CAN STOP US.
LET'S MAKE THIS CITY *OURS.*
YOU CAN DO IT...
...CAN'T YOU?
OF COURSE.
GREAT!
AND YOU?

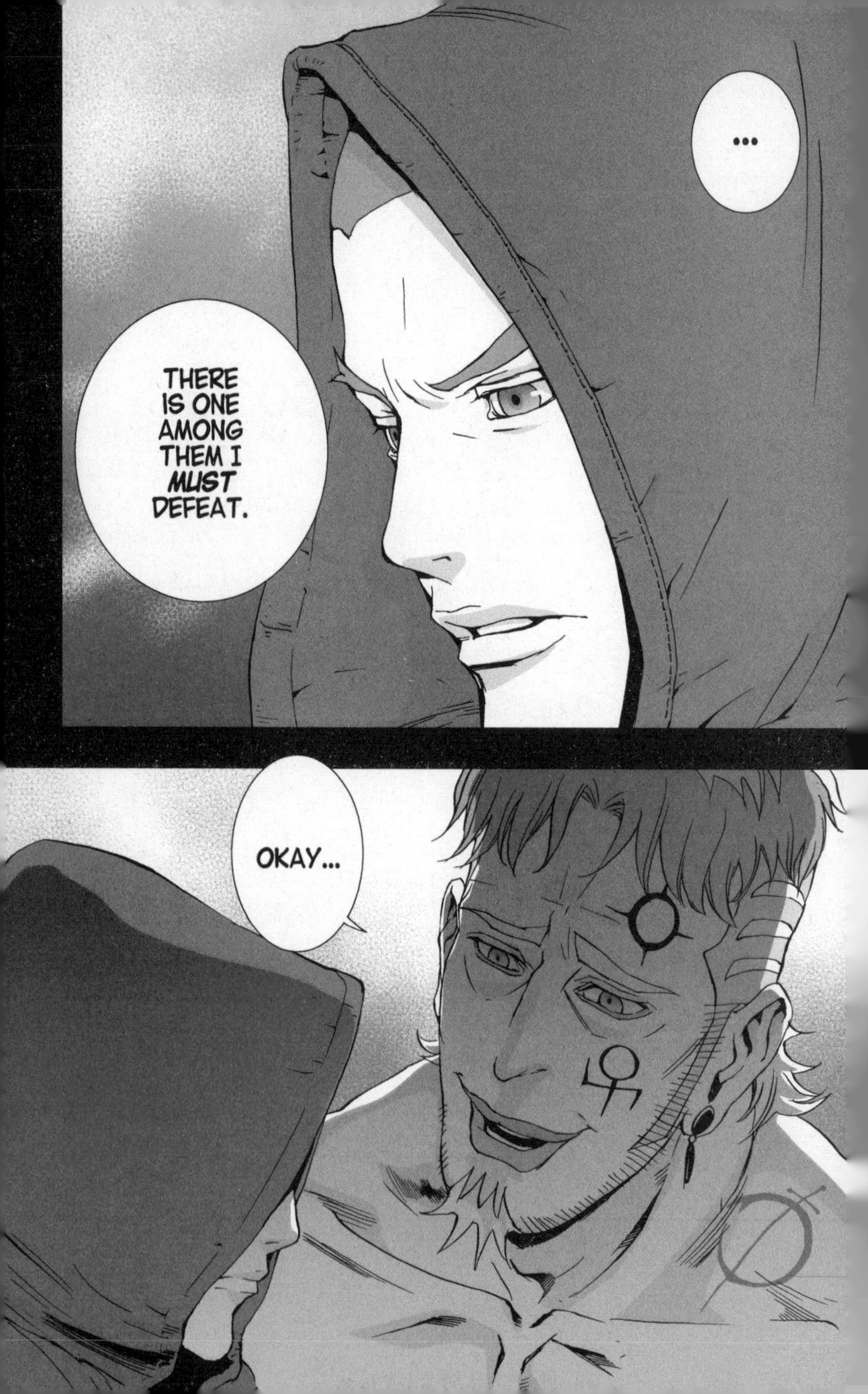
...
THERE IS ONE AMONG THEM I MUST DEFEAT.
OKAY...

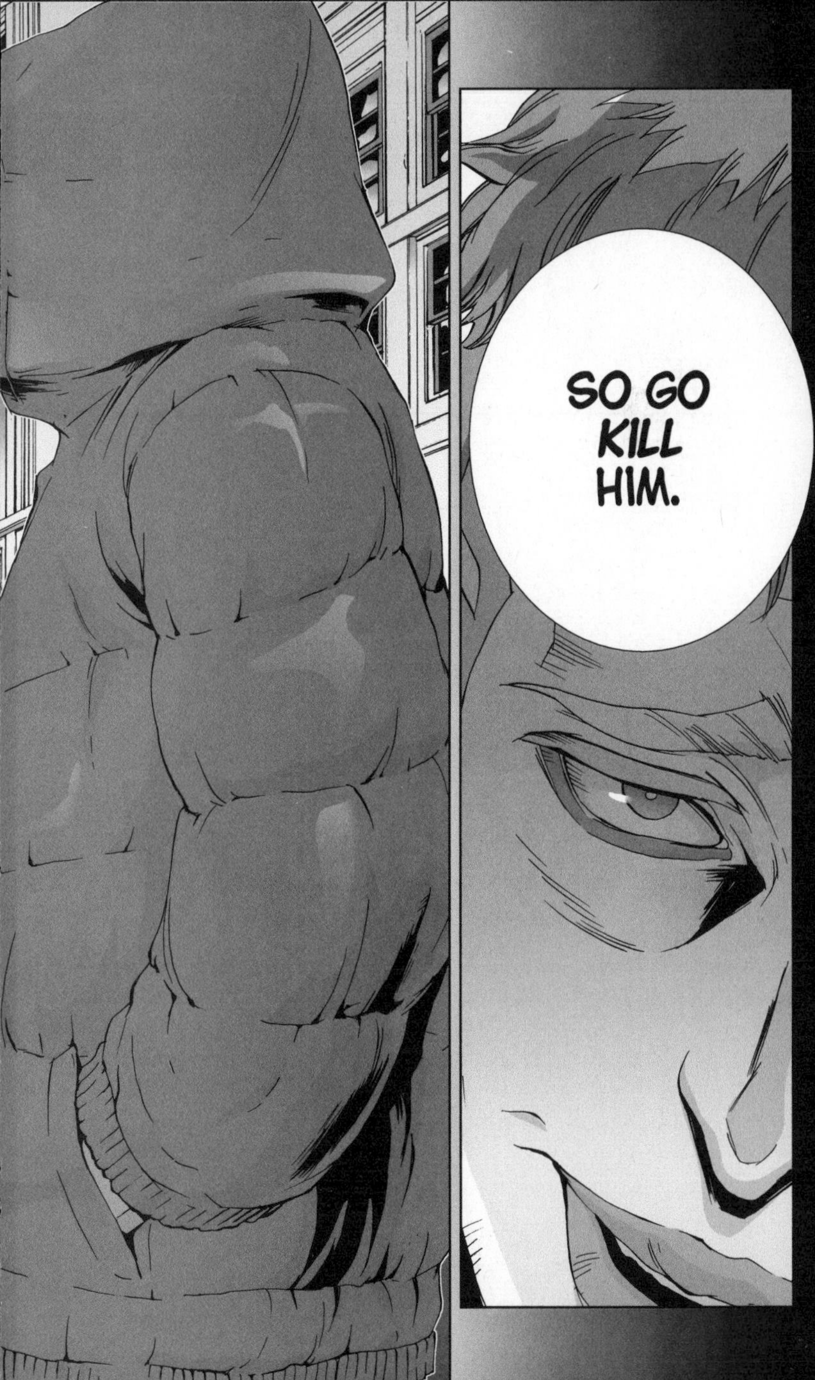
SO GO KILL HIM.

# #22 Take Heed of the Snake in the Grass, Part 2

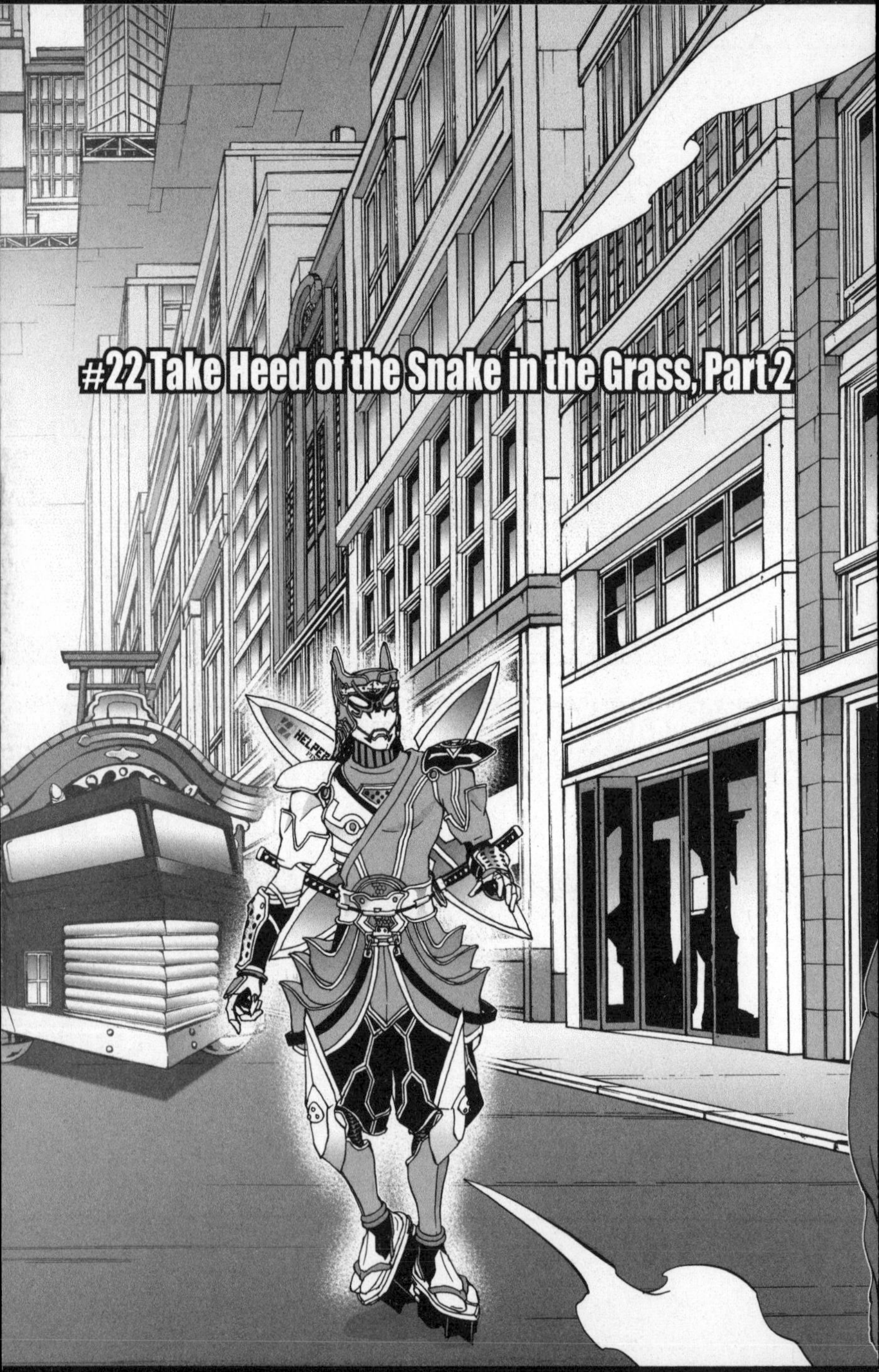
HELPER

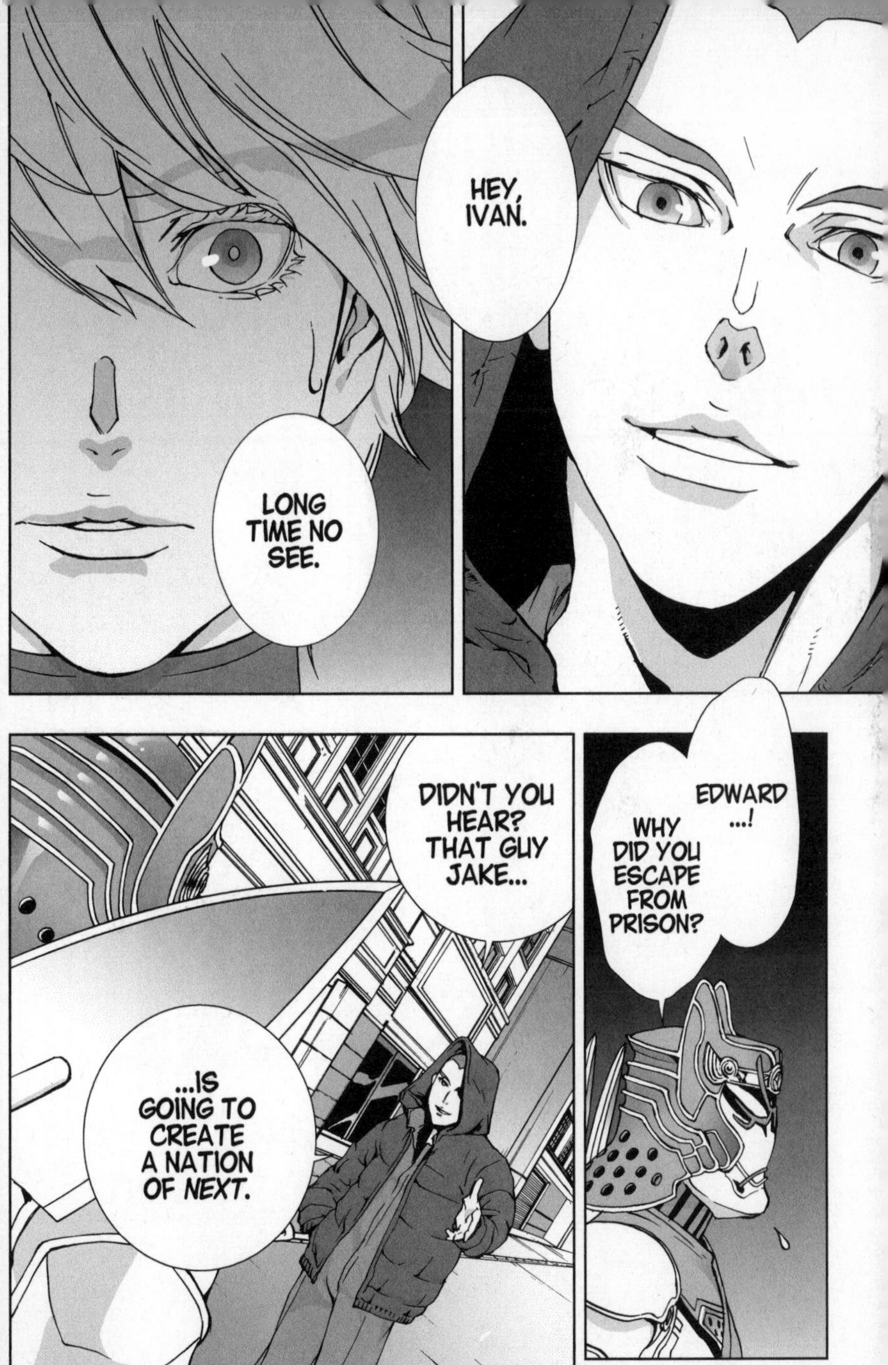
HEY, IVAN.
LONG TIME NO SEE.
EDWARD ...!
WHY DID YOU ESCAPE FROM PRISON?
DIDN'T YOU HEAR? THAT GUY JAKE...
...IS GOING TO CREATE A NATION OF NEXT.

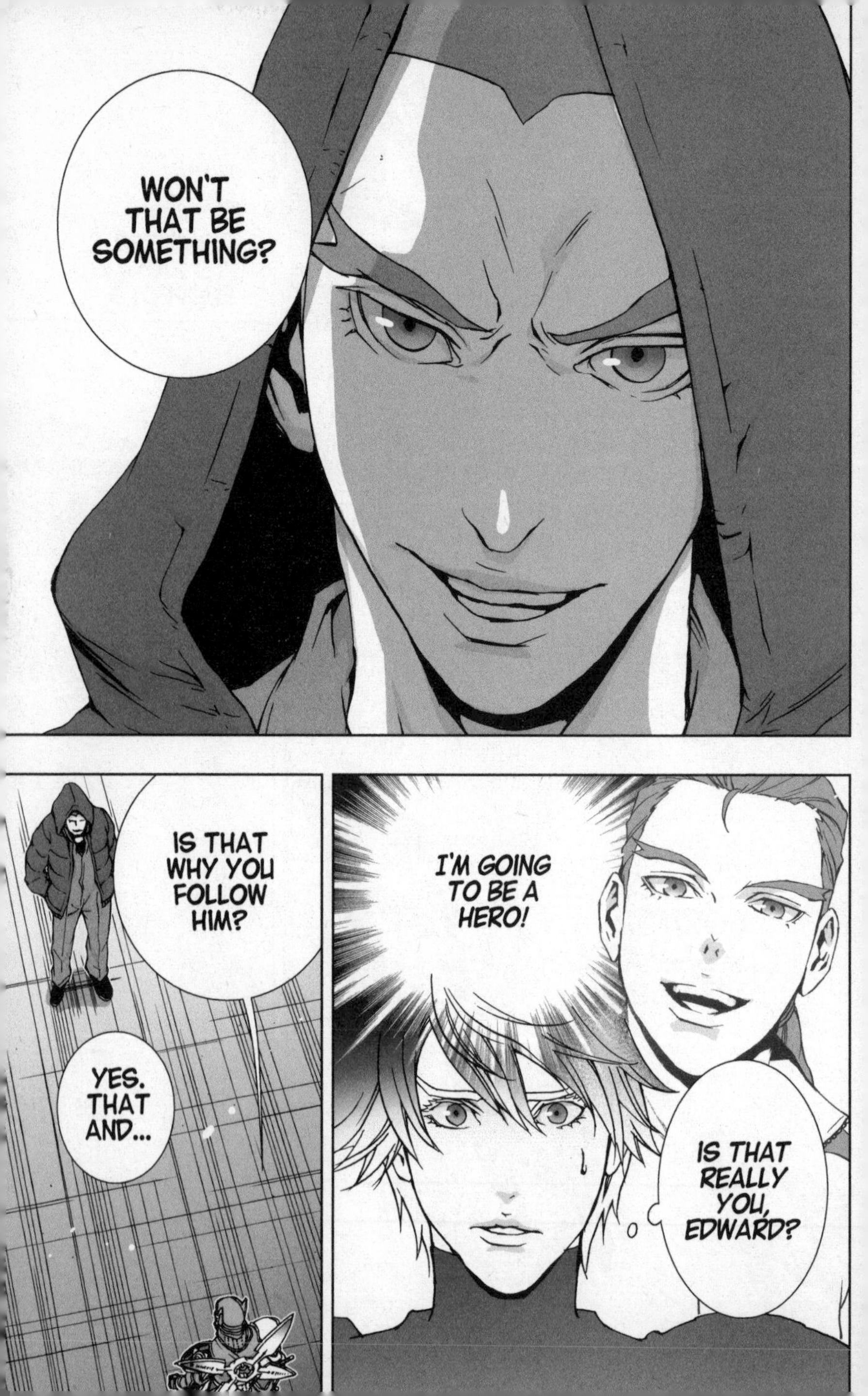
WON'T THAT BE SOMETHING?
I'M GOING TO BE A HERO!
IS THAT REALLY YOU, EDWARD?
IS THAT WHY YOU FOLLOW HIM?
YES. THAT AND...

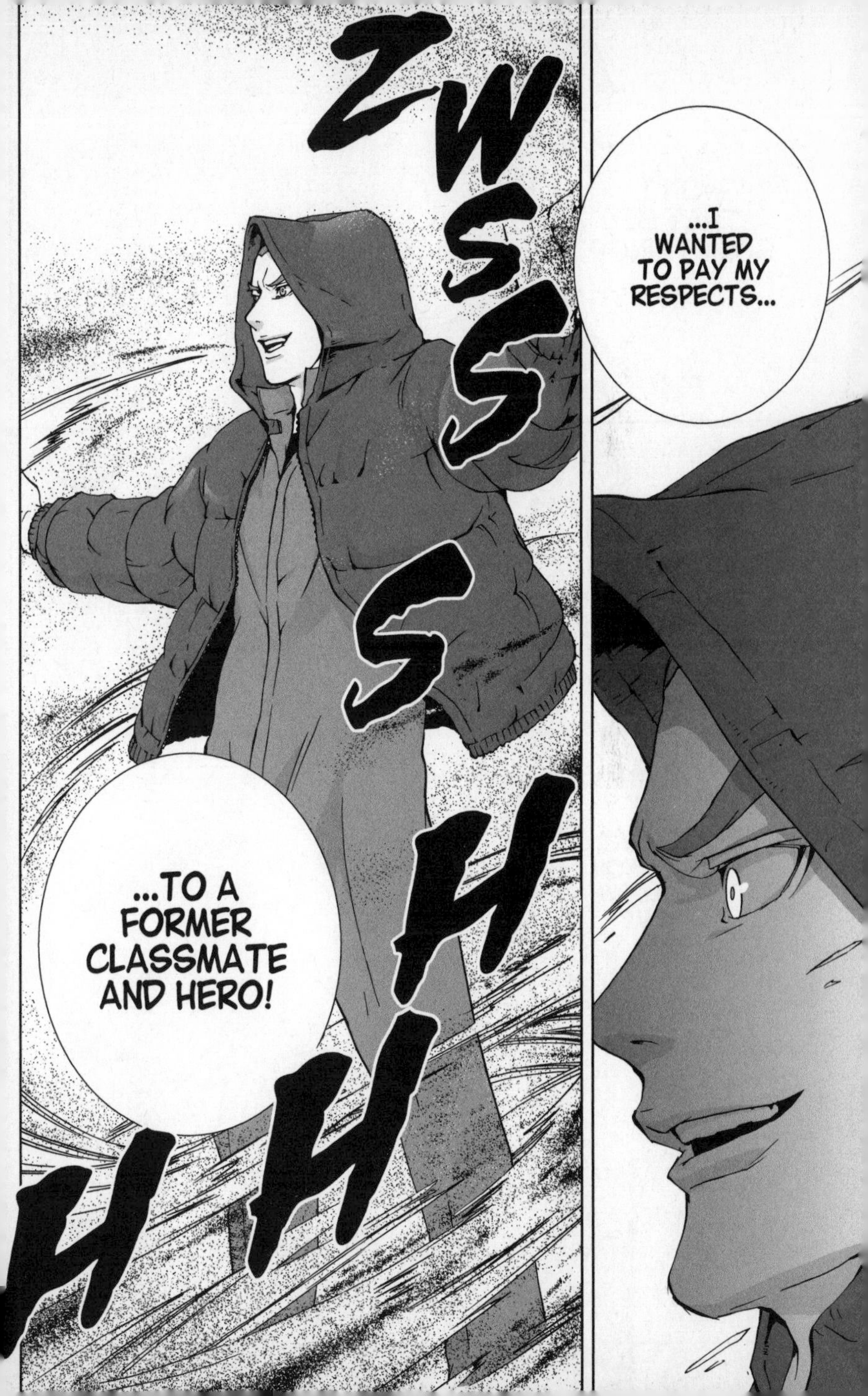
...I WANTED TO PAY MY RESPECTS...
ZWSSSHHHH
...TO A FORMER CLASSMATE AND HERO!

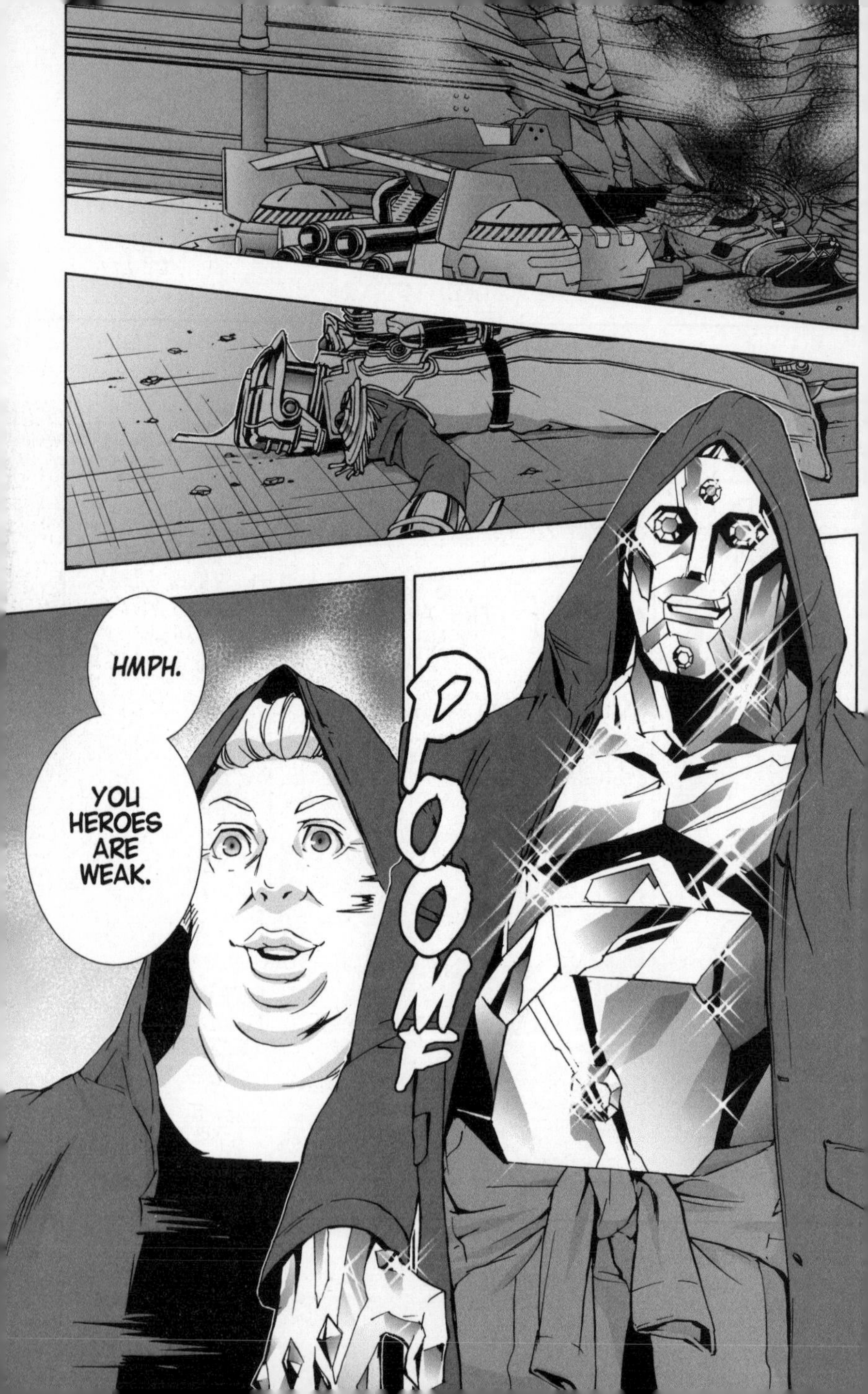
HMPH.
YOU HEROES ARE WEAK.
POOMF

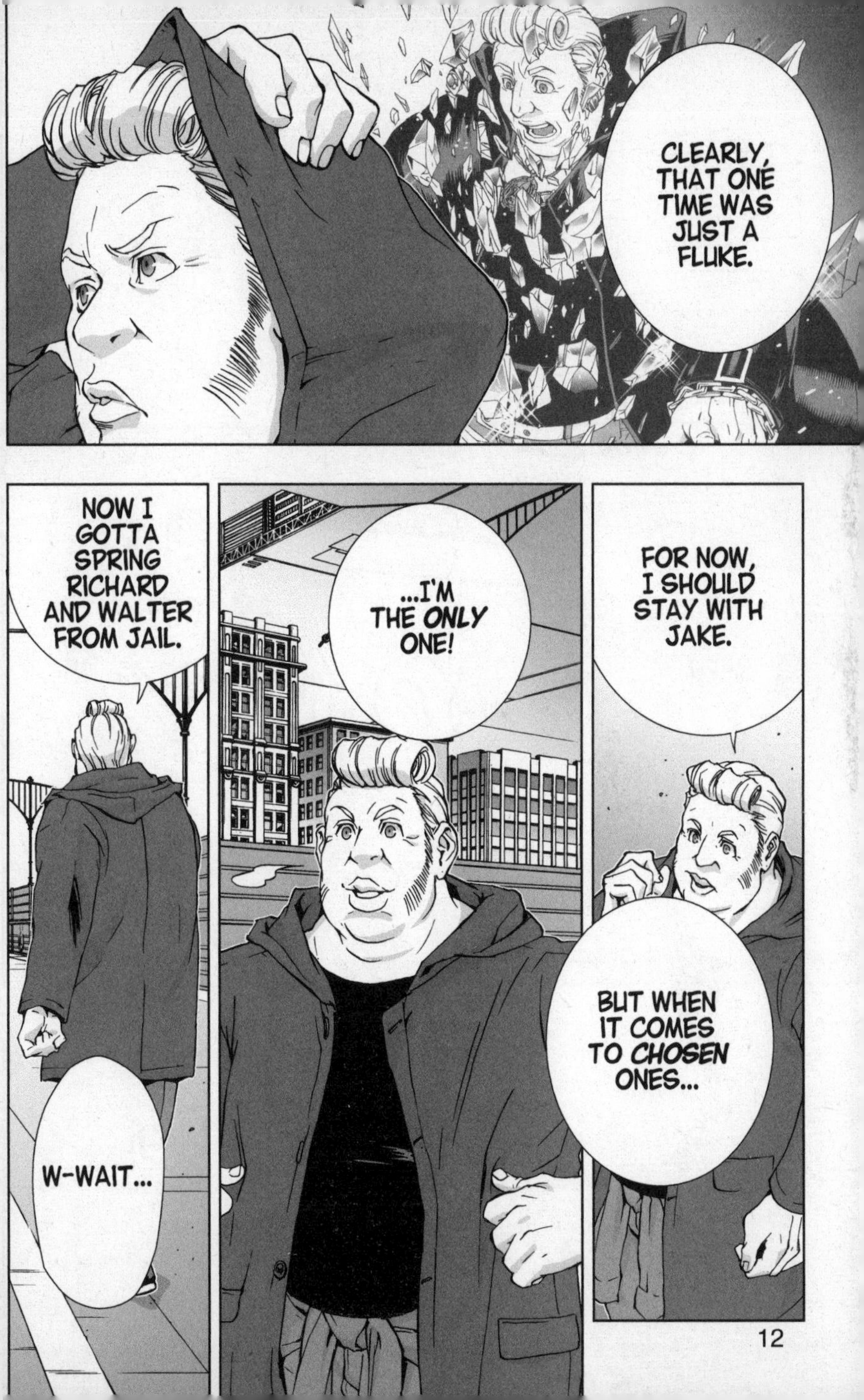
CLEARLY, THAT ONE TIME WAS JUST A FLUKE.
FOR NOW, I SHOULD STAY WITH JAKE.
BUT WHEN IT COMES TO *CHOSEN* ONES...
...I'M THE *ONLY* ONE!
NOW I GOTTA SPRING RICHARD AND WALTER FROM JAIL.
W-WAIT...

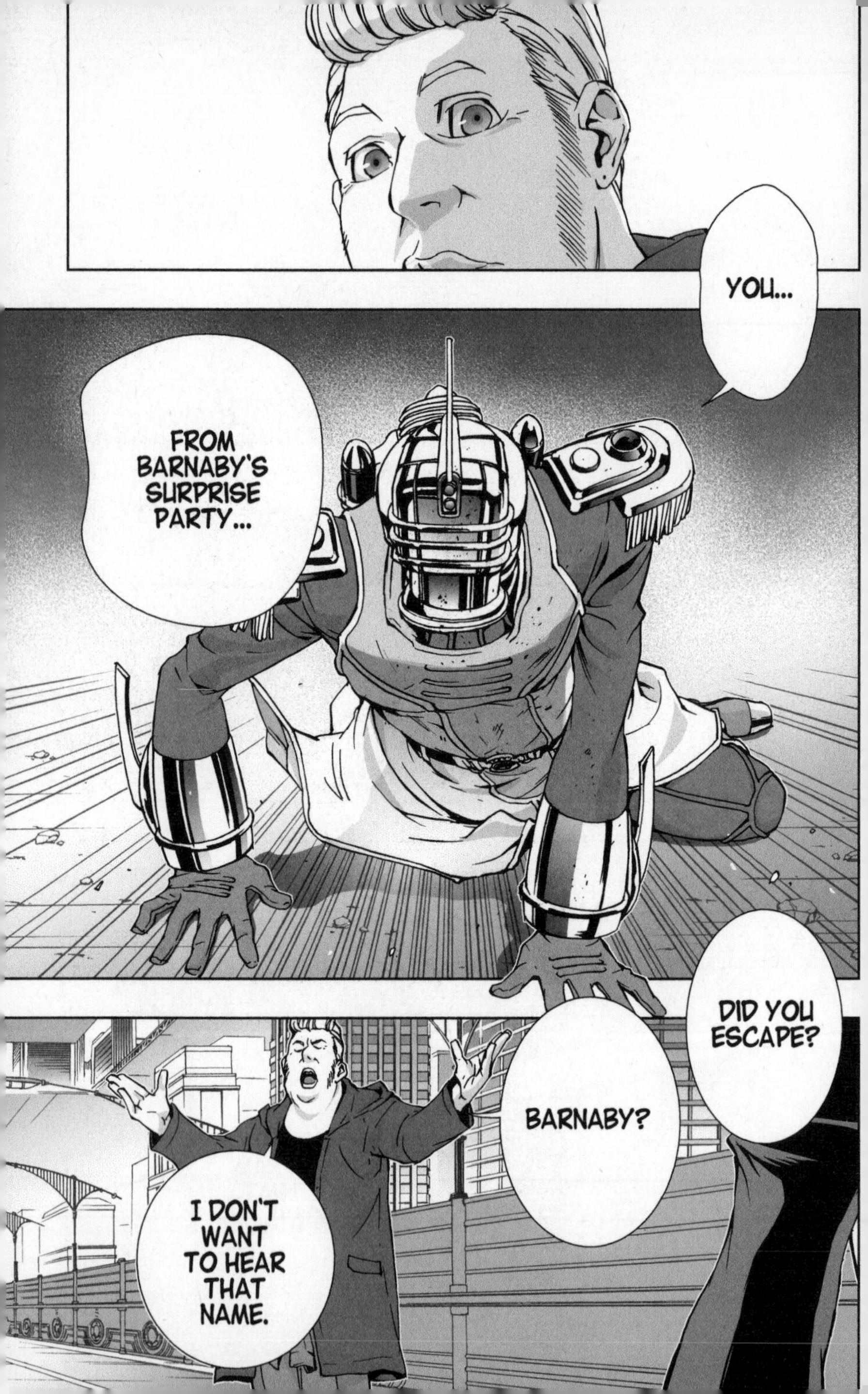
YOU...
FROM BARNABY'S SURPRISE PARTY...
DID YOU ESCAPE?
BARNABY?
I DON'T WANT TO HEAR THAT NAME.

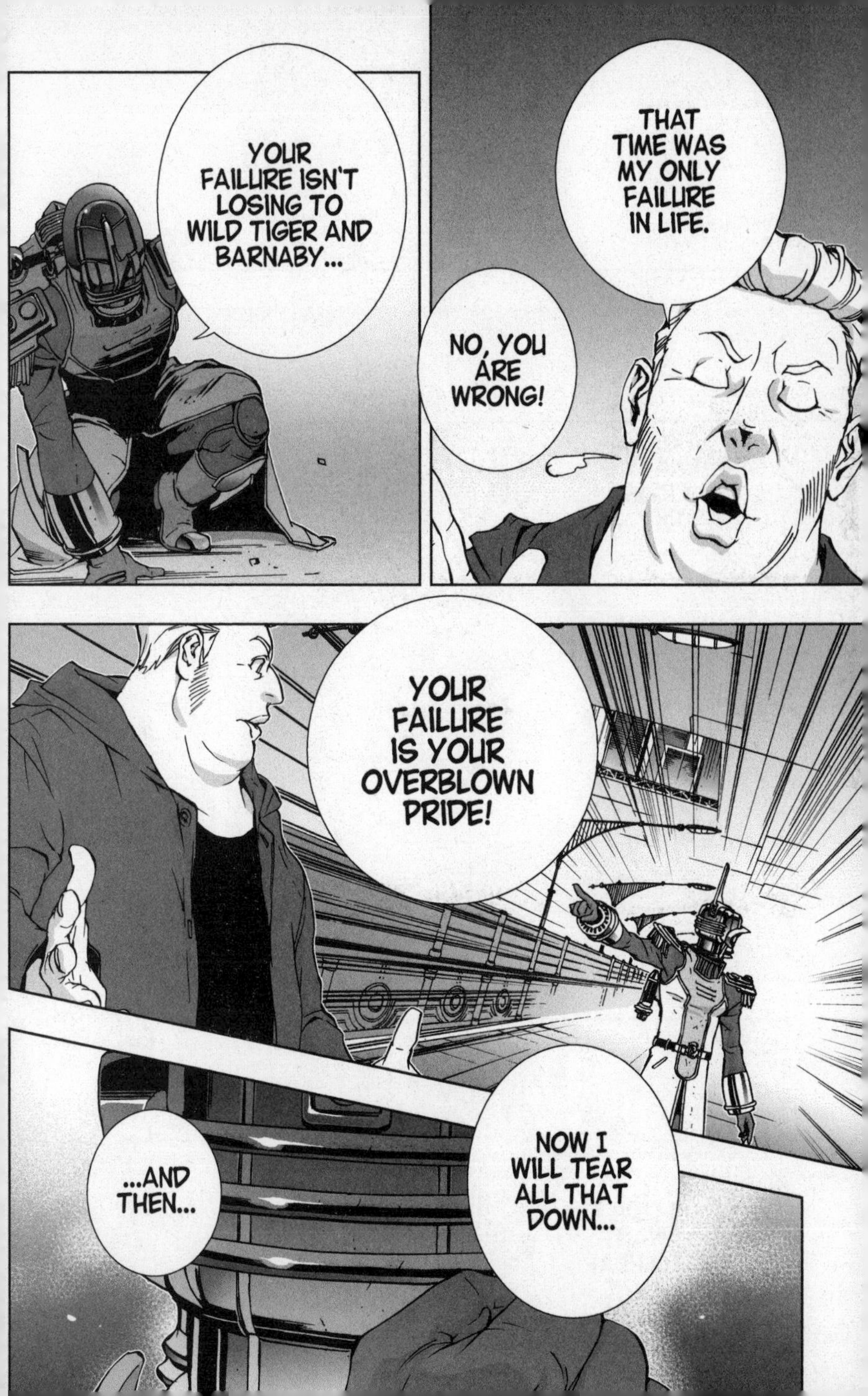
THAT TIME WAS MY ONLY FAILURE IN LIFE.
NO, YOU ARE WRONG!
YOUR FAILURE ISN'T LOSING TO WILD TIGER AND BARNABY...
YOUR FAILURE IS YOUR OVERBLOWN PRIDE!
NOW I WILL TEAR ALL THAT DOWN...
...AND THEN...

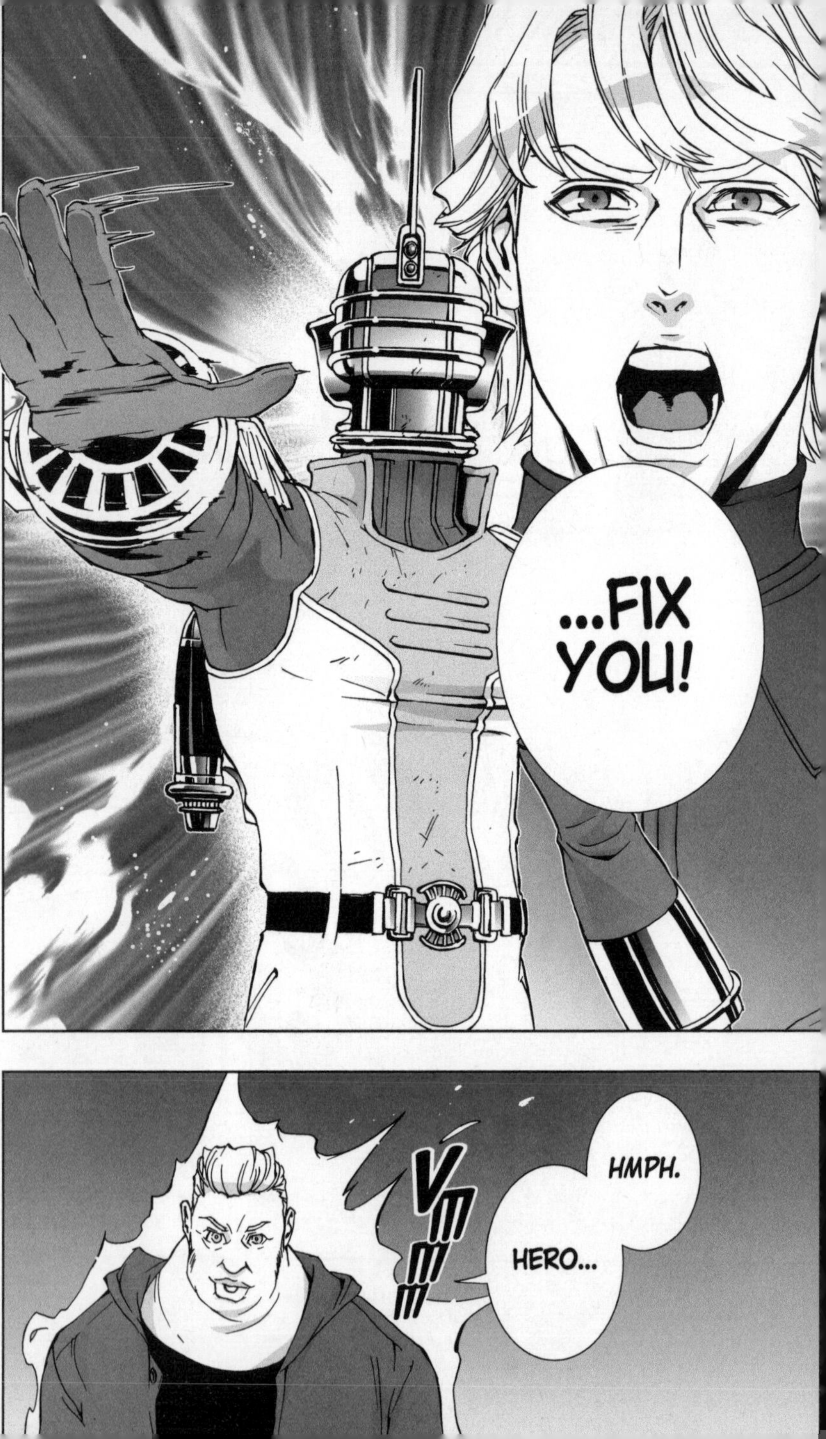
...FIX YOU!
HMPH.
HERO...
VMMM

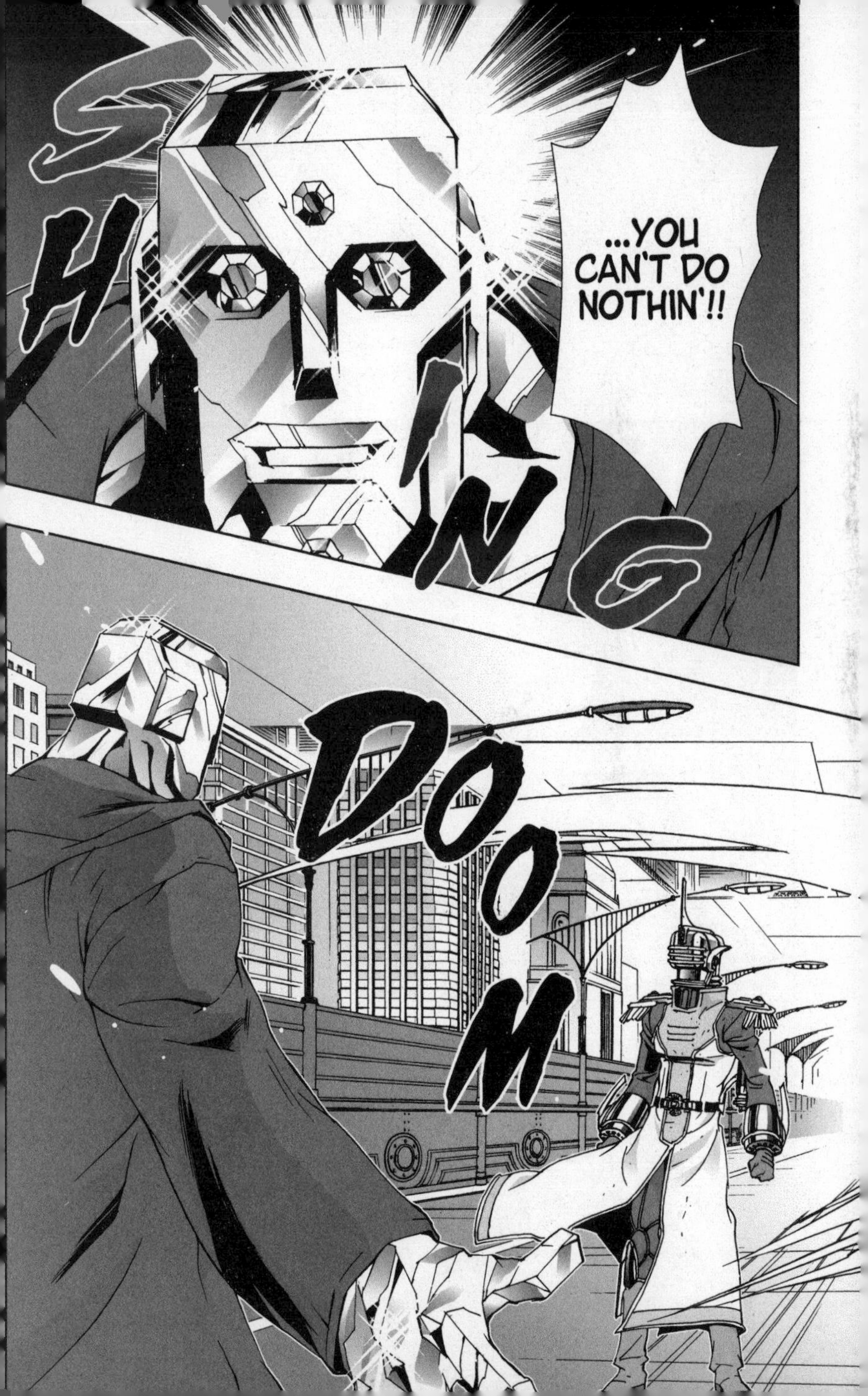
SHING
...YOU CAN'T DO NOTHIN'!!
DOOOM

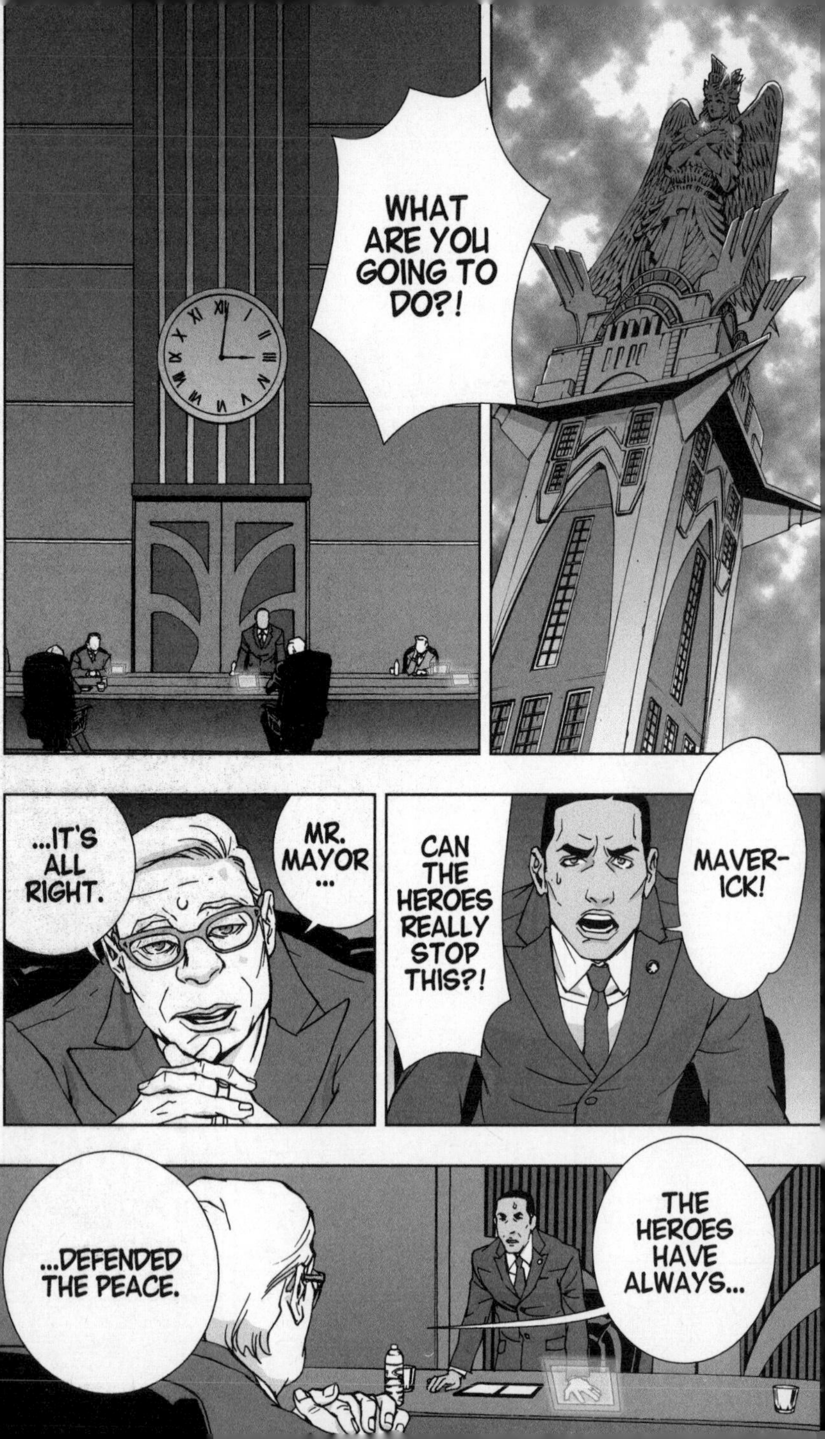
WHAT ARE YOU GOING TO DO?!
MAVER-ICK!
CAN THE HEROES REALLY STOP THIS?!
MR. MAYOR...
...IT'S ALL RIGHT.
THE HEROES HAVE ALWAYS...
...DEFENDED THE PEACE.

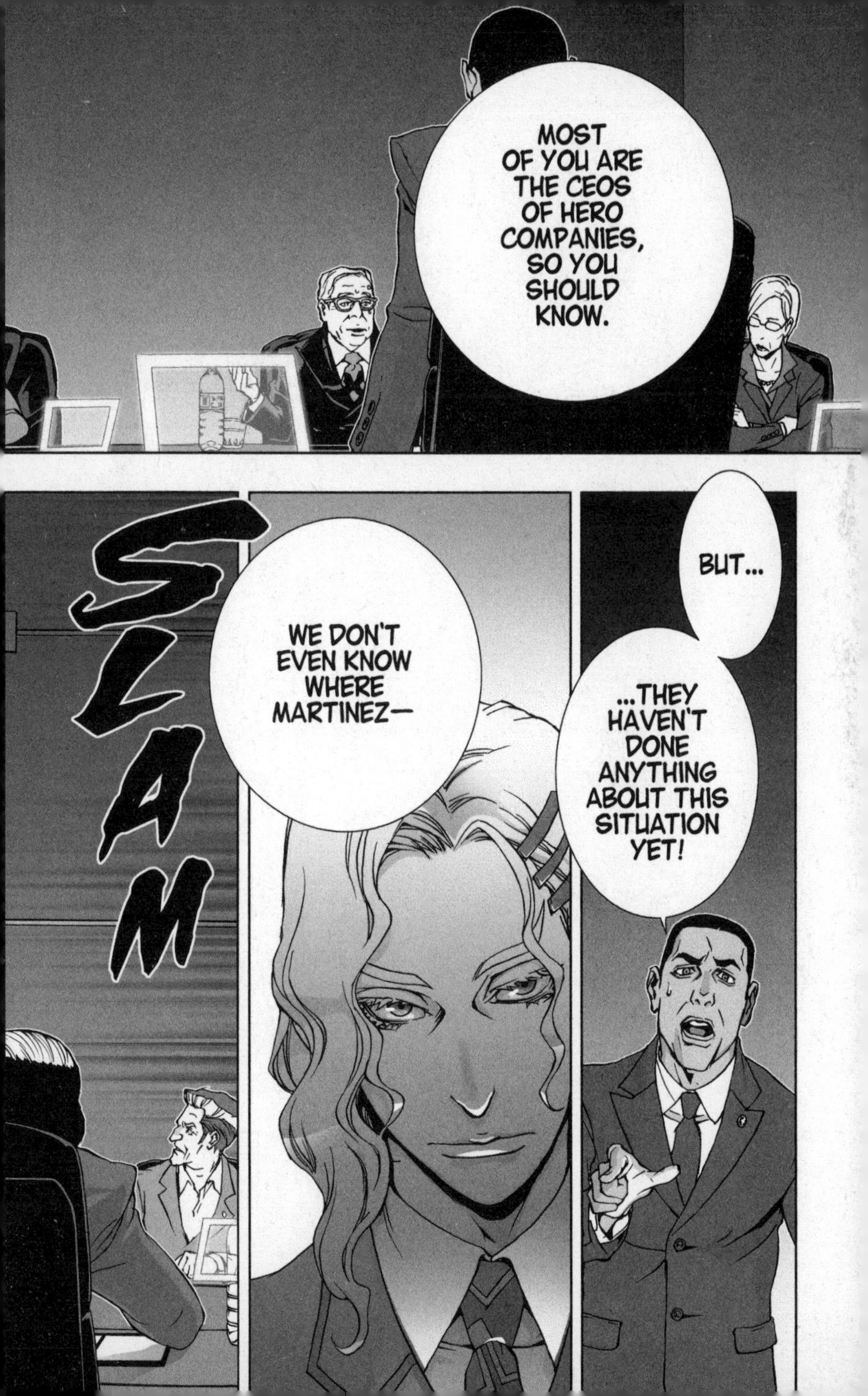
MOST OF YOU ARE THE CEOS OF HERO COMPANIES, SO YOU SHOULD KNOW.
BUT...
...THEY HAVEN'T DONE ANYTHING ABOUT THIS SITUATION YET!
WE DON'T EVEN KNOW WHERE MARTINEZ—
SLAM

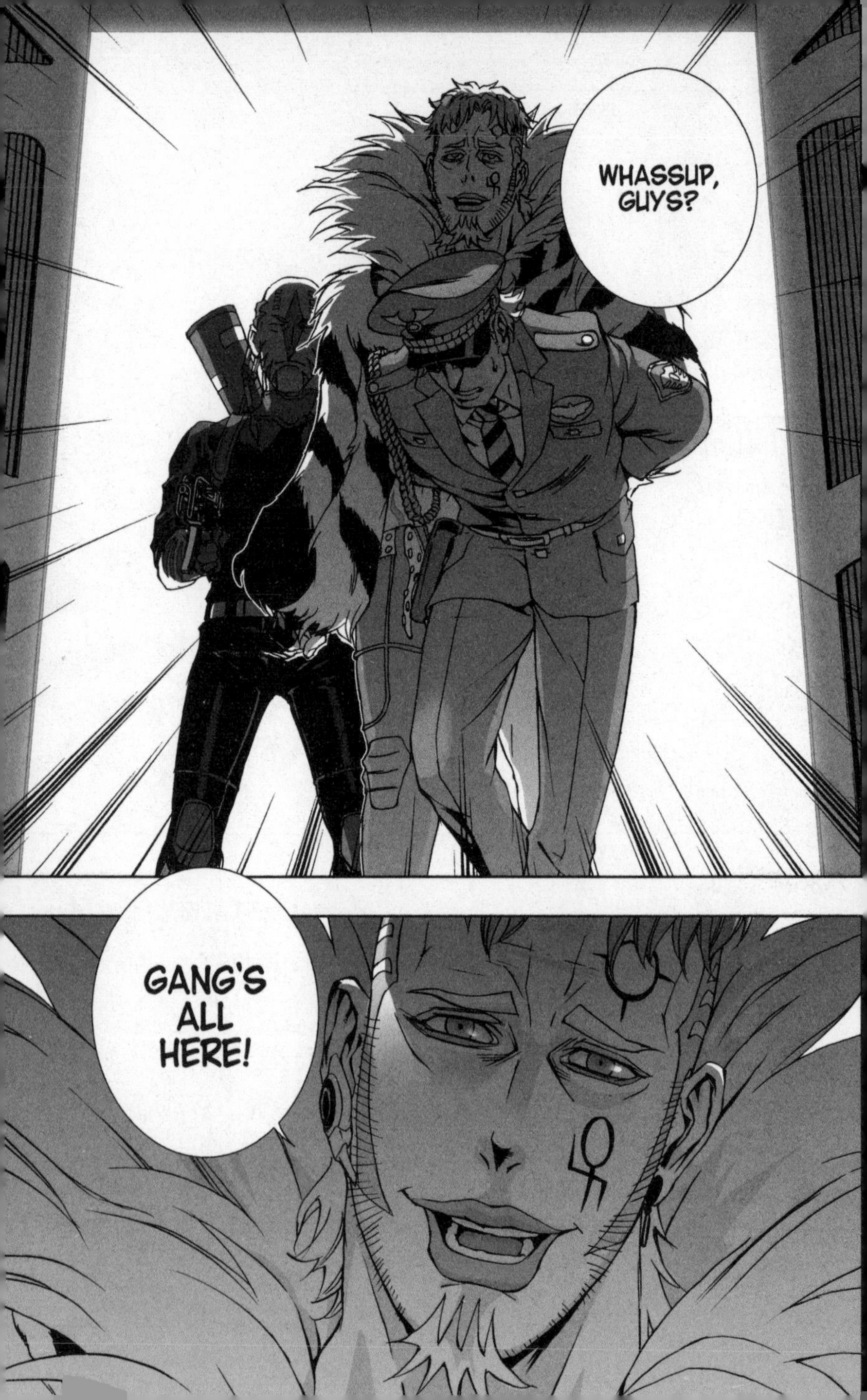
WHASSUP, GUYS?
GANG'S ALL HERE!

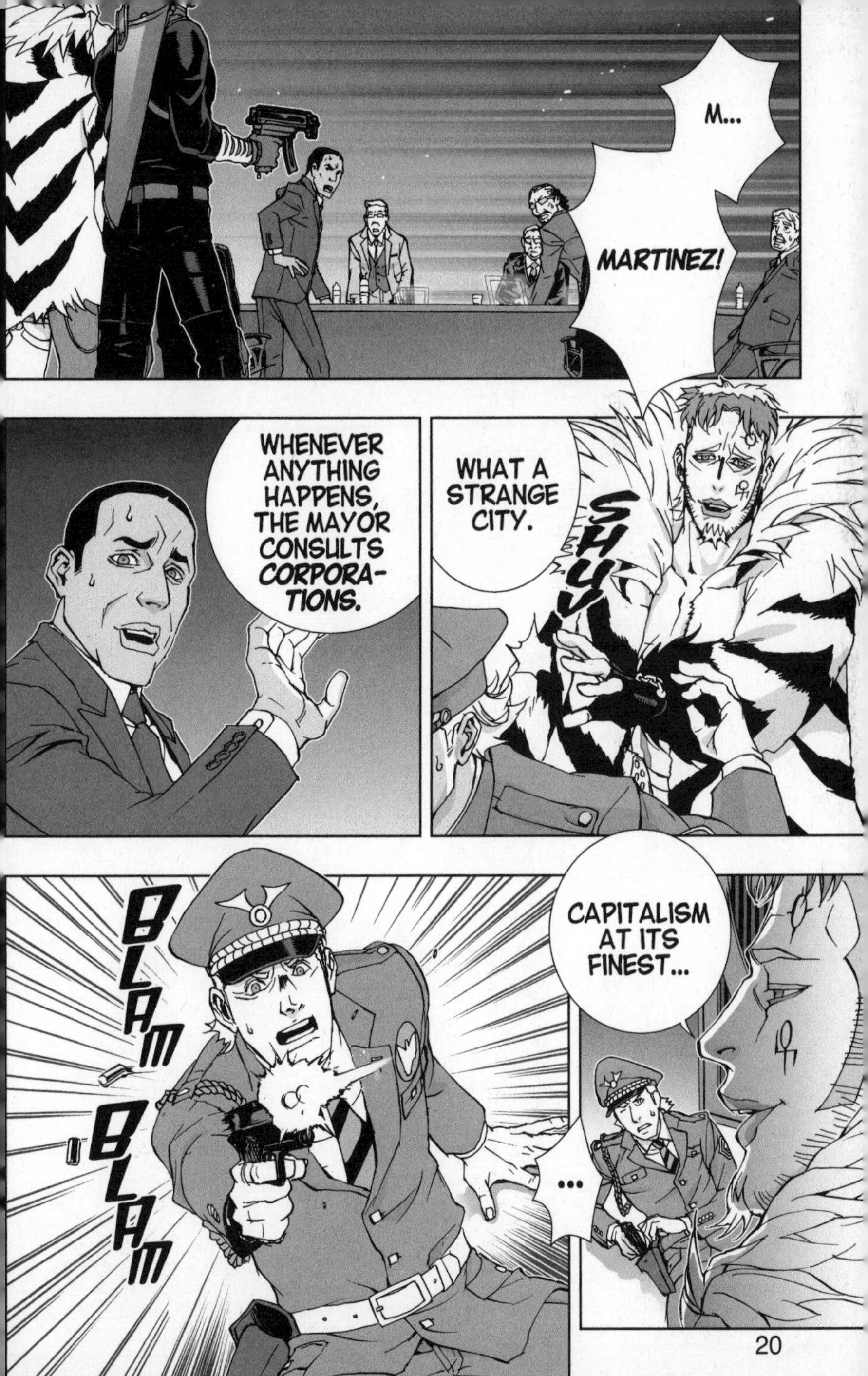
M...
MARTINEZ!
WHAT A STRANGE CITY.
WHENEVER ANYTHING HAPPENS, THE MAYOR CONSULTS CORPORATIONS.
CAPITALISM AT ITS FINEST...
...
BLAM
BLAM
BLAM

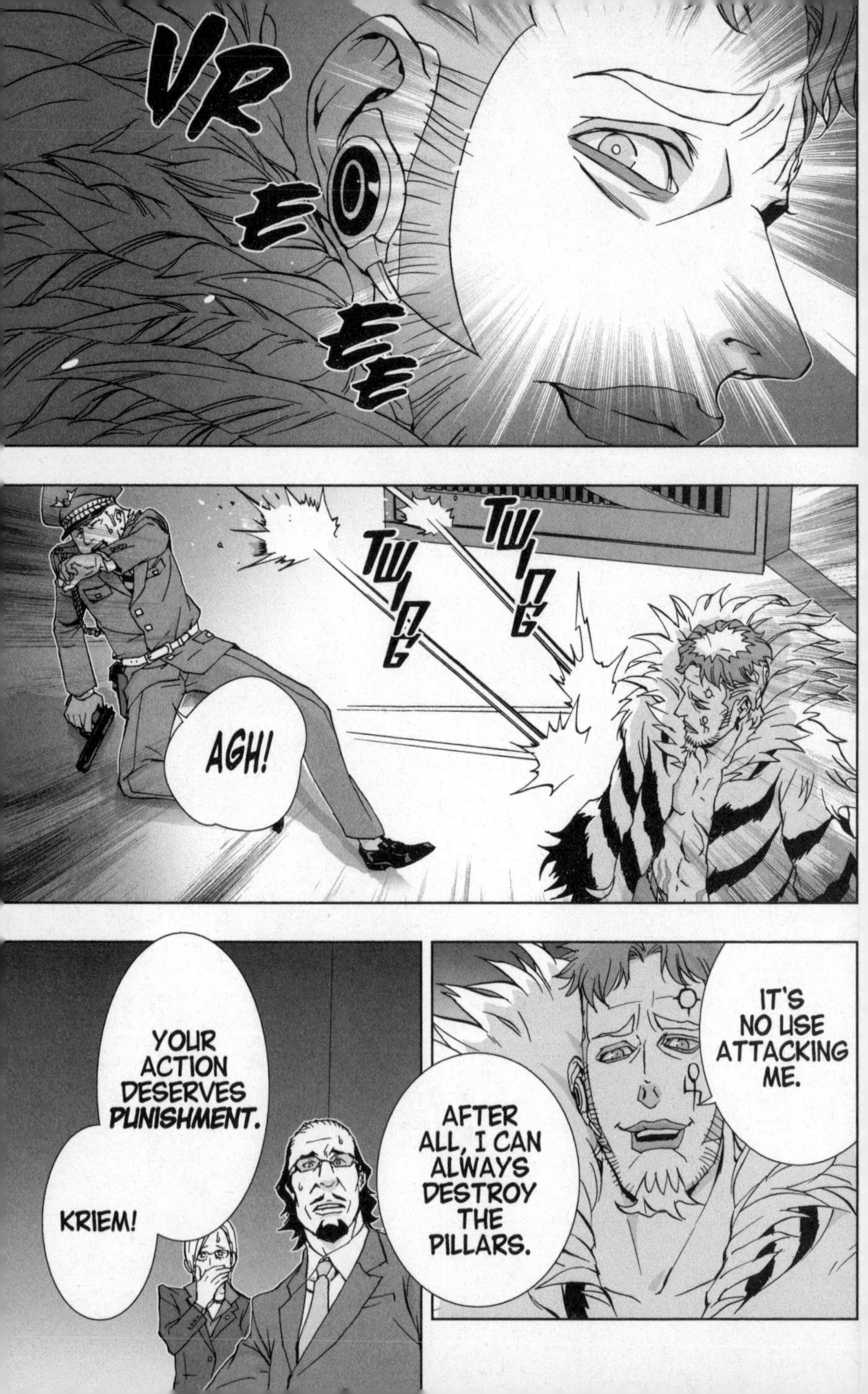
VREEEE
TWING
TWING
AGH!
IT'S NO USE ATTACKING ME.
AFTER ALL, I CAN ALWAYS DESTROY THE PILLARS.
YOUR ACTION DESERVES PUNISHMENT.
KRIEM!

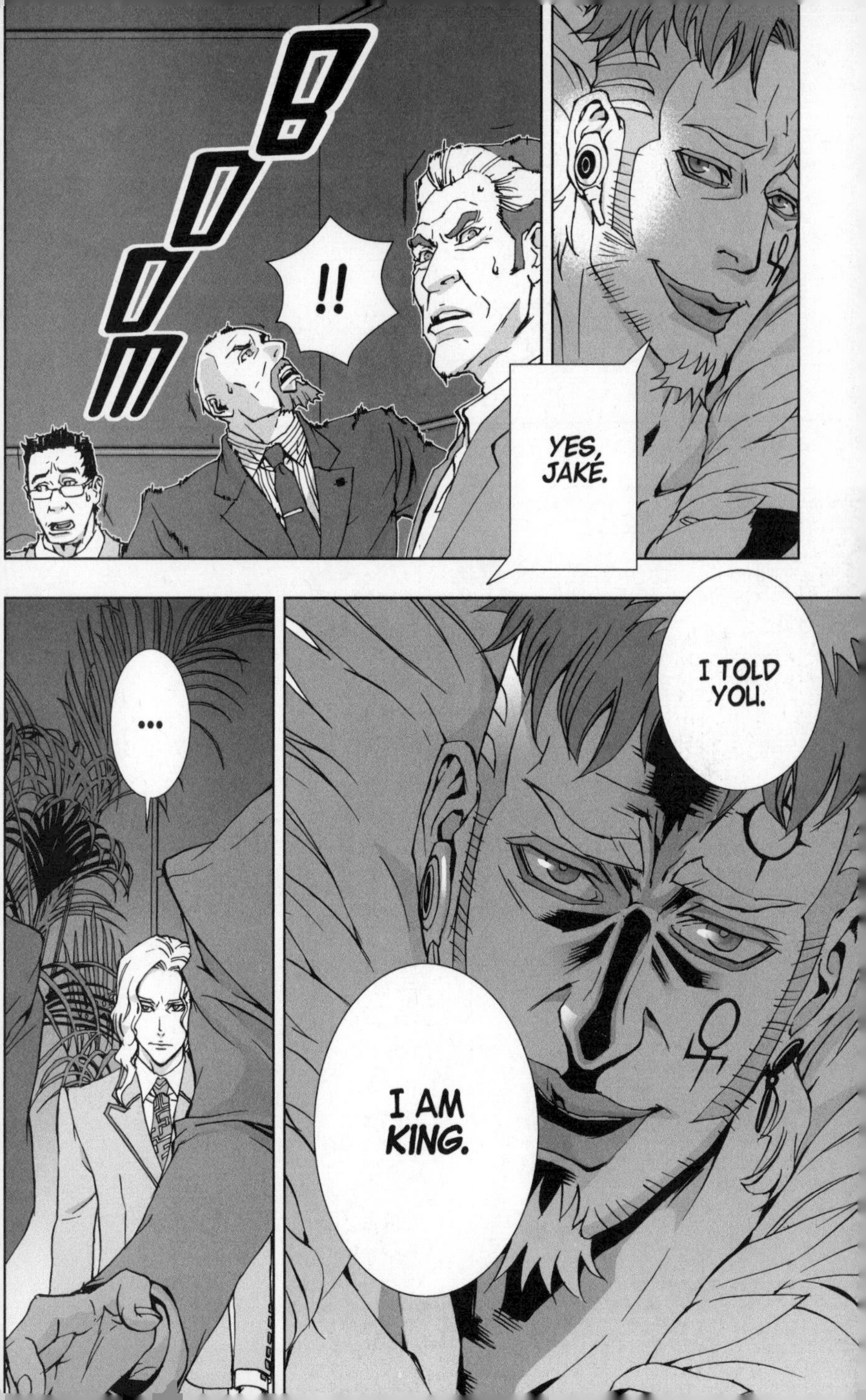
YES, JAKE.
BOOM
!!
I TOLD YOU.
I AM KING.
...

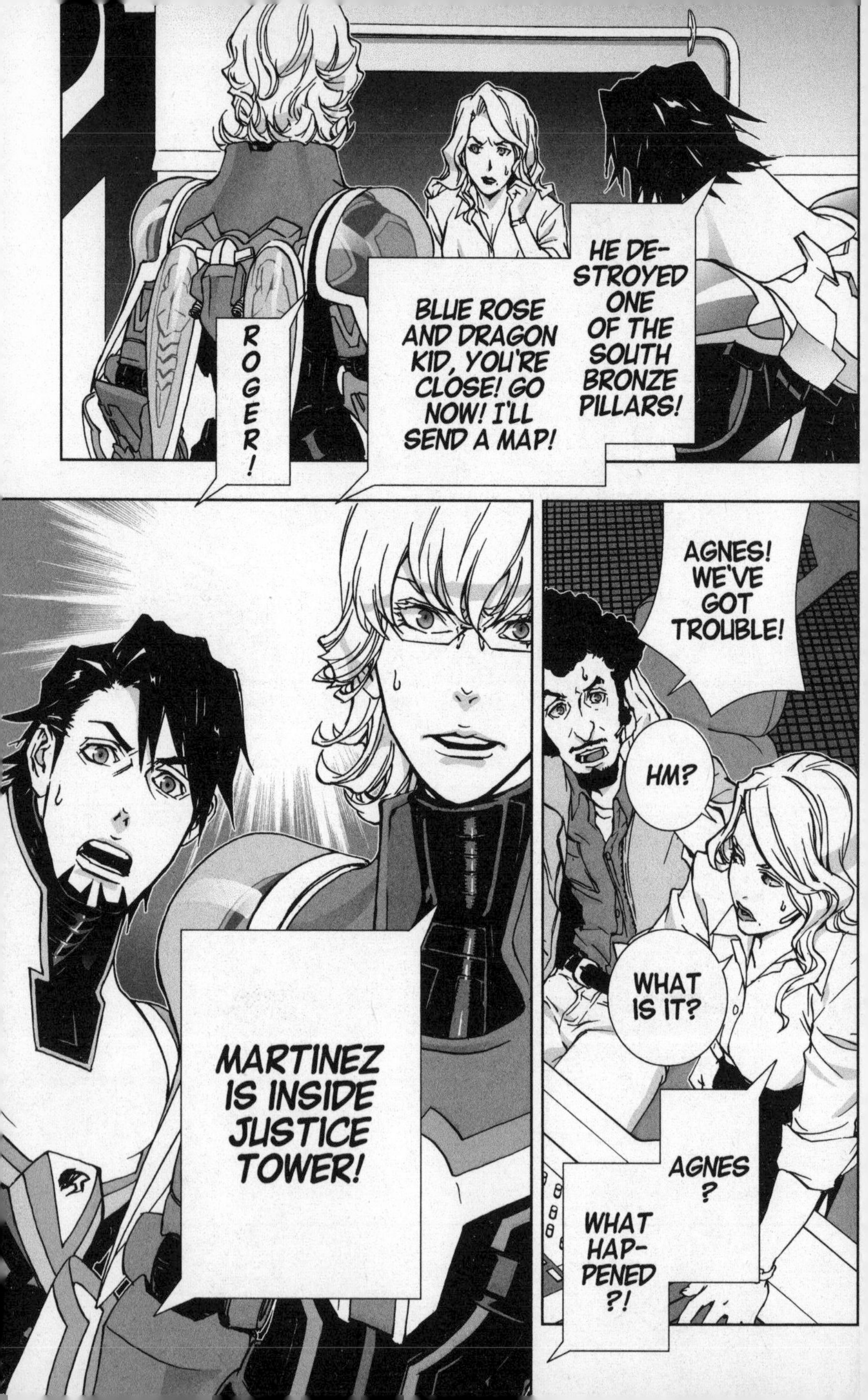
HE DE-
STROYED
ONE
OF THE
SOUTH
BRONZE
PILLARS!
BLUE ROSE
AND DRAGON
KID, YOU'RE
CLOSE! GO
NOW! I'LL
SEND A MAP!
ROGER!
AGNES!
WE'VE
GOT
TROUBLE!
HM?
WHAT
IS IT?
AGNES
?
WHAT
HAP-
PENED
?!
MARTINEZ
IS INSIDE
JUSTICE
TOWER!

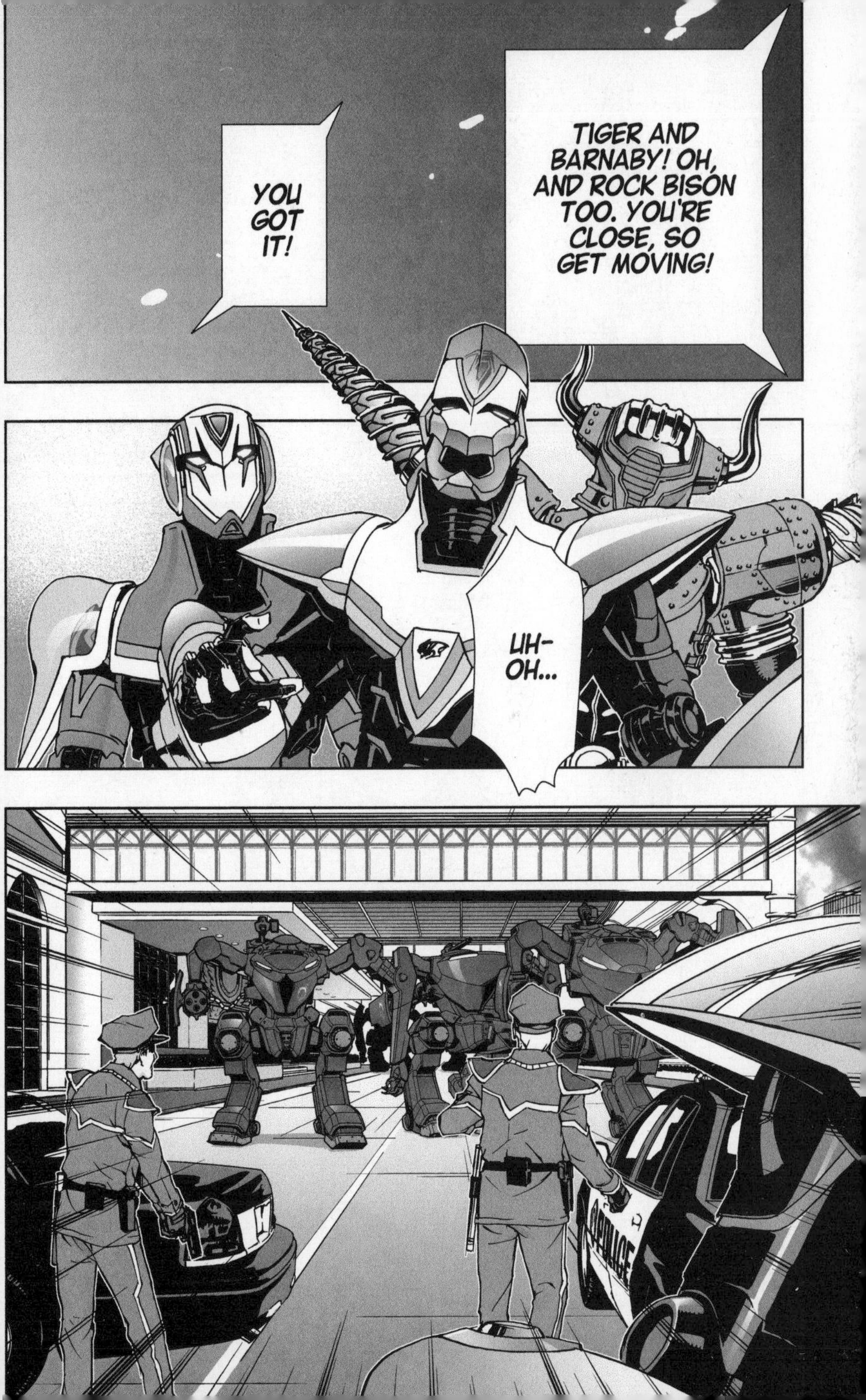
TIGER AND BARNABY! OH, AND ROCK BISON TOO. YOU'RE CLOSE, SO GET MOVING!
YOU GOT IT!
UH-OH...
POLICE

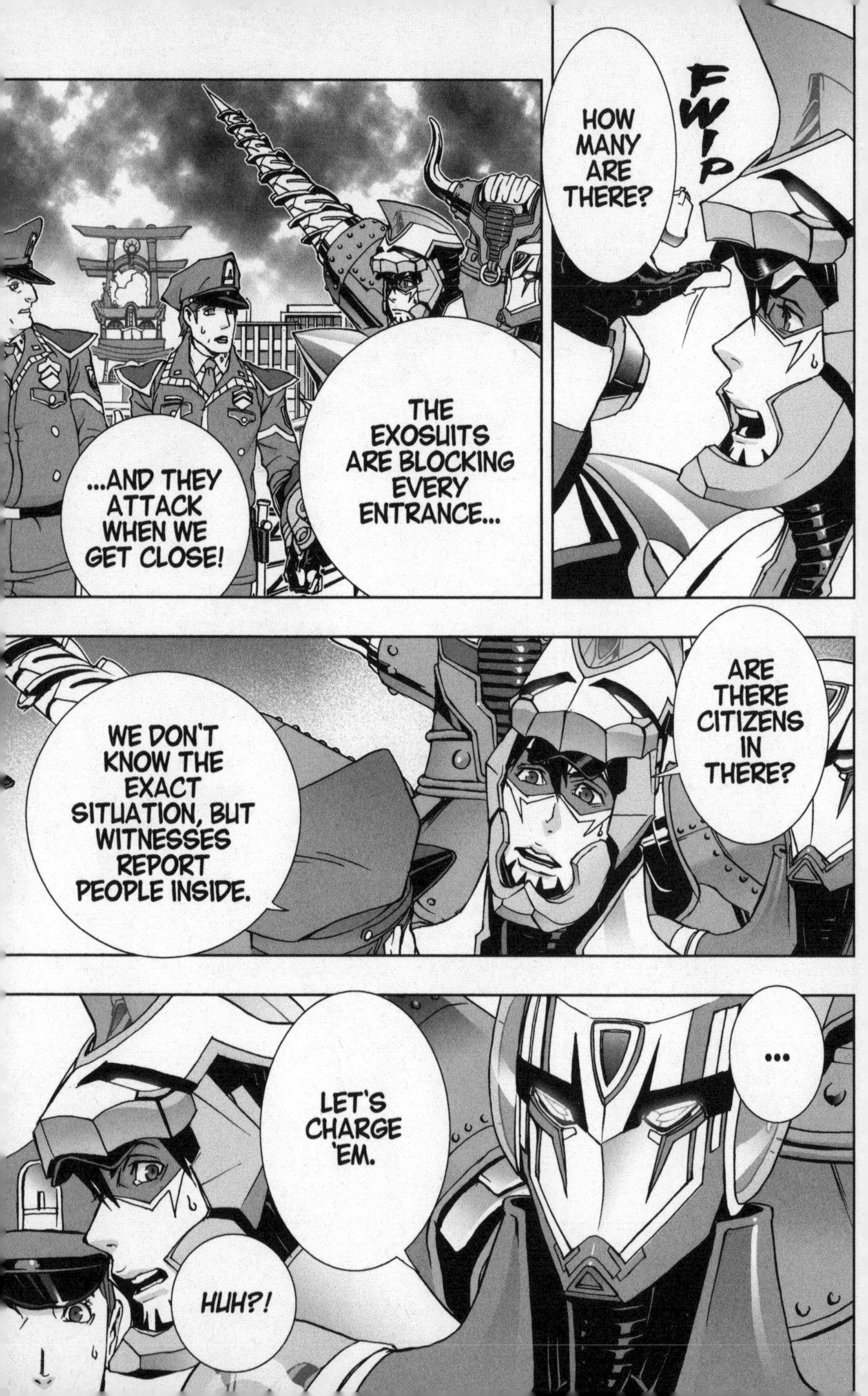
FWIP
HOW MANY ARE THERE?
THE EXOSUITS ARE BLOCKING EVERY ENTRANCE...
...AND THEY ATTACK WHEN WE GET CLOSE!
ARE THERE CITIZENS IN THERE?
WE DON'T KNOW THE EXACT SITUATION, BUT WITNESSES REPORT PEOPLE INSIDE.
...
LET'S CHARGE 'EM.
HUH?!

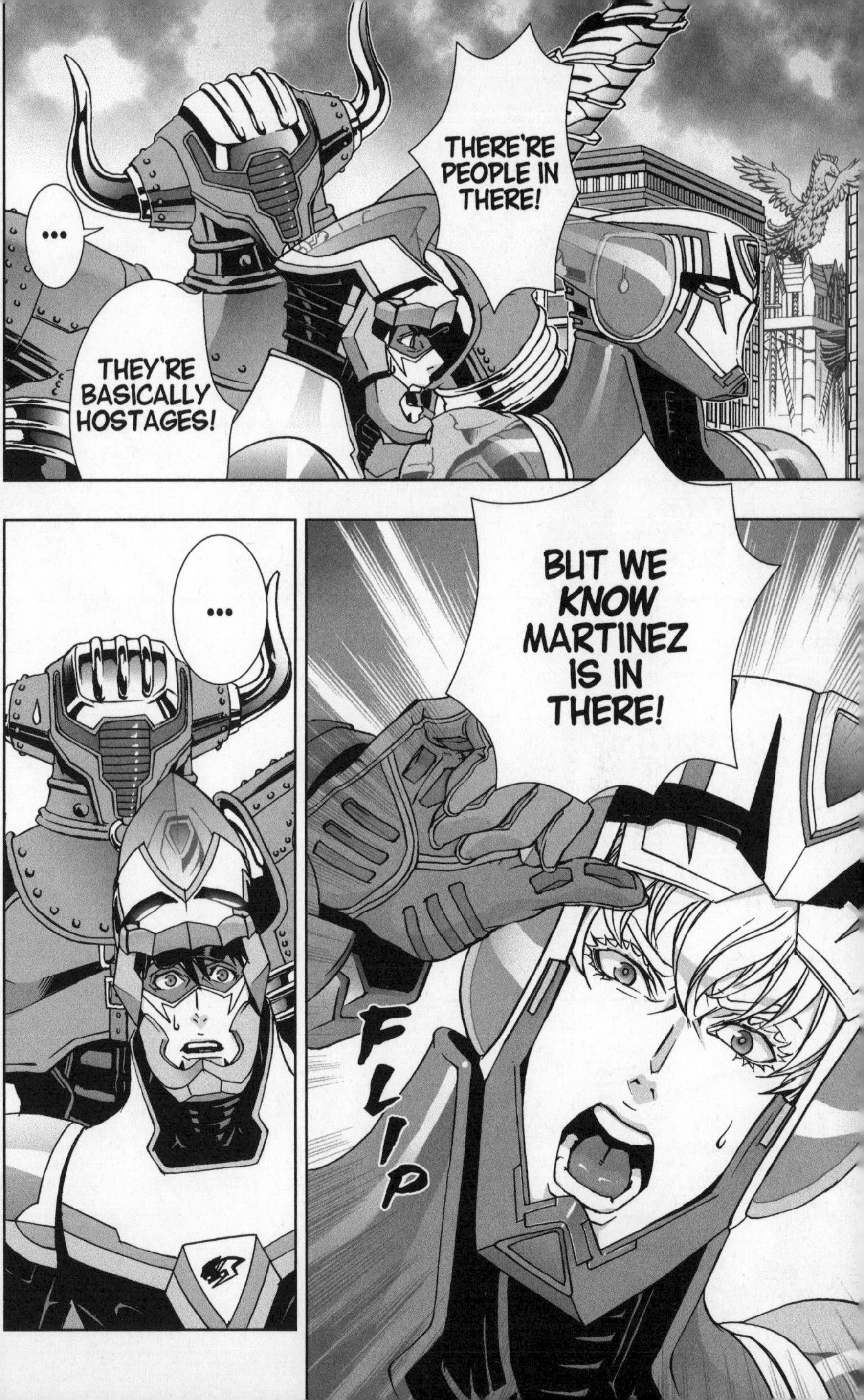
THERE'RE PEOPLE IN THERE!
...
THEY'RE BASICALLY HOSTAGES!
BUT WE KNOW MARTINEZ IS IN THERE!
FLIP
...

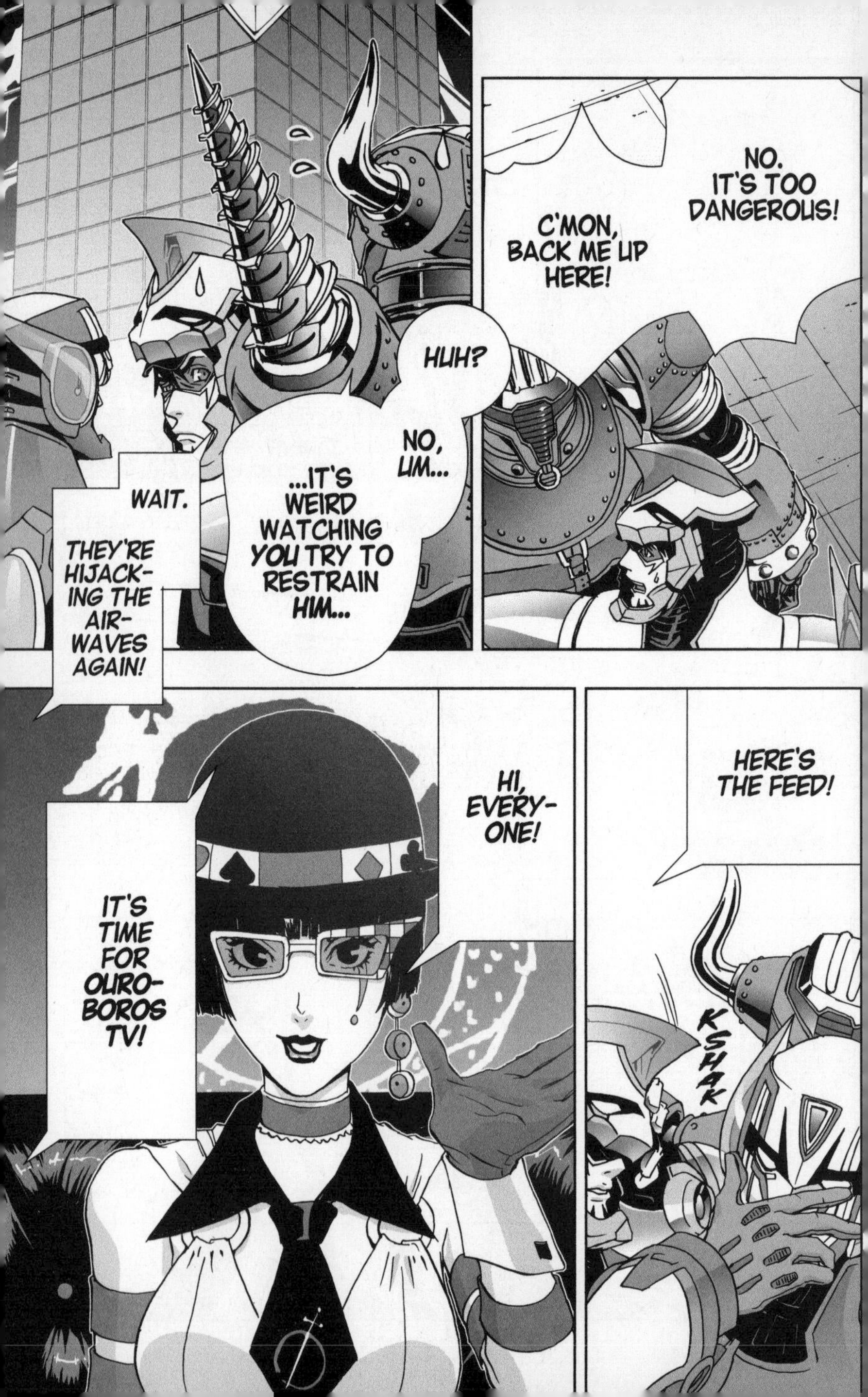
NO. IT'S TOO DANGEROUS!
C'MON, BACK ME UP HERE!
HUH?
NO, UM...
...IT'S WEIRD WATCHING YOU TRY TO RESTRAIN HIM...
WAIT.
THEY'RE HIJACKING THE AIRWAVES AGAIN!
HERE'S THE FEED!
KSHAK
HI, EVERYONE!
IT'S TIME FOR OUROBOROS TV!

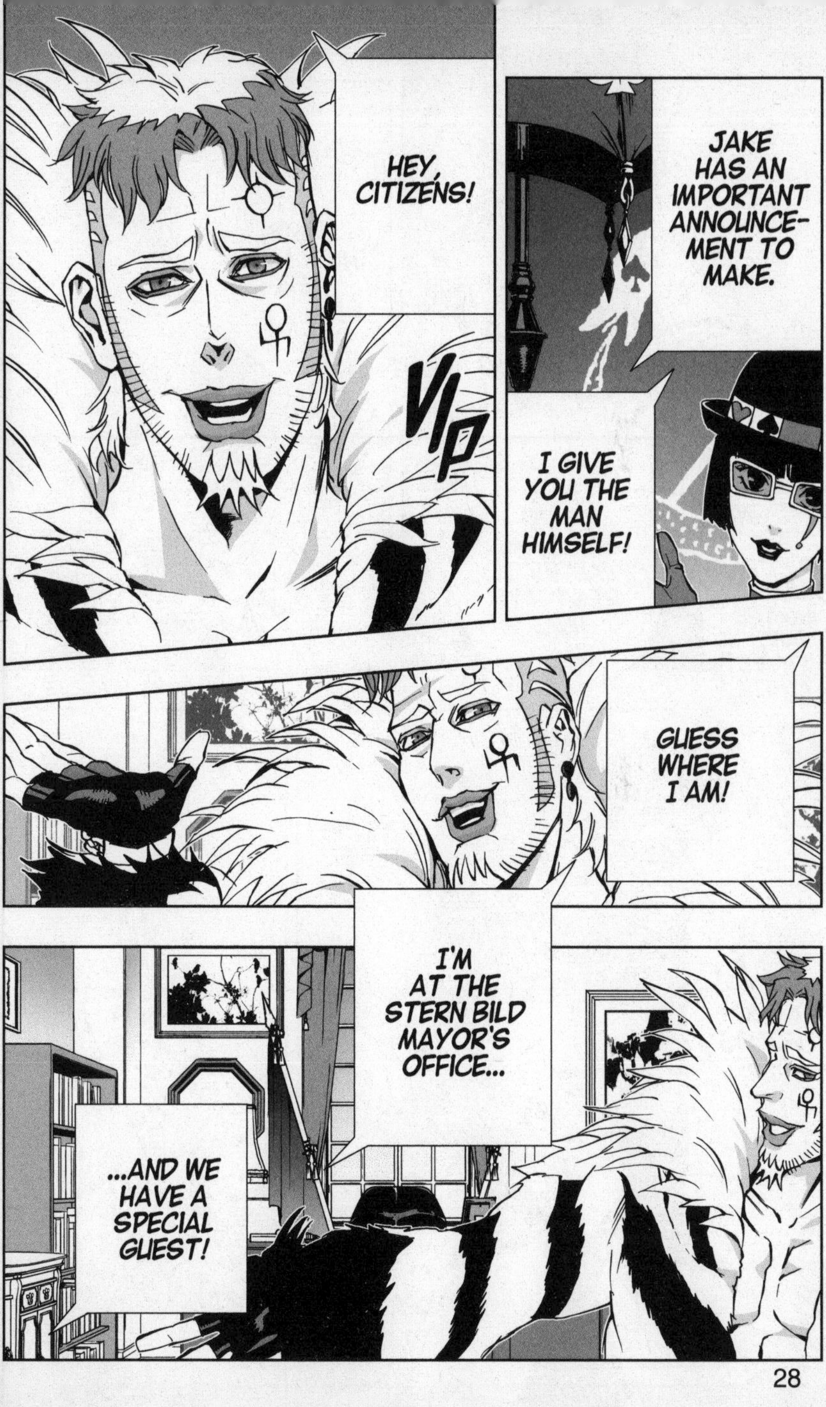
JAKE HAS AN IMPORTANT ANNOUNCE-MENT TO MAKE.
I GIVE YOU THE MAN HIMSELF!
HEY, CITIZENS!
VIP
GUESS WHERE I AM!
I'M AT THE STERN BILD MAYOR'S OFFICE...
...AND WE HAVE A SPECIAL GUEST!

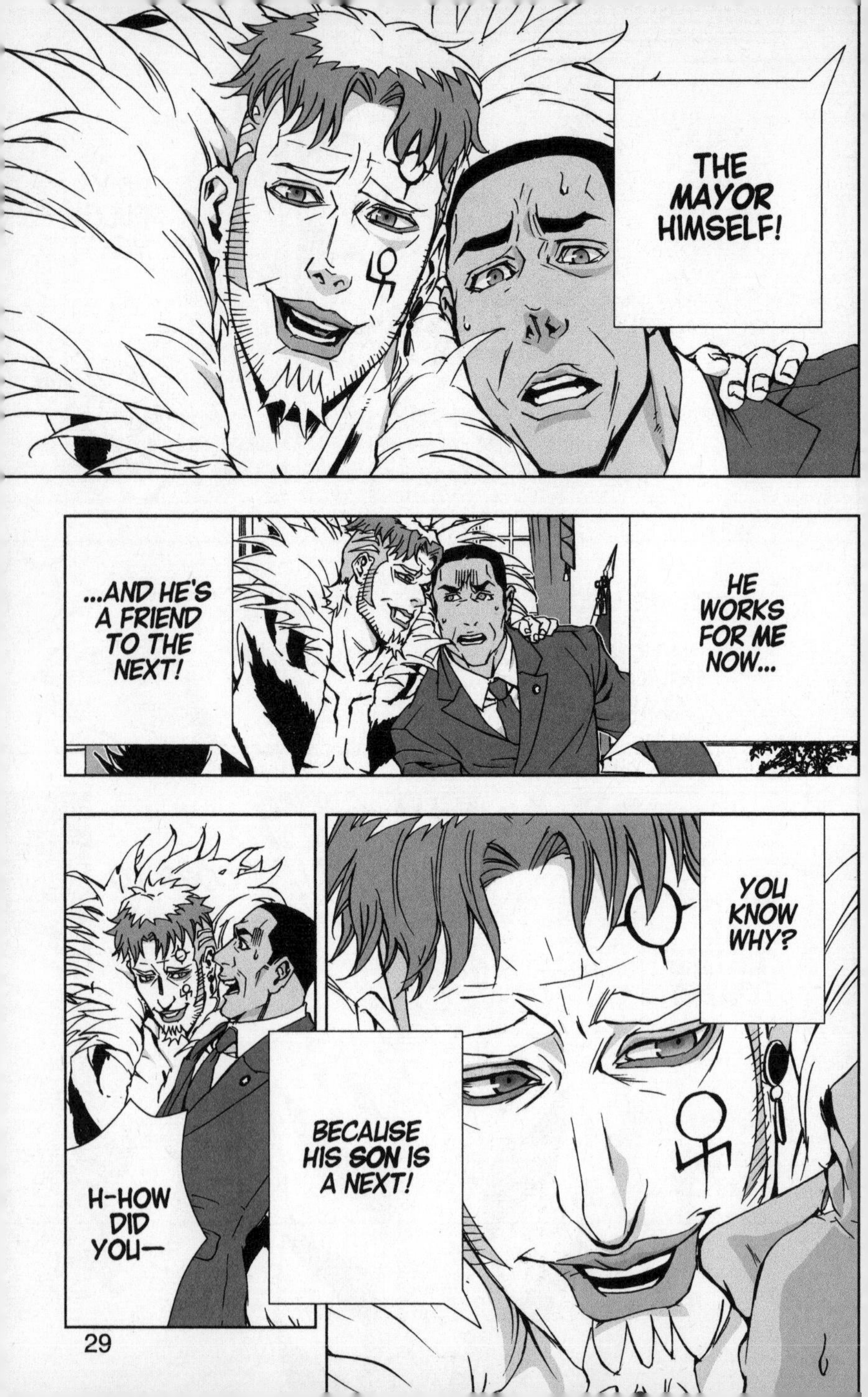
THE MAYOR HIMSELF!
HE WORKS FOR ME NOW...
...AND HE'S A FRIEND TO THE NEXT!
YOU KNOW WHY?
BECAUSE HIS SON IS A NEXT!
H-HOW DID YOU—

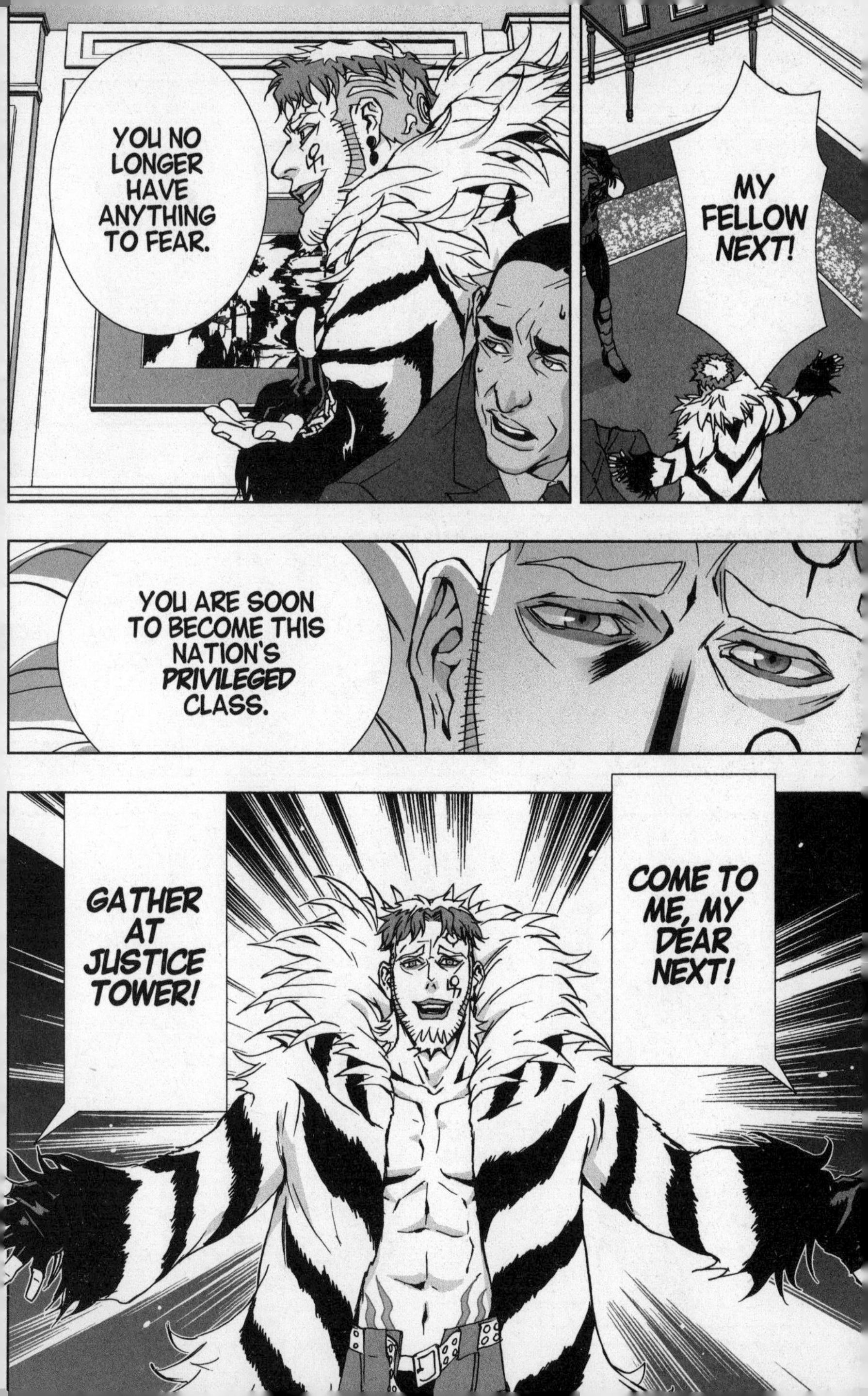
MY FELLOW NEXT!
YOU NO LONGER HAVE ANYTHING TO FEAR.
YOU ARE SOON TO BECOME THIS NATION'S PRIVILEGED CLASS.
COME TO ME, MY DEAR NEXT!
GATHER AT JUSTICE TOWER!

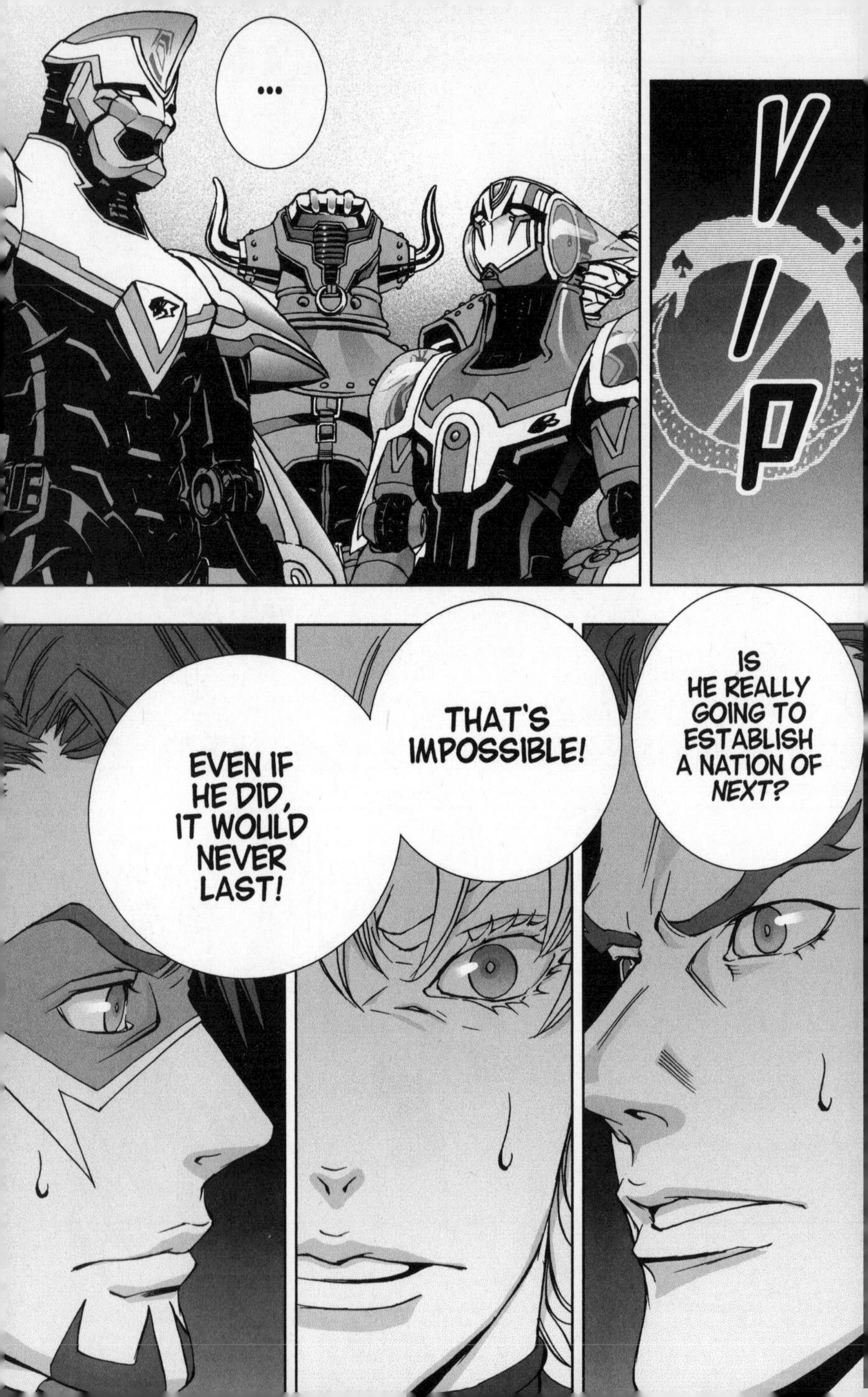
VIP
...
IS HE REALLY GOING TO ESTABLISH A NATION OF NEXT?
THAT'S IMPOSSIBLE!
EVEN IF HE DID, IT WOULD NEVER LAST!

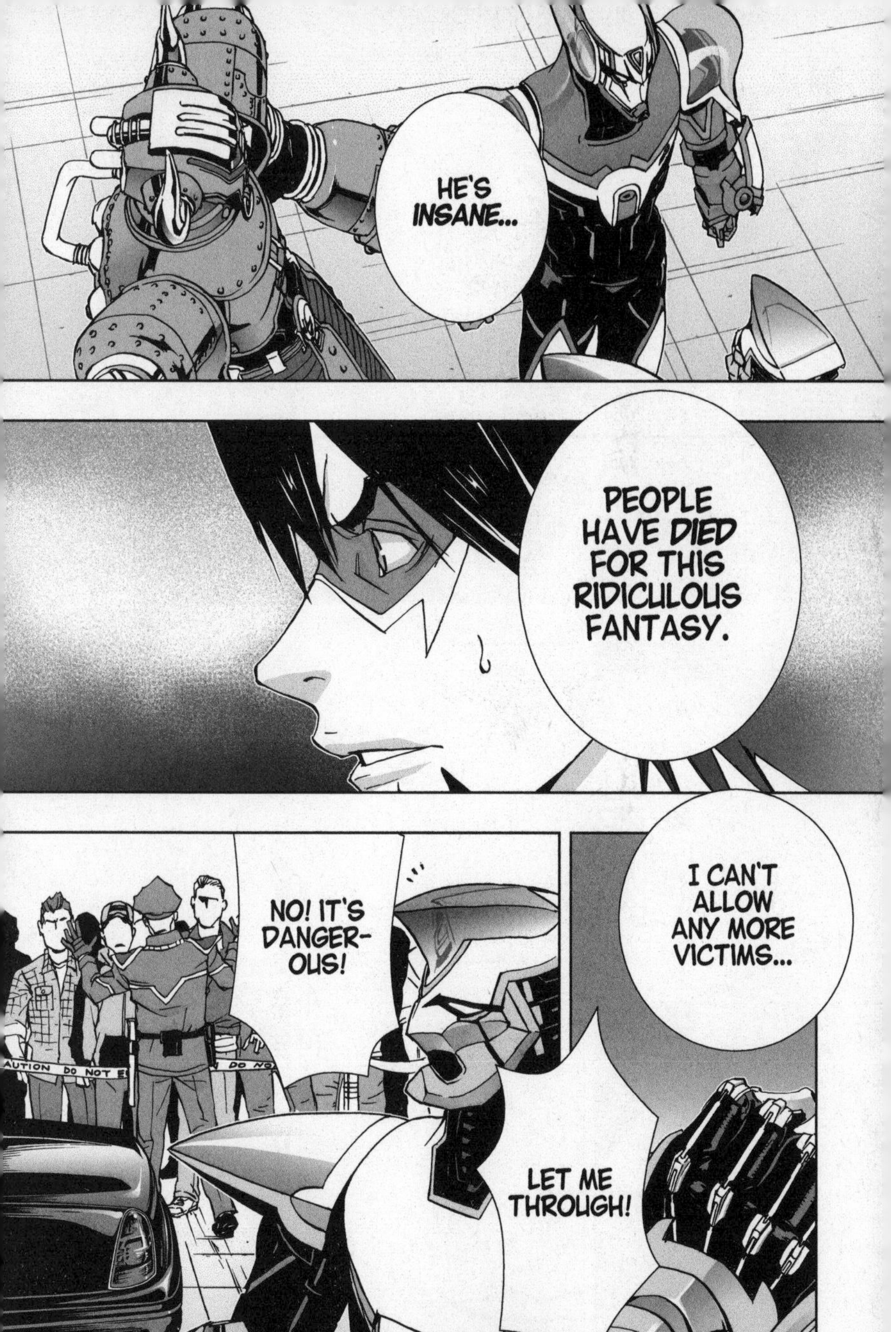
HE'S INSANE...
PEOPLE HAVE DIED FOR THIS RIDICULOUS FANTASY.
I CAN'T ALLOW ANY MORE VICTIMS...
NO! IT'S DANGER-OUS!
LET ME THROUGH!

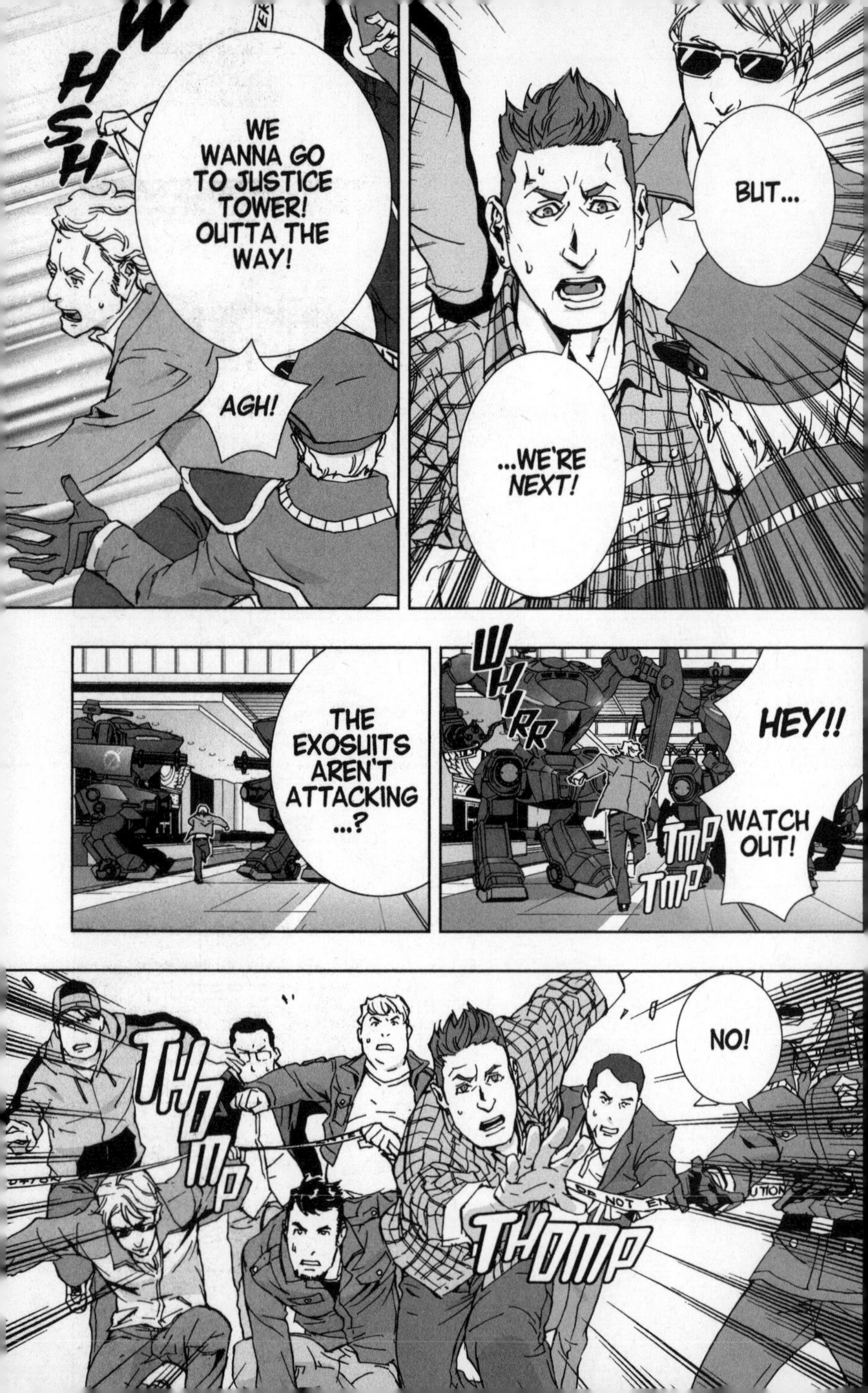
BUT...
...WE'RE NEXT!
WHSH
WE WANNA GO TO JUSTICE TOWER! OUTTA THE WAY!
AGH!
WHIRR
HEY!!
WATCH OUT!
TMP
TMP
THE EXOSUITS AREN'T ATTACKING ...?
NO!
THOMP
THOMP

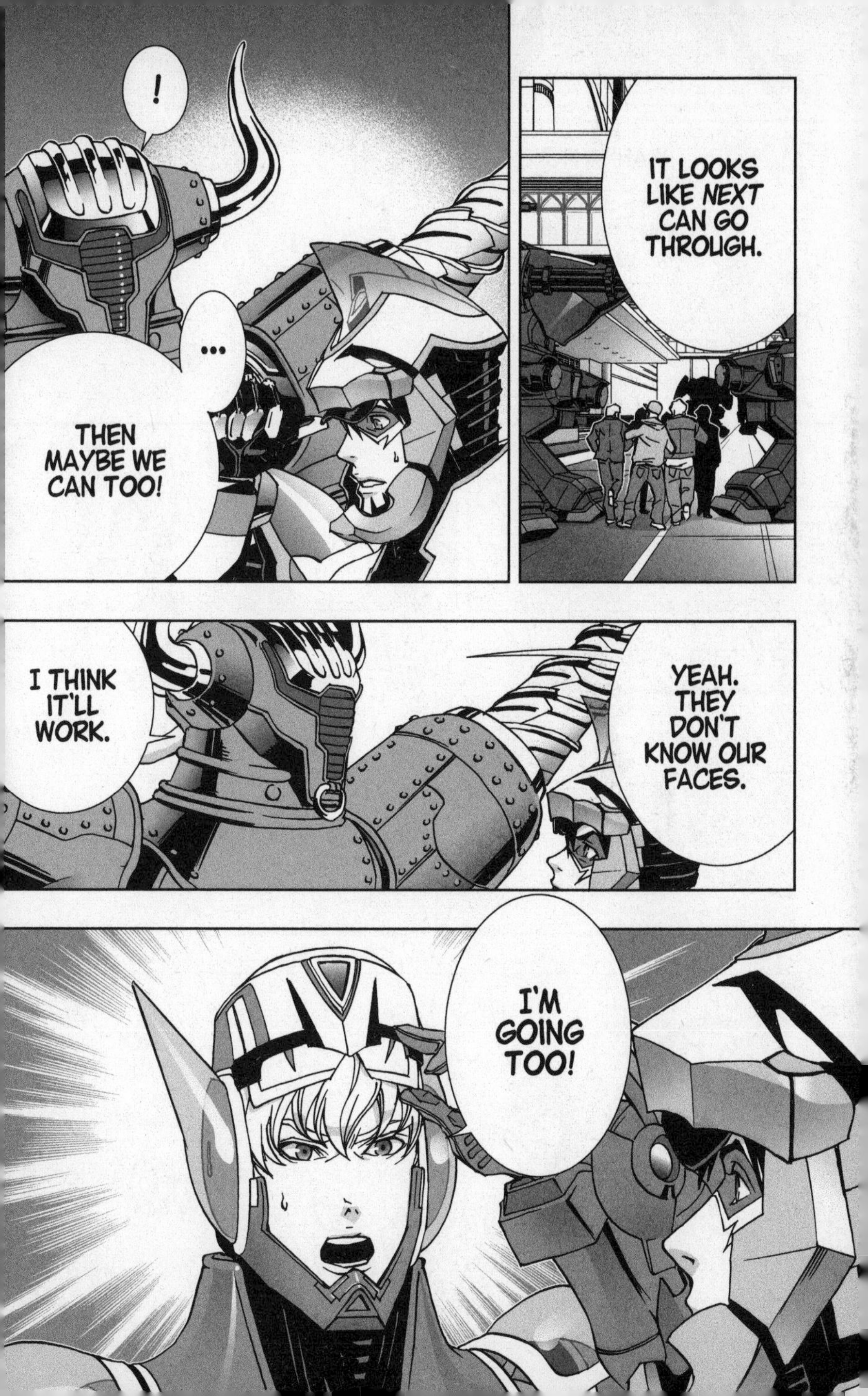
IT LOOKS LIKE NEXT CAN GO THROUGH.
!
...
THEN MAYBE WE CAN TOO!
YEAH. THEY DON'T KNOW OUR FACES.
I THINK IT'LL WORK.
I'M GOING TOO!

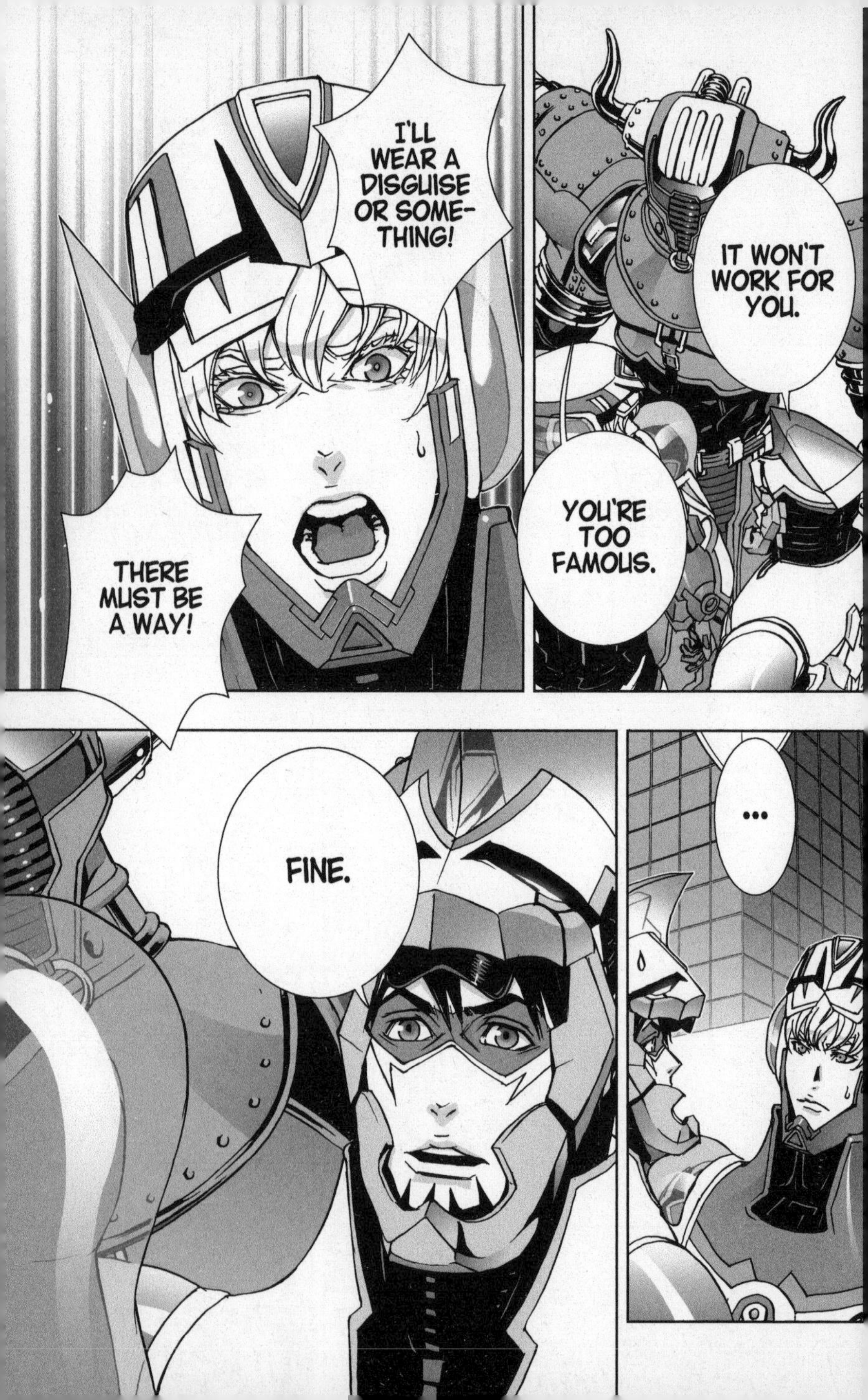
IT WON'T WORK FOR YOU.
YOU'RE TOO FAMOUS.
I'LL WEAR A DISGUISE OR SOME-THING!
THERE MUST BE A WAY!
...
FINE.

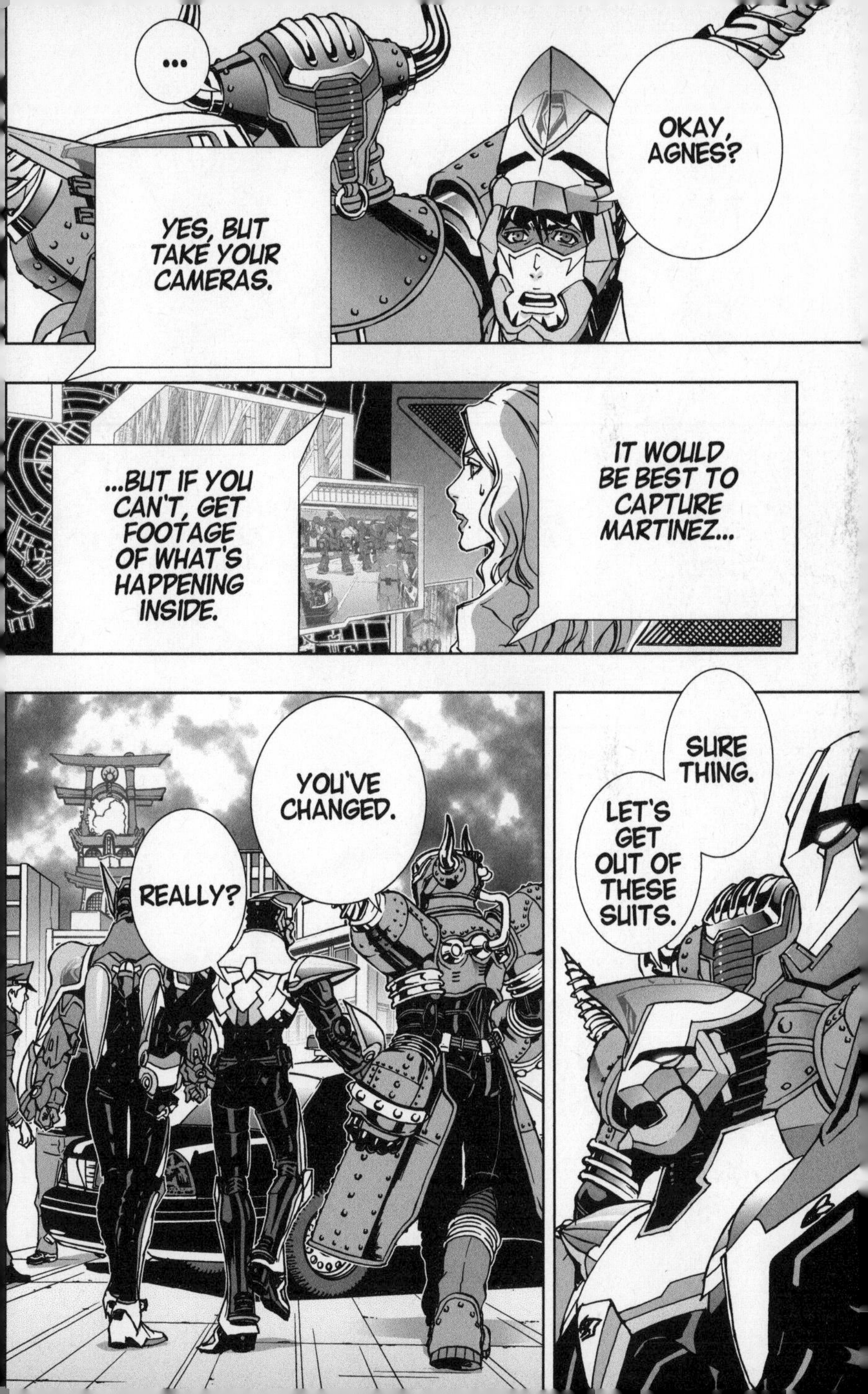
OKAY, AGNES?
...
YES, BUT TAKE YOUR CAMERAS.
IT WOULD BE BEST TO CAPTURE MARTINEZ...
...BUT IF YOU CAN'T, GET FOOTAGE OF WHAT'S HAPPENING INSIDE.
SURE THING.
LET'S GET OUT OF THESE SUITS.
YOU'VE CHANGED.
REALLY?

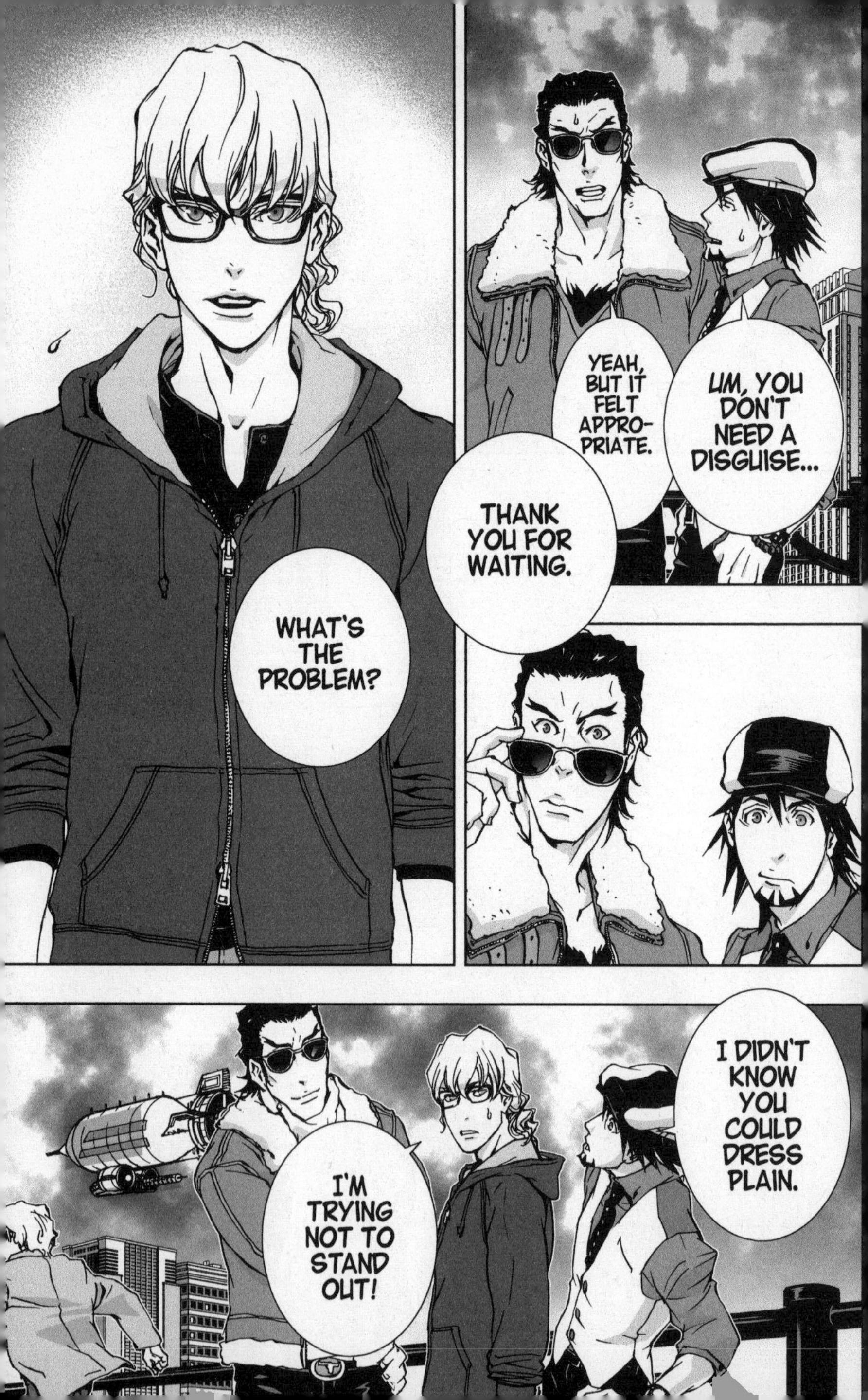
UM, YOU DON'T NEED A DISGUISE...
YEAH, BUT IT FELT APPRO-PRIATE.
THANK YOU FOR WAITING.
WHAT'S THE PROBLEM?
I DIDN'T KNOW YOU COULD DRESS PLAIN.
I'M TRYING NOT TO STAND OUT!

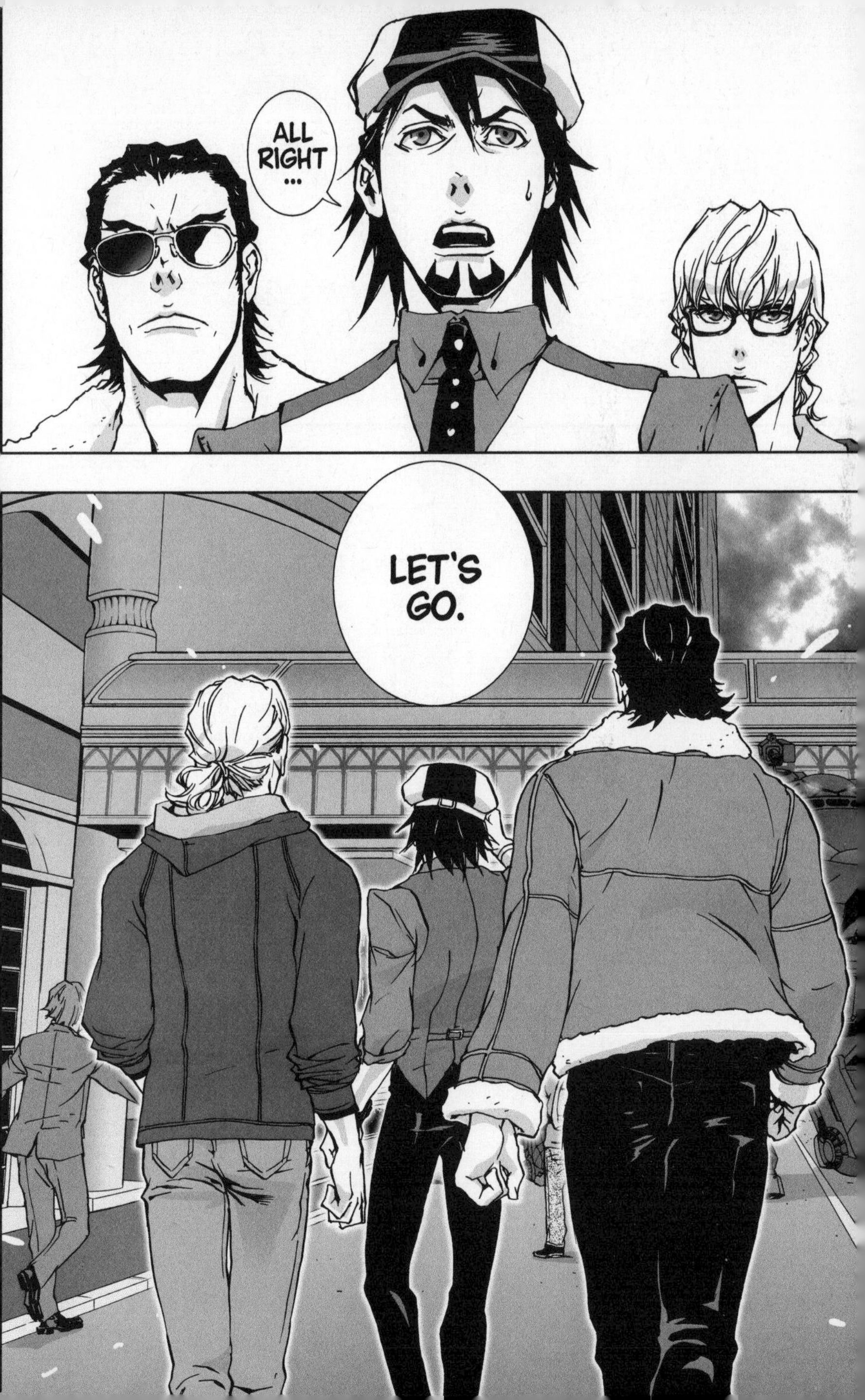
ALL RIGHT ...
LET'S GO.

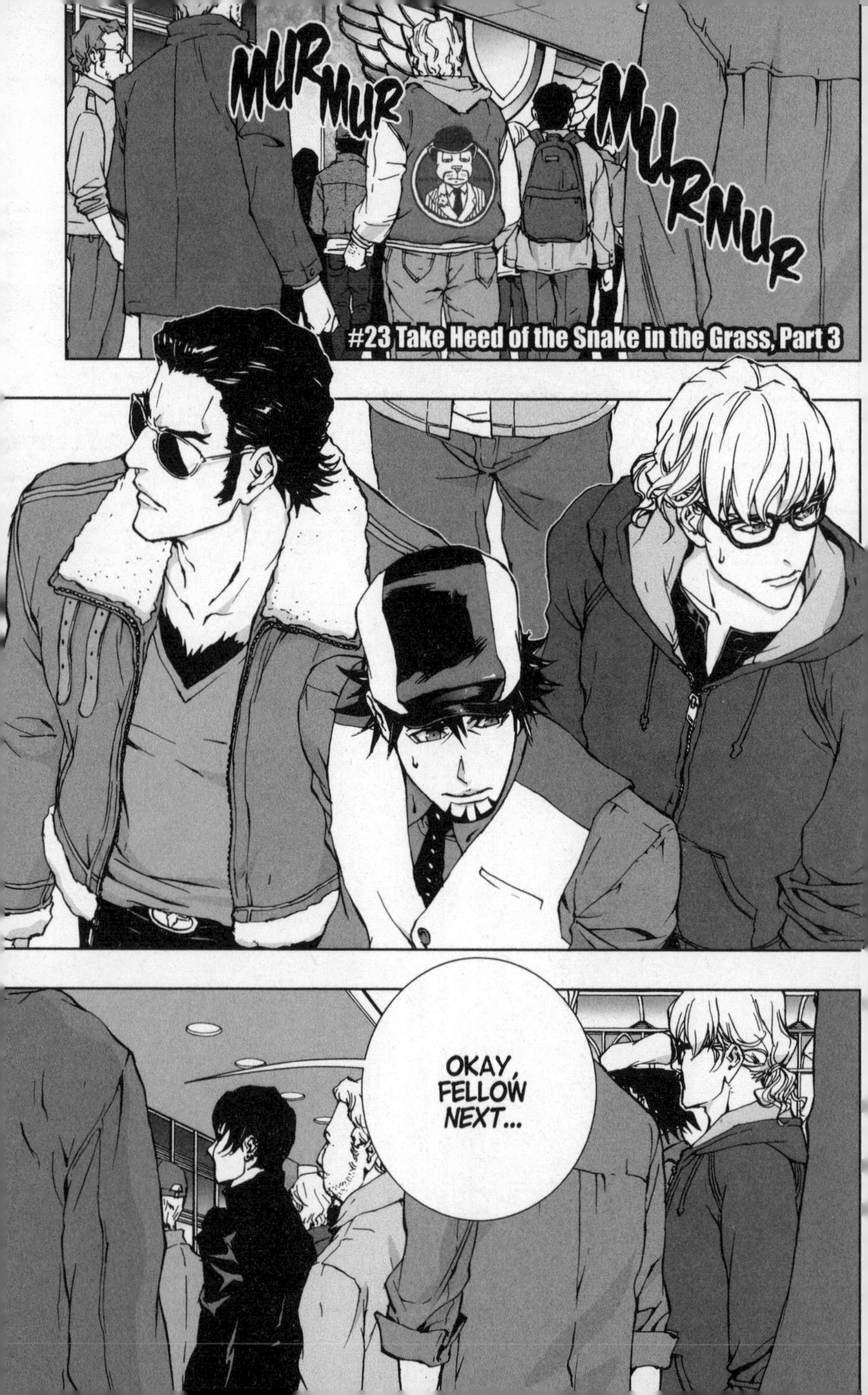
MURMUR
MURMUR
#23 Take Heed of the Snake in the Grass, Part 3
OKAY, FELLOW NEXT...

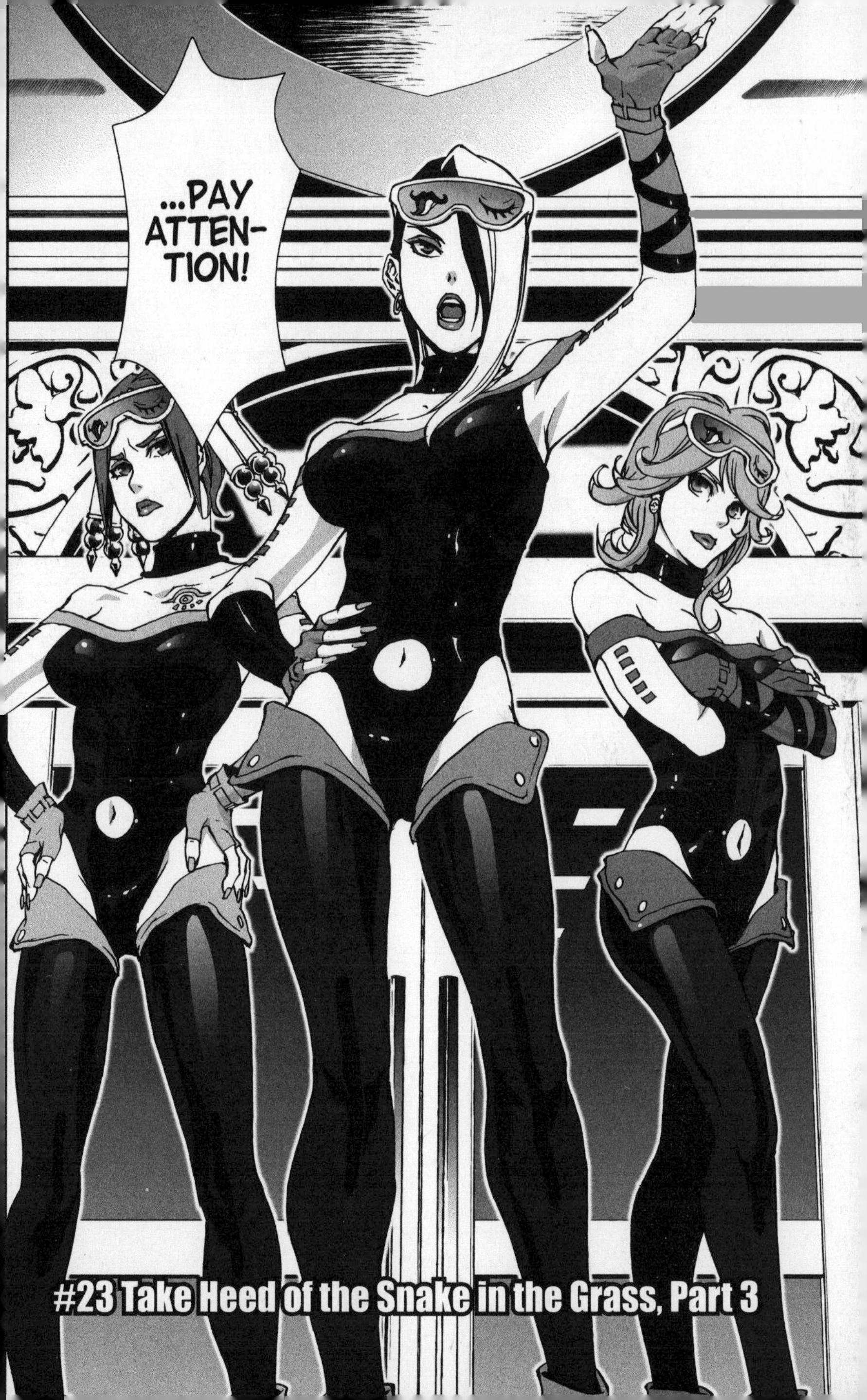
...PAY ATTEN- TION!

## #23 Take Heed of the Snake in the Grass, Part 3

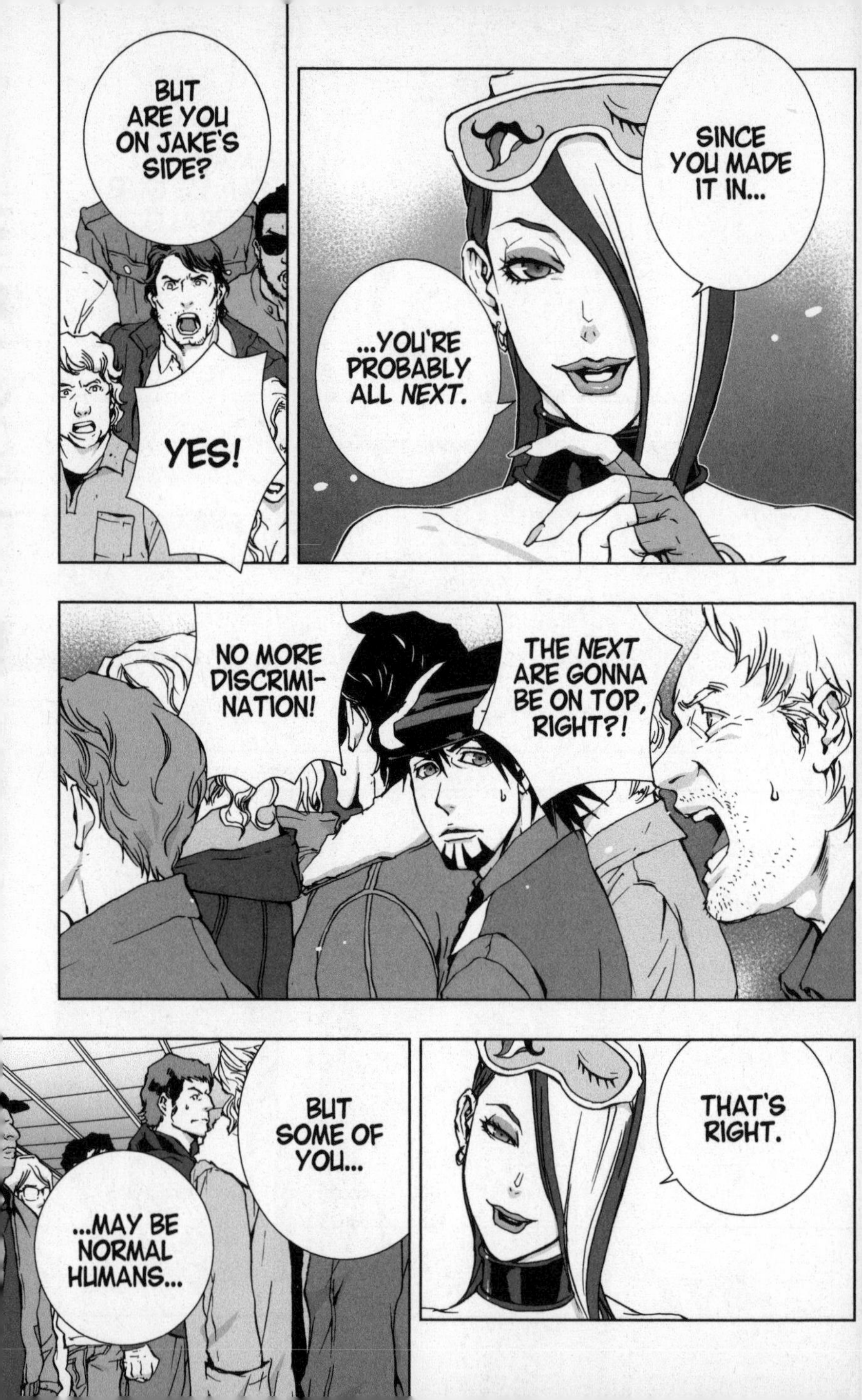
SINCE YOU MADE IT IN...
...YOU'RE PROBABLY ALL NEXT.
BUT ARE YOU ON JAKE'S SIDE?
YES!
THE NEXT ARE GONNA BE ON TOP, RIGHT?!
NO MORE DISCRIMINATION!
THAT'S RIGHT.
BUT SOME OF YOU...
...MAY BE NORMAL HUMANS...

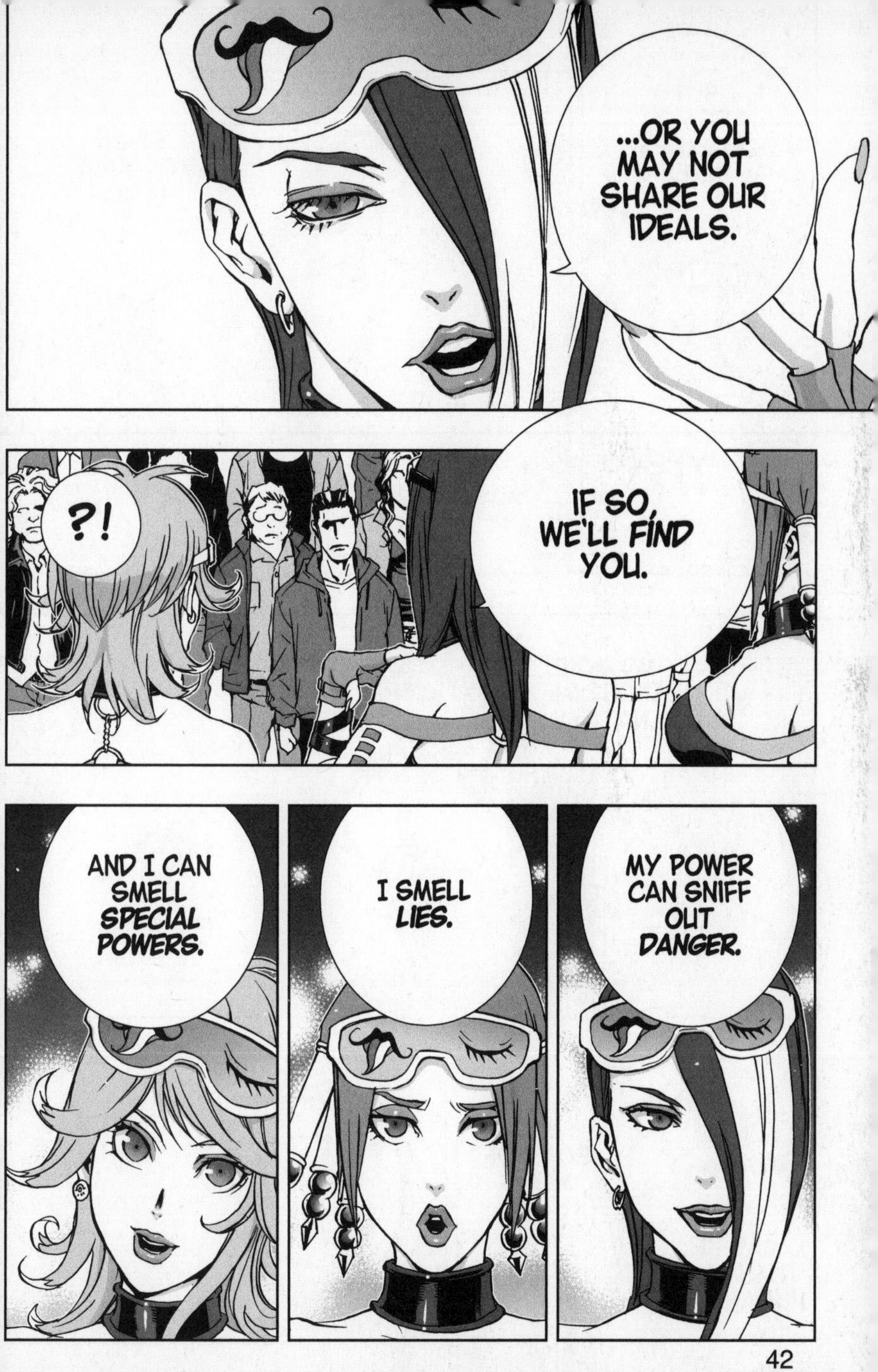
...OR YOU MAY NOT SHARE OUR IDEALS.
IF SO, WE'LL FIND YOU.
?!
MY POWER CAN SNIFF OUT DANGER.
I SMELL LIES.
AND I CAN SMELL SPECIAL POWERS.

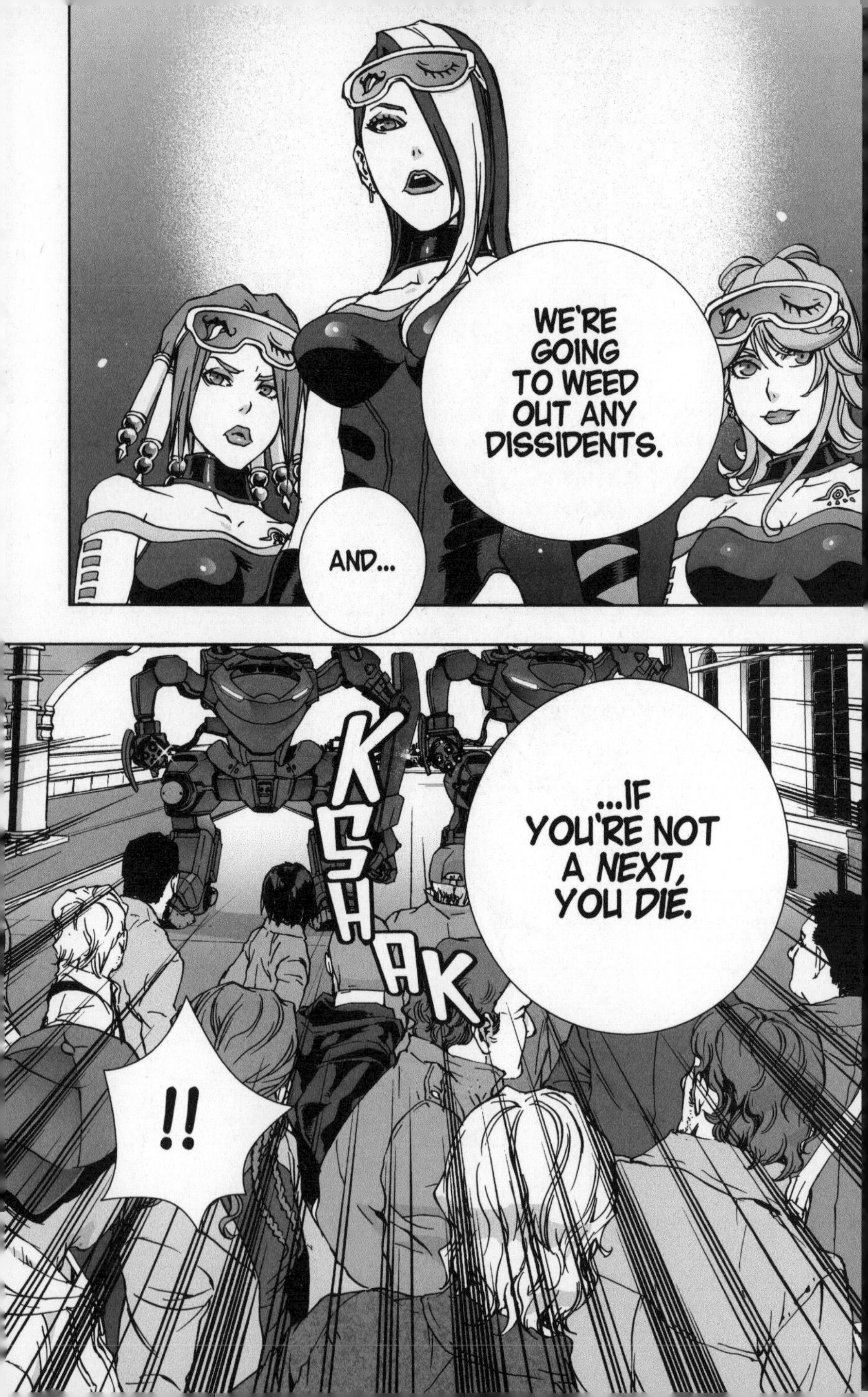
WE'RE GOING TO WEED OUT ANY DISSIDENTS.
AND...
...IF YOU'RE NOT A *NEXT*, YOU DIE.
KSHAK
!!

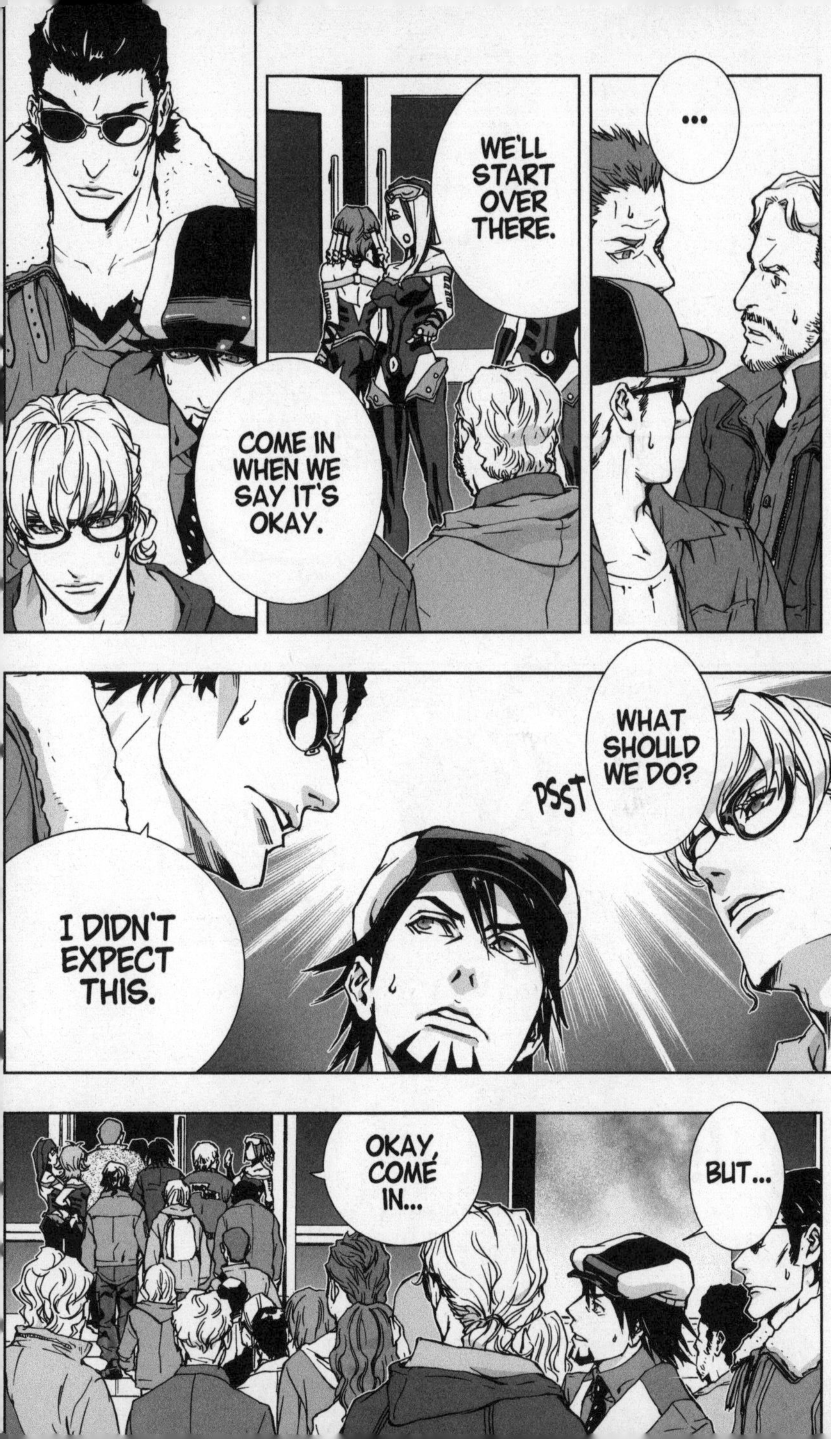
...
WE'LL START OVER THERE.
COME IN WHEN WE SAY IT'S OKAY.
WHAT SHOULD WE DO?
PSST
I DIDN'T EXPECT THIS.
OKAY, COME IN...
BUT...

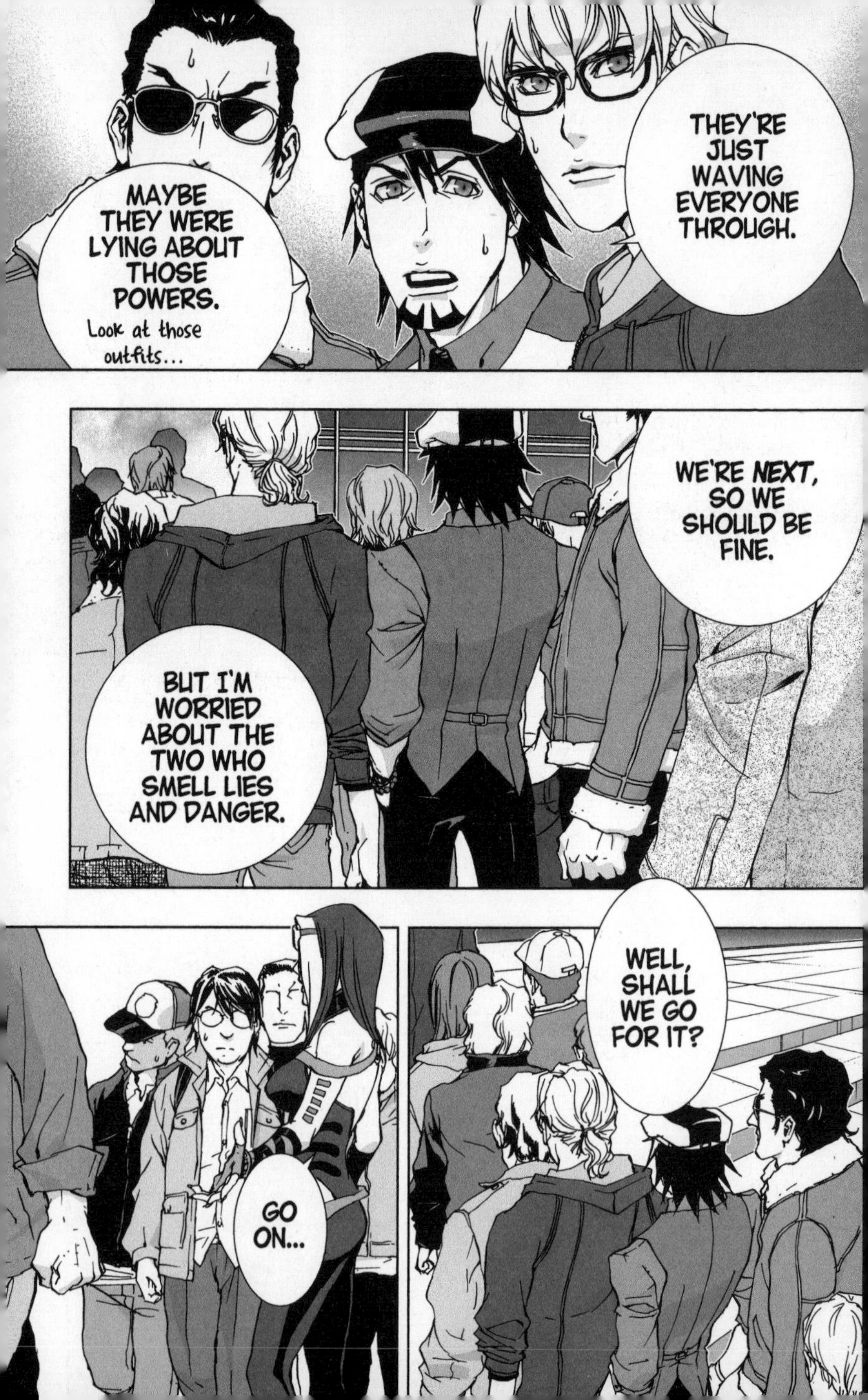
THEY'RE JUST WAVING EVERYONE THROUGH.
MAYBE THEY WERE LYING ABOUT THOSE POWERS.
Look at those outfits...
WE'RE *NEXT*, SO WE SHOULD BE FINE.
BUT I'M WORRIED ABOUT THE TWO WHO SMELL LIES AND DANGER.
WELL, SHALL WE GO FOR IT?
GO ON...

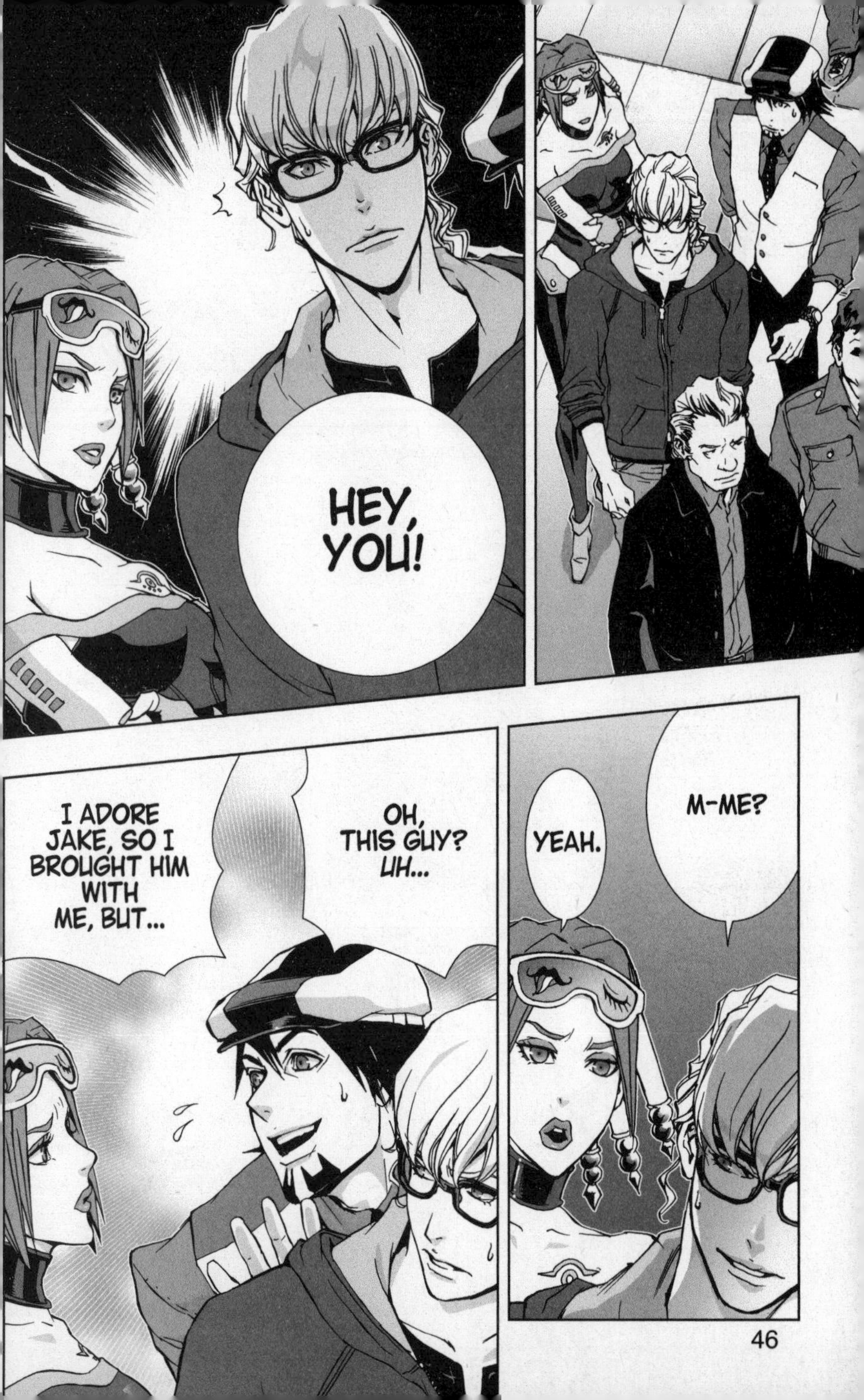
HEY, YOU!
M-ME?
YEAH.
OH, THIS GUY? UH...
I ADORE JAKE, SO I BROUGHT HIM WITH ME, BUT...

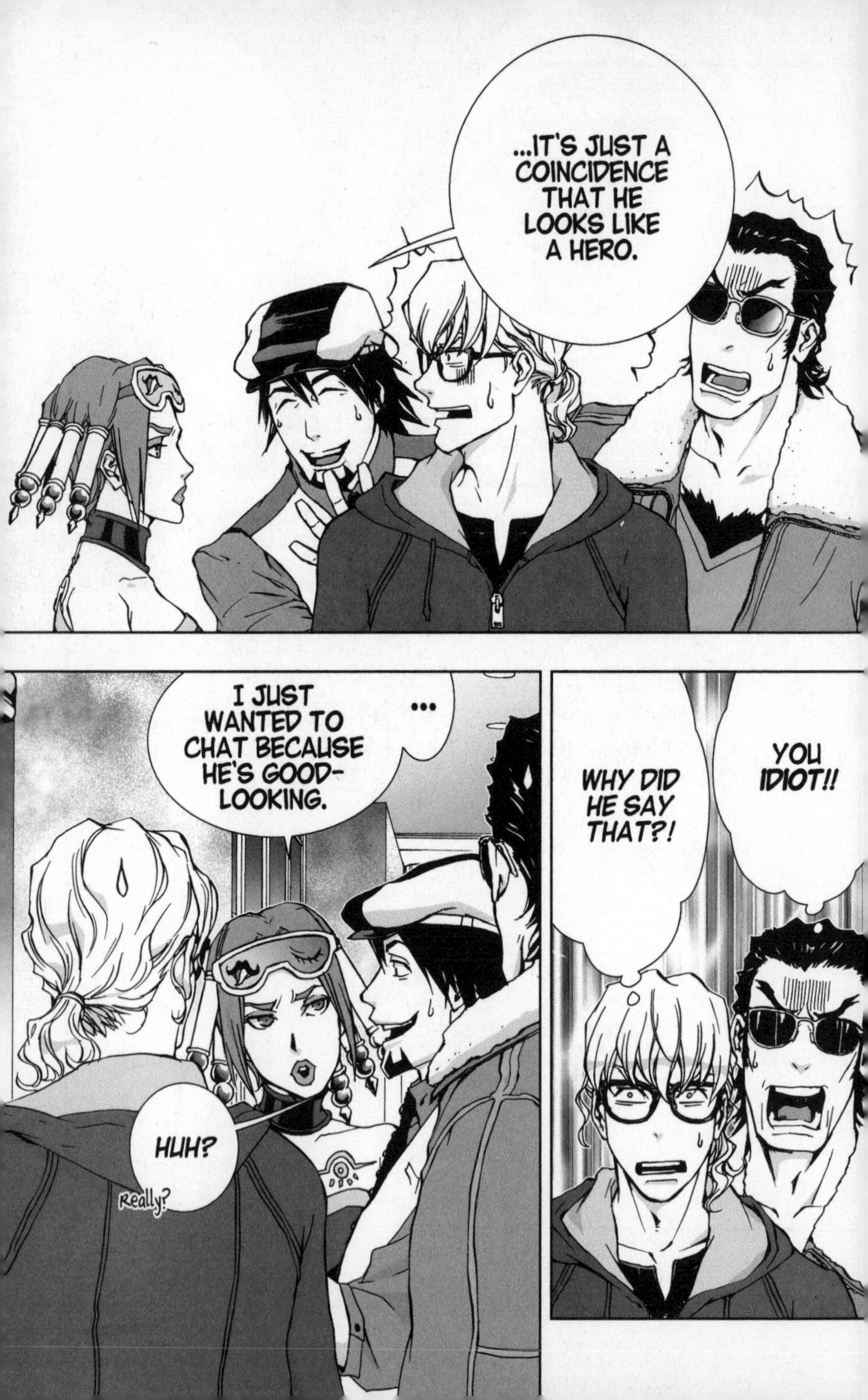
...IT'S JUST A COINCIDENCE THAT HE LOOKS LIKE A HERO.
YOU IDIOT!!
WHY DID HE SAY THAT?!
...
I JUST WANTED TO CHAT BECAUSE HE'S GOOD-LOOKING.
HUH?
Really?

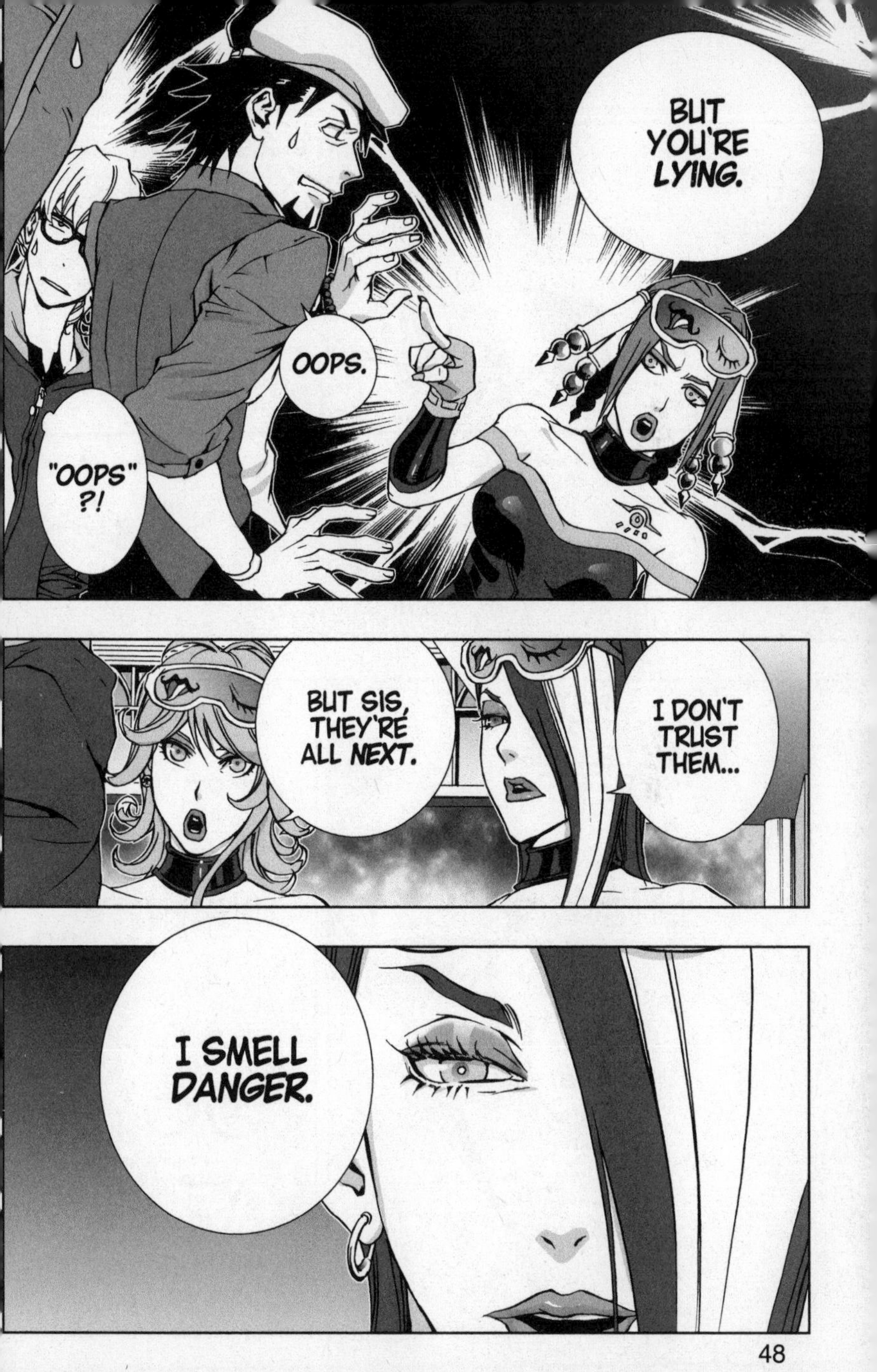
BUT YOU'RE LYING.
OOPS.
"OOPS" ?!
I DON'T TRUST THEM...
BUT SIS, THEY'RE ALL NEXT.
I SMELL DANGER.

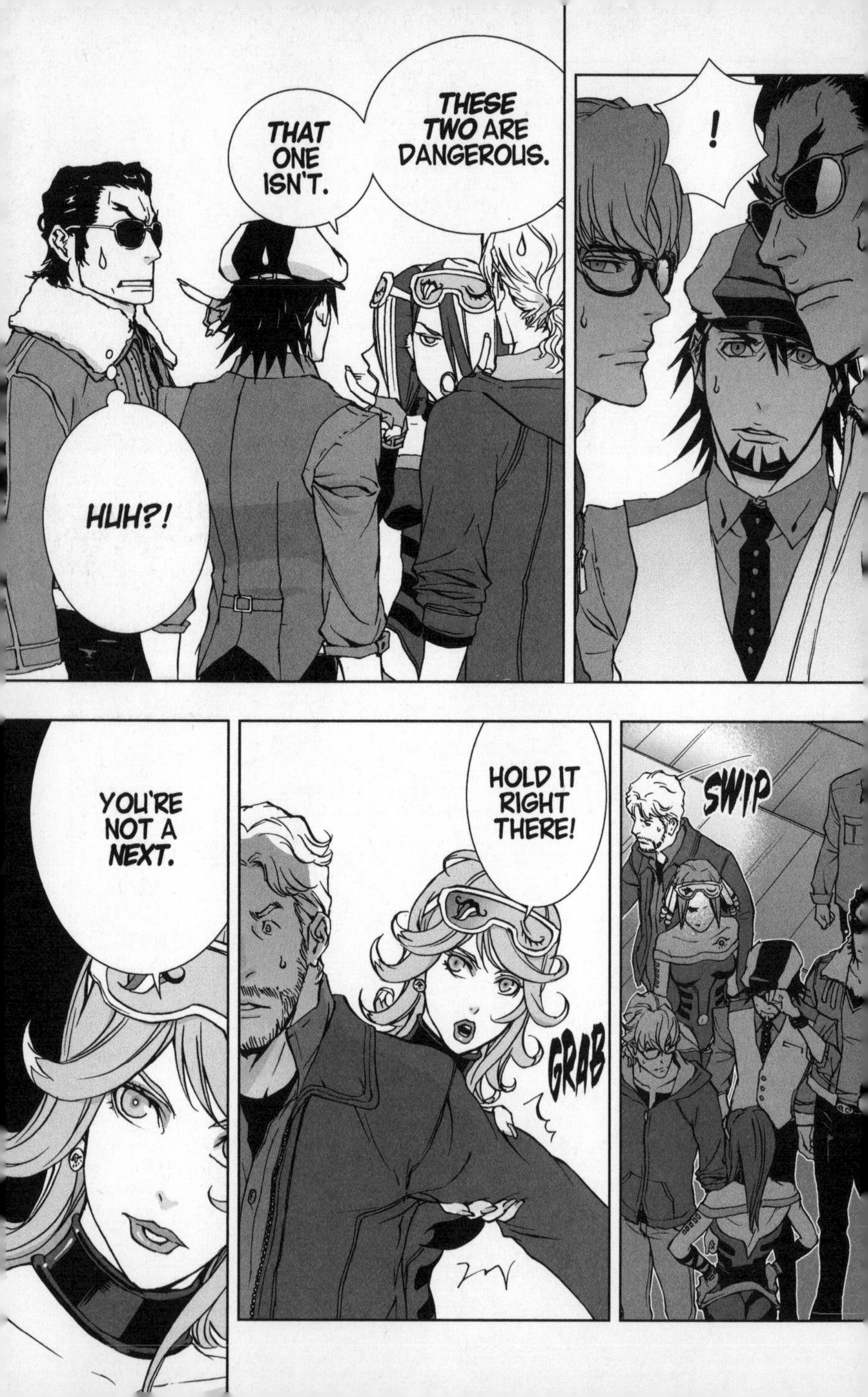
!
THESE TWO ARE DANGEROUS.
THAT ONE ISN'T.
HUH?!
SWIP
HOLD IT RIGHT THERE!
GRAB
YOU'RE NOT A NEXT.

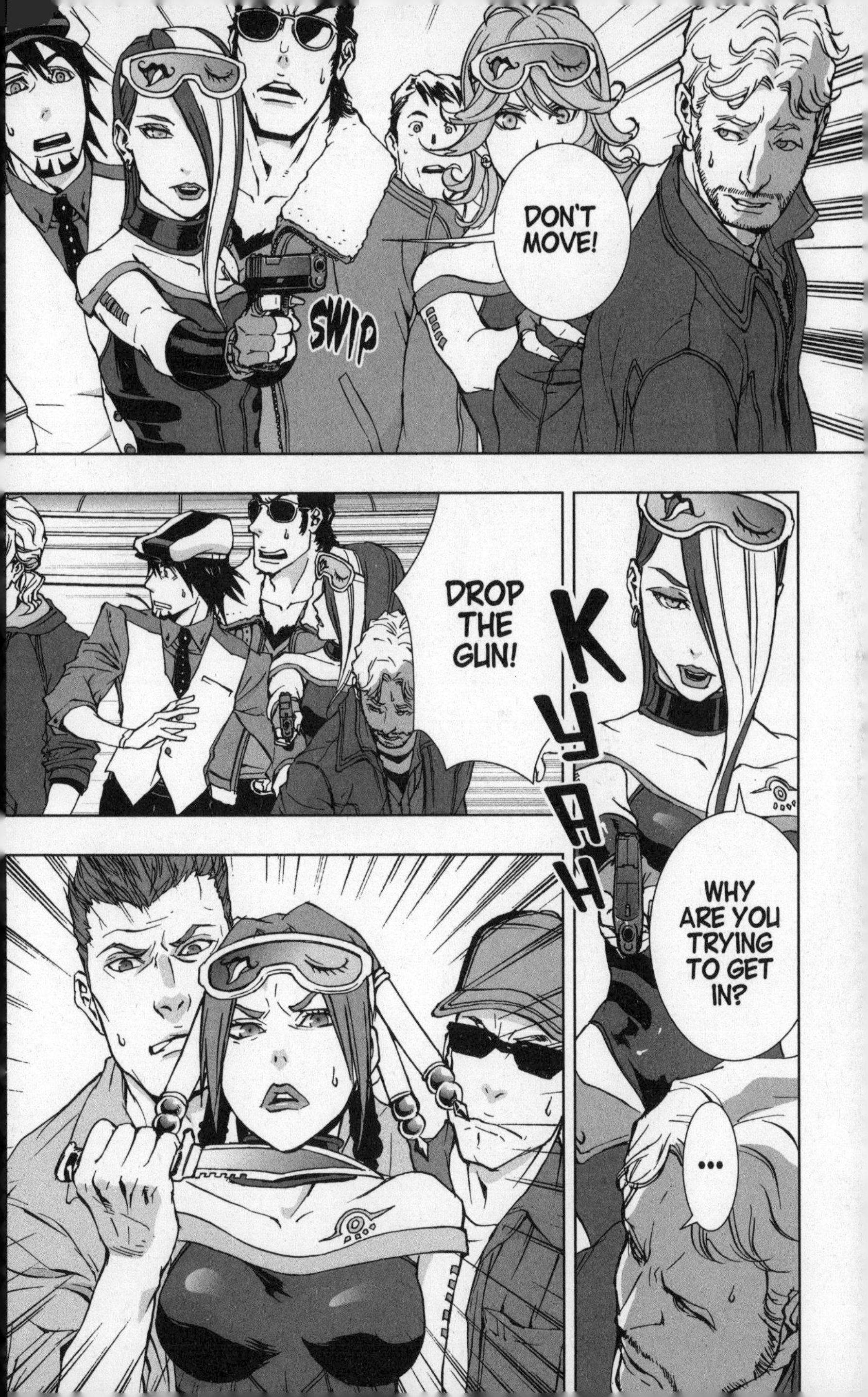
DON'T MOVE!
SWIP
KYAAH
WHY ARE YOU TRYING TO GET IN?
...
DROP THE GUN!

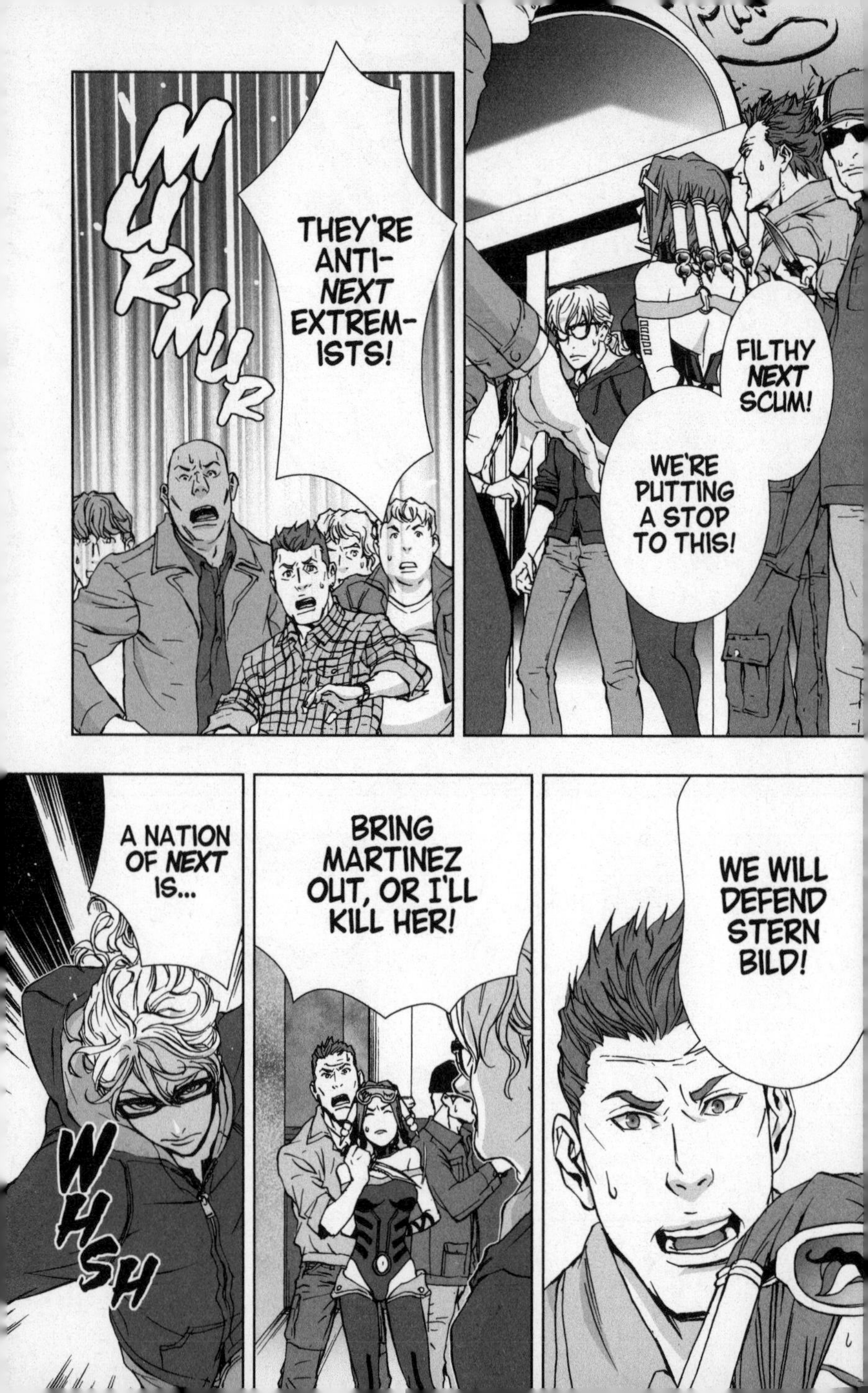
FILTHY NEXT SCUM!
WE'RE PUTTING A STOP TO THIS!
THEY'RE ANTI-NEXT EXTREMISTS!
MURMUR
WE WILL DEFEND STERN BILD!
BRING MARTINEZ OUT, OR I'LL KILL HER!
A NATION OF NEXT IS...
WHSH

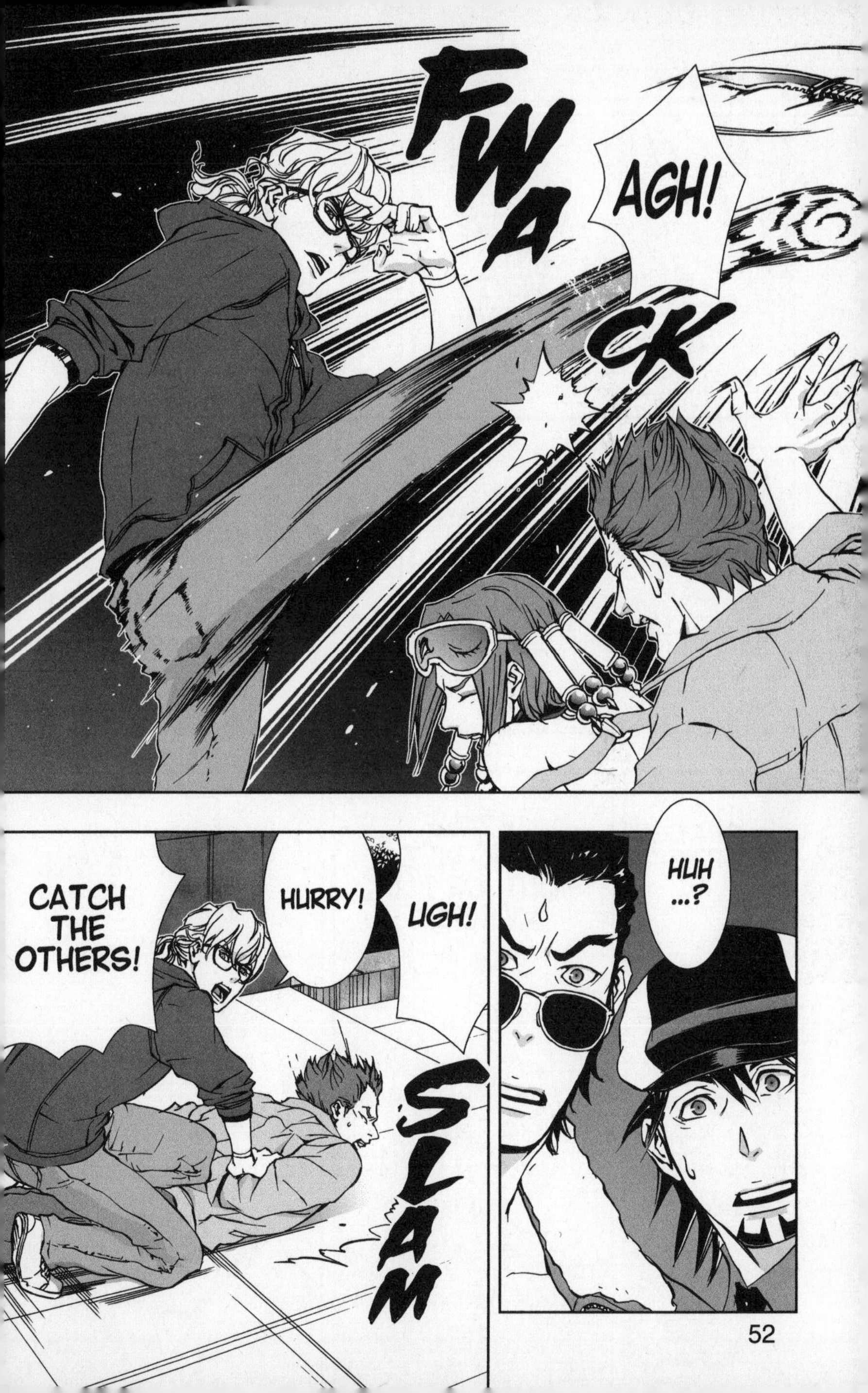
AGH!
FWACK
HUH ...?
UGH!
HURRY!
CATCH THE OTHERS!
SLAM

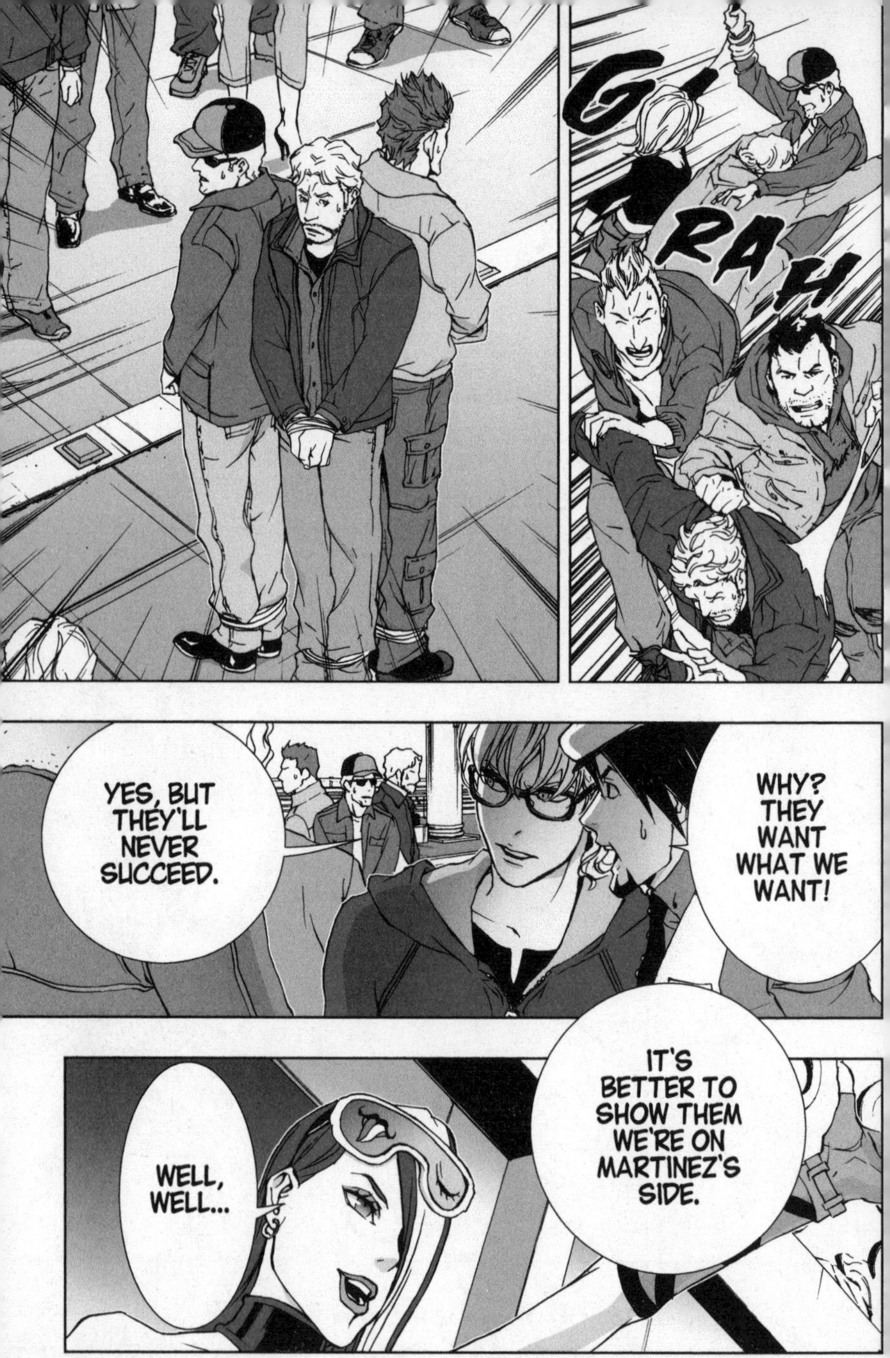
GRAH
WHY? THEY WANT WHAT WE WANT!
YES, BUT THEY'LL NEVER SUCCEED.
IT'S BETTER TO SHOW THEM WE'RE ON MARTINEZ'S SIDE.
WELL, WELL...

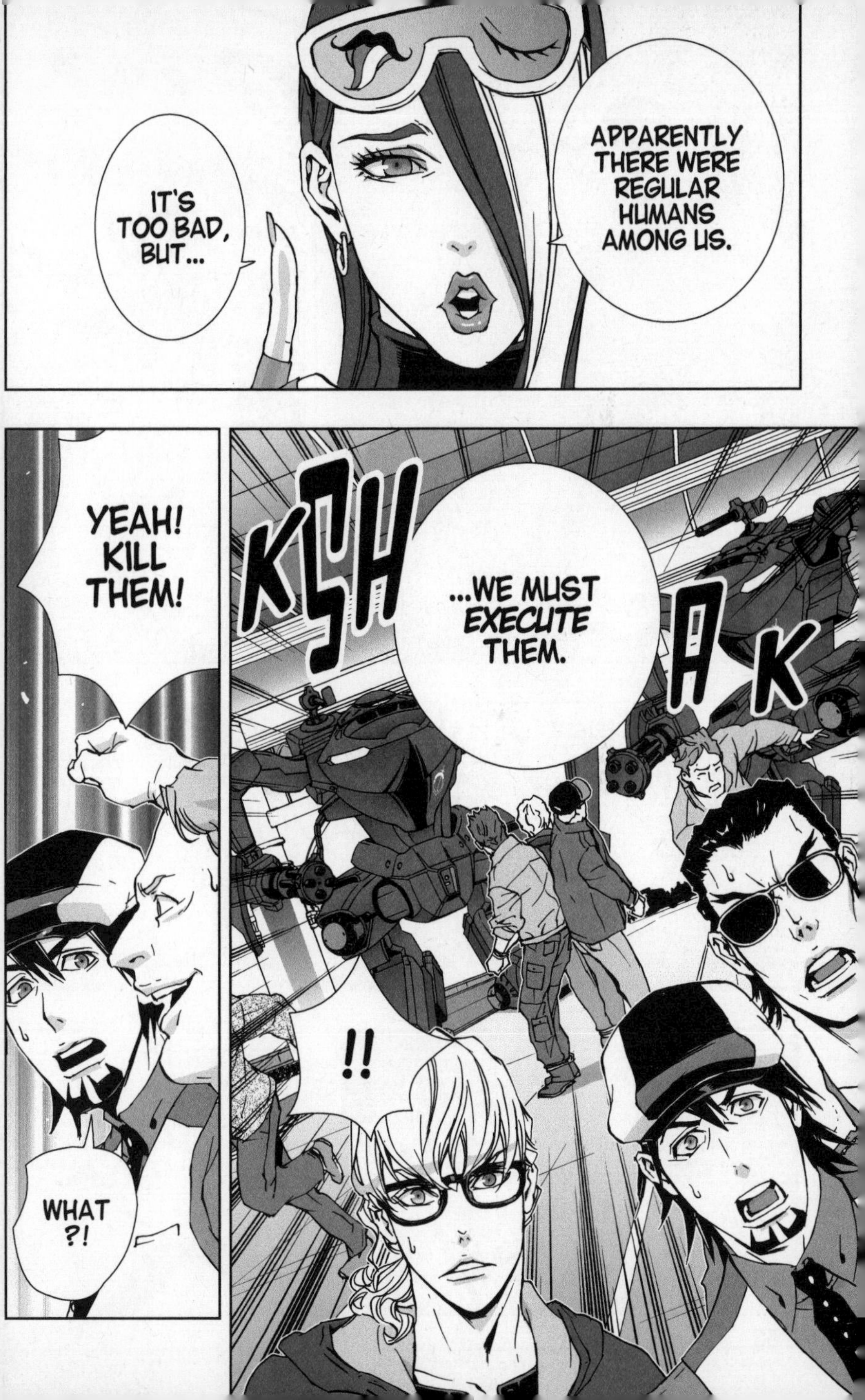
APPARENTLY THERE WERE REGULAR HUMANS AMONG US.
IT'S TOO BAD, BUT...
KSH
...WE MUST *EXECUTE* THEM.
AK
!!
YEAH! KILL THEM!
WHAT?!

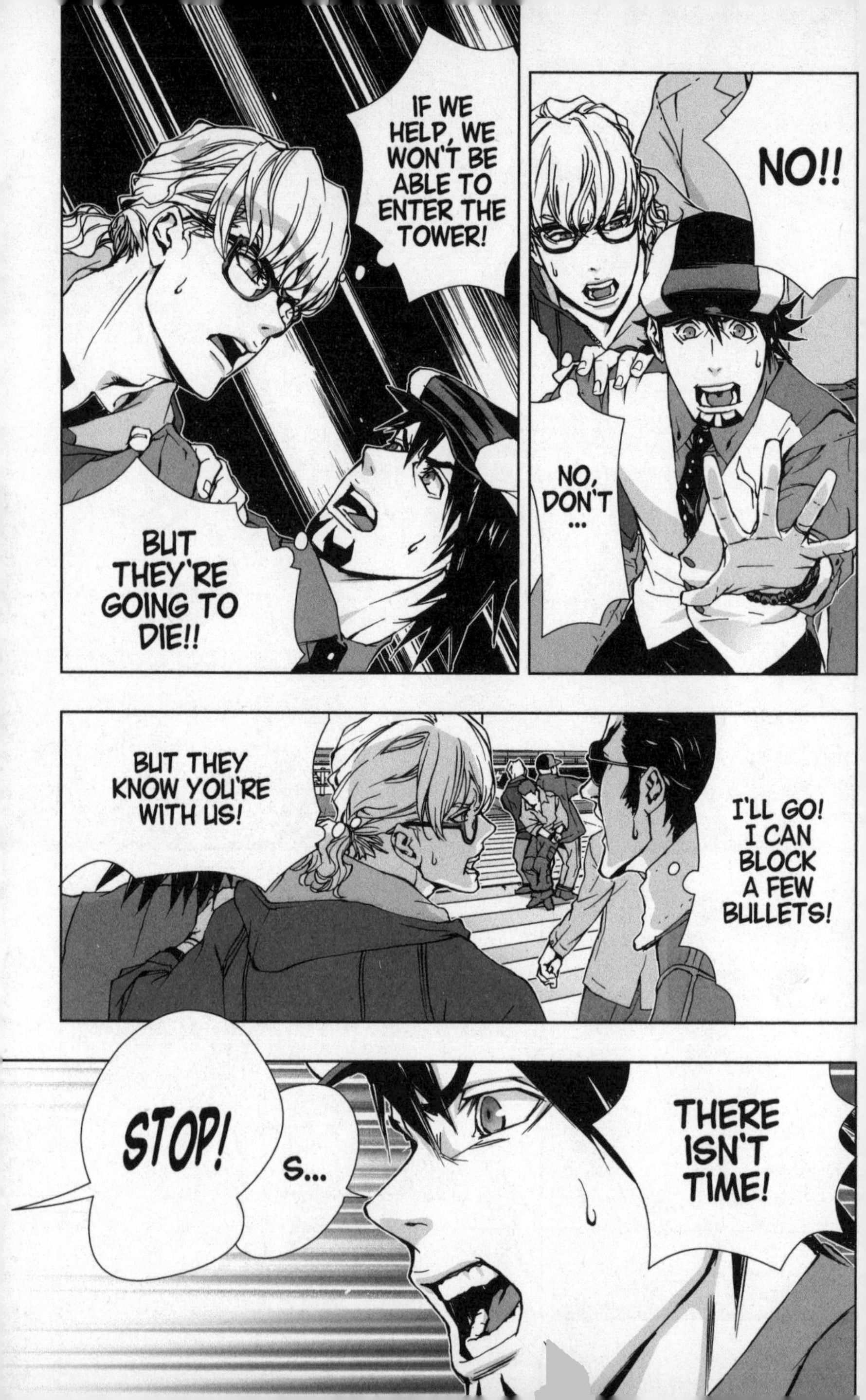
NO!!
NO, DON'T ...
IF WE HELP, WE WON'T BE ABLE TO ENTER THE TOWER!
BUT THEY'RE GOING TO DIE!!
I'LL GO! I CAN BLOCK A FEW BULLETS!
BUT THEY KNOW YOU'RE WITH US!
THERE ISN'T TIME!
S...
STOP!

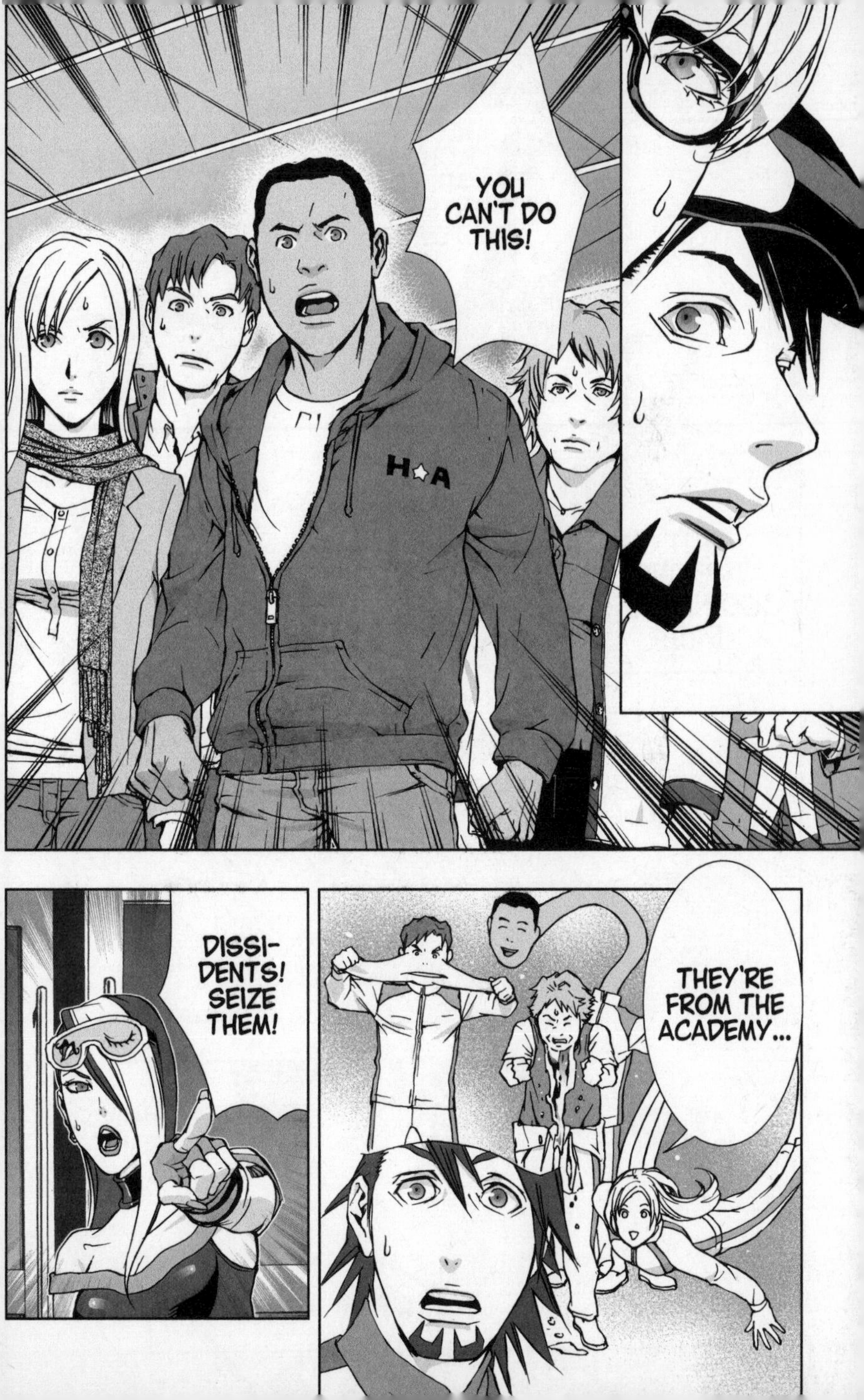
YOU CAN'T DO THIS!
THEY'RE FROM THE ACADEMY...
DISSI-DENTS! SEIZE THEM!

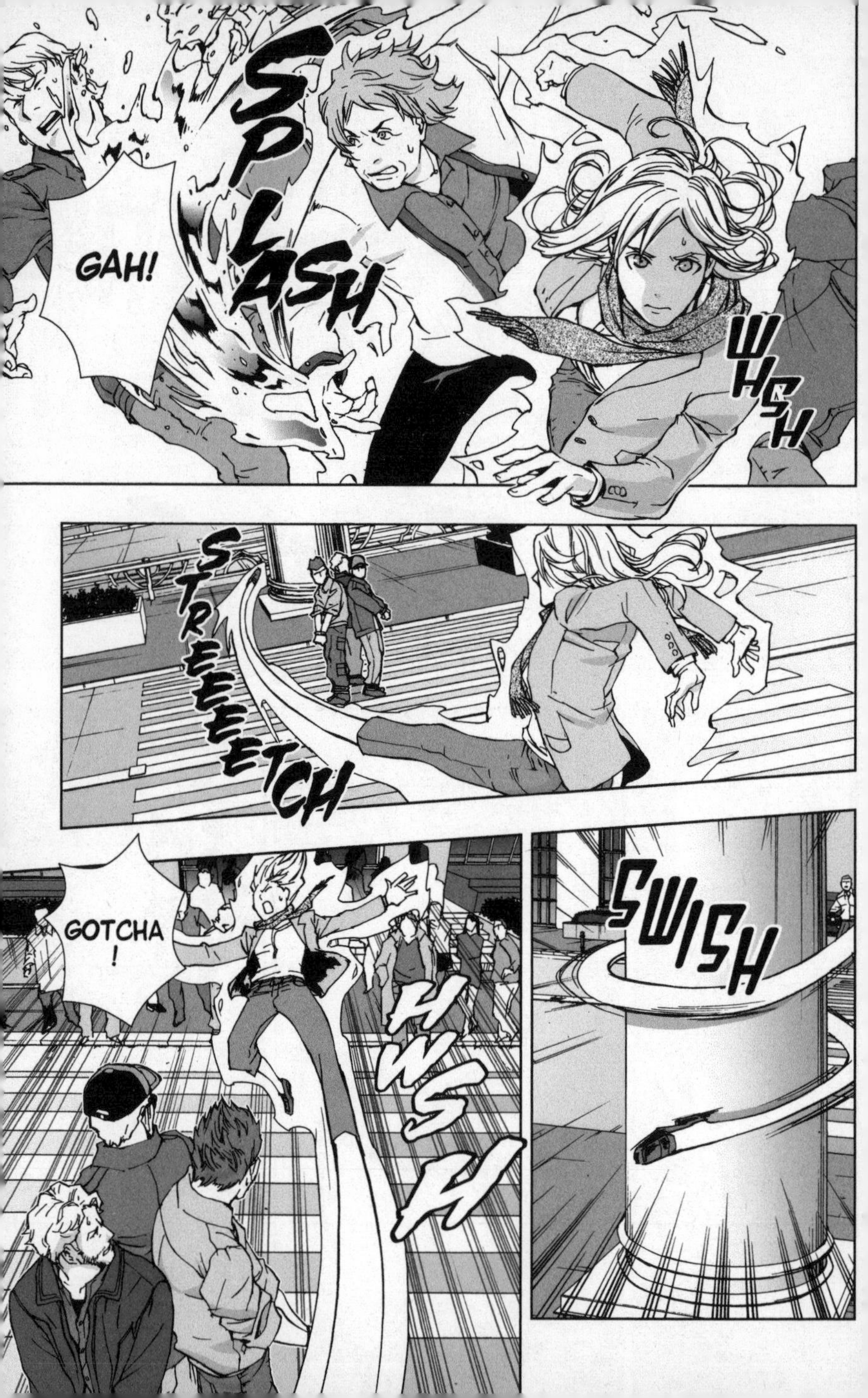
WHSH
SPLASH
GAH!
STREEEEETCH
SWISH
HWSH
GOTCHA!

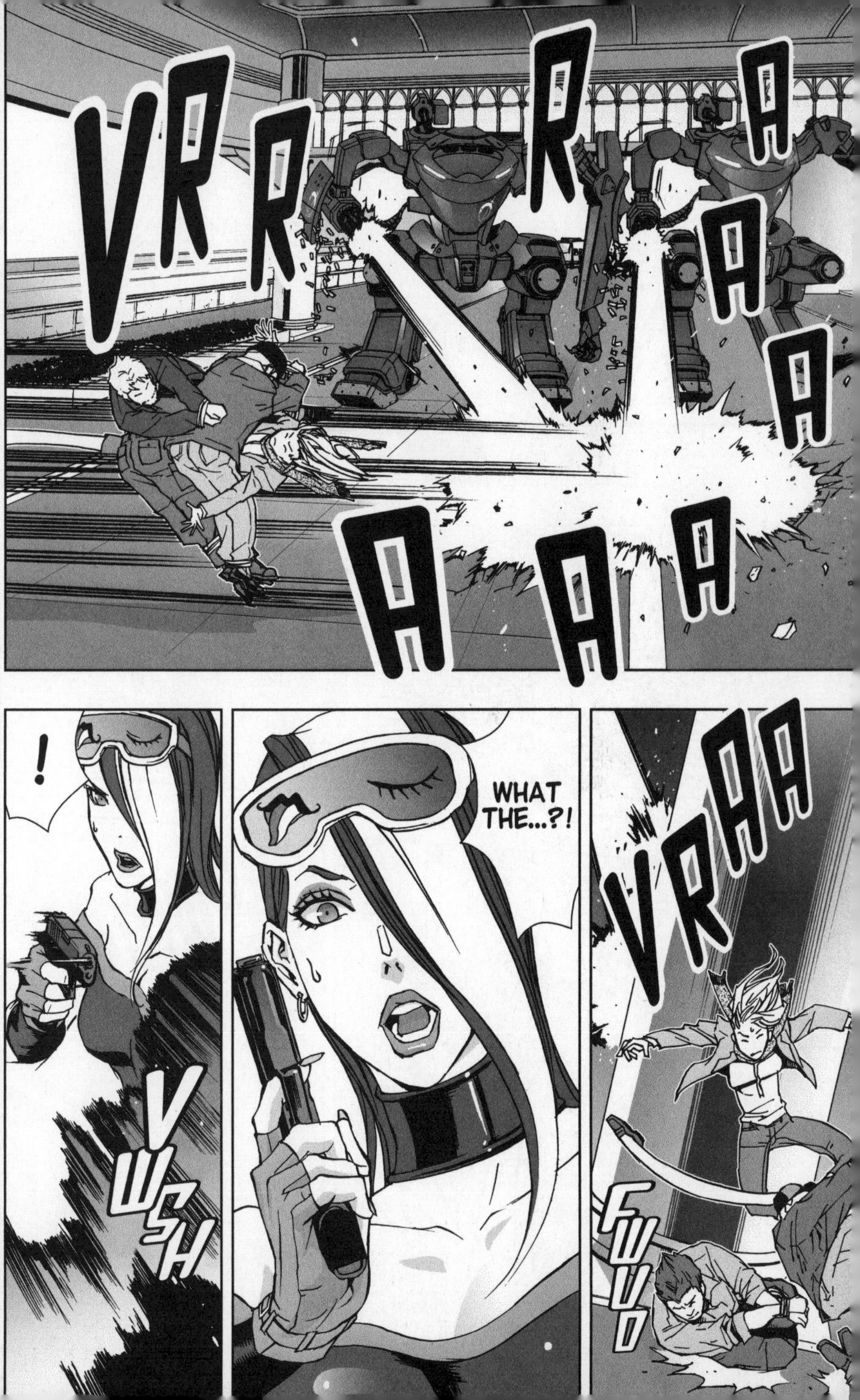
VRRRAAAAAA
VRAA
FWUD
WHAT THE...?!
!
VWSH

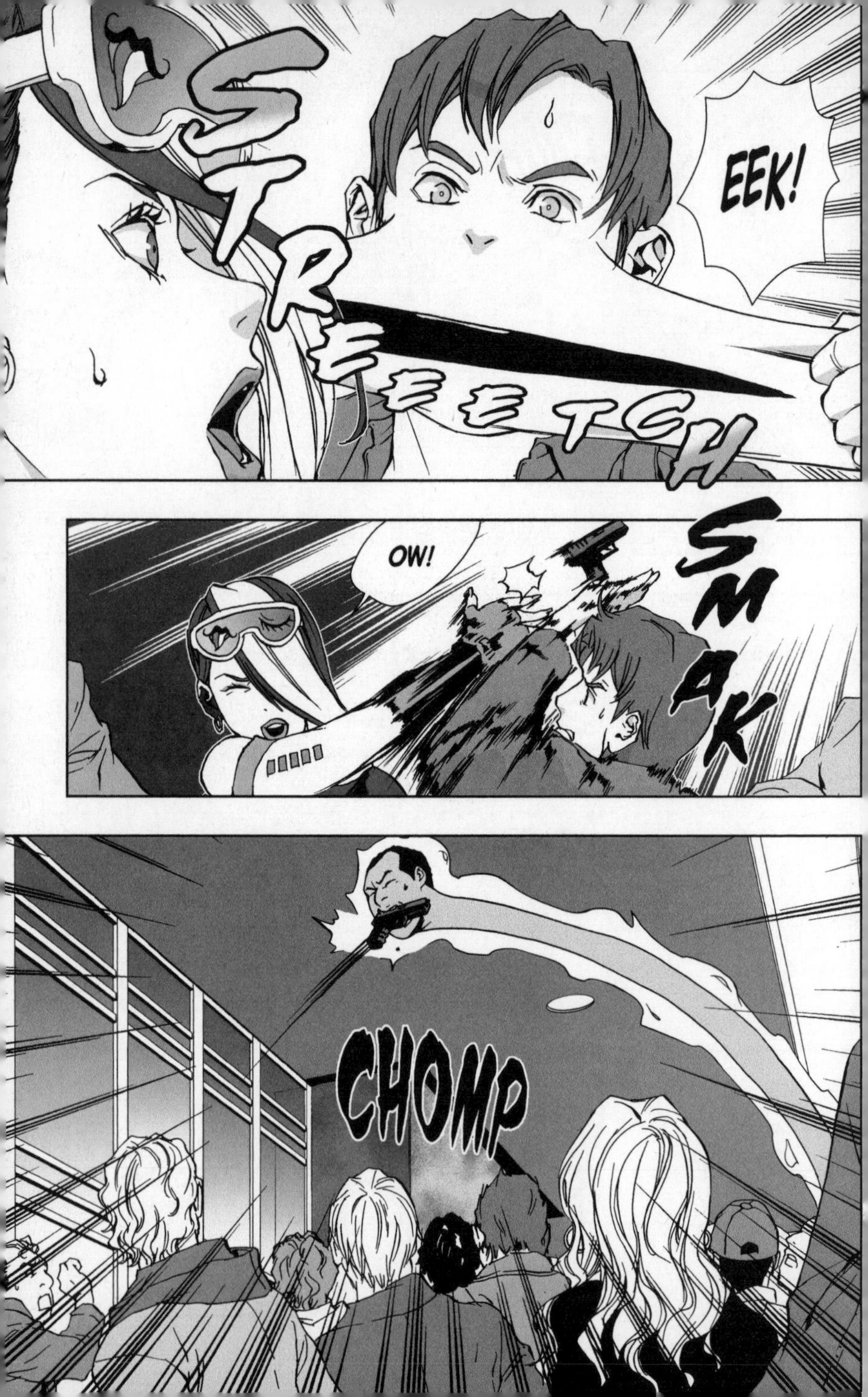
EEK!
STREEETCH
SMAK
OW!
CHOMP

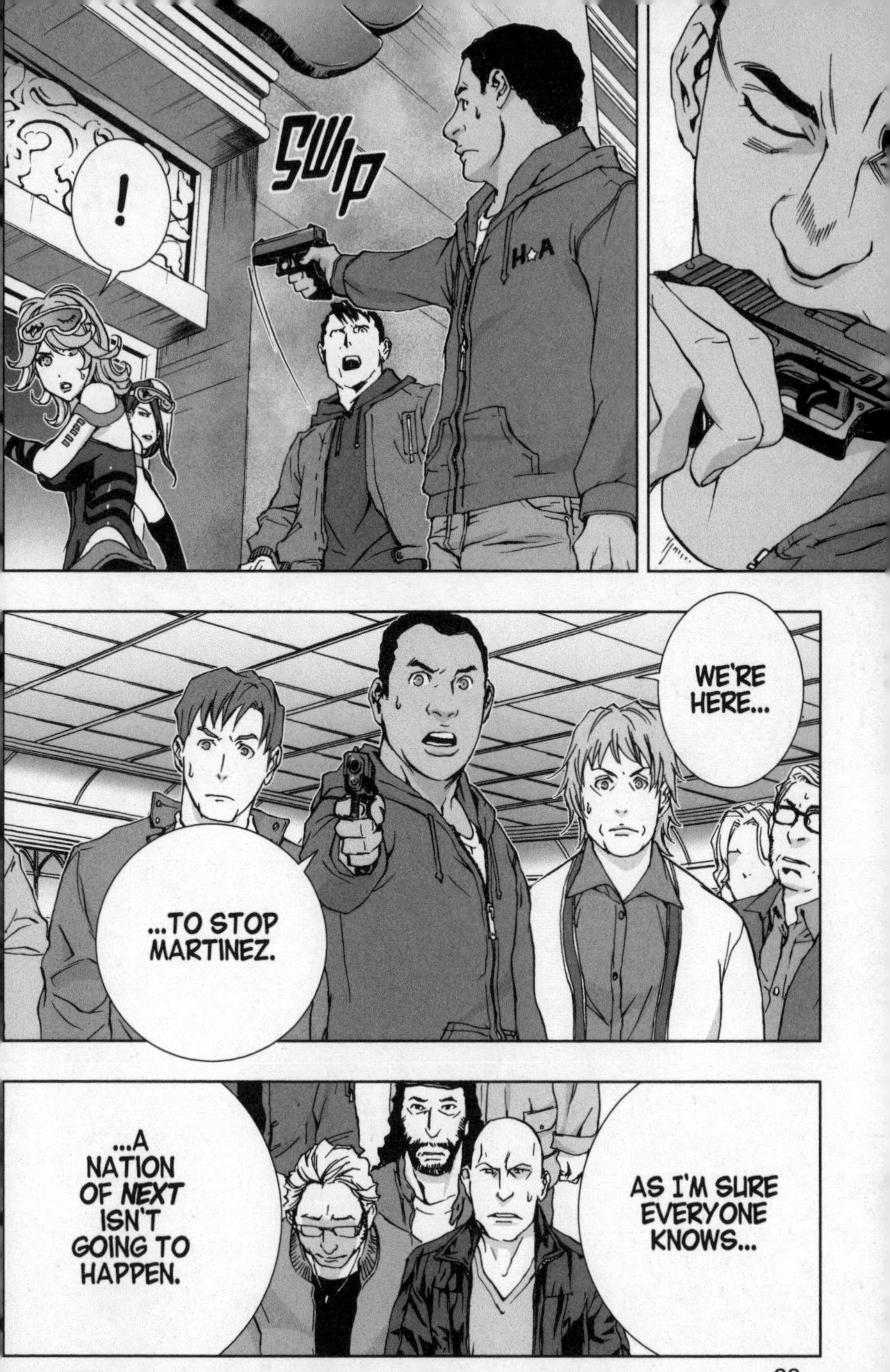
SWIP
!
WE'RE HERE...
...TO STOP MARTINEZ.
AS I'M SURE EVERYONE KNOWS...
...A NATION OF *NEXT* ISN'T GOING TO HAPPEN.

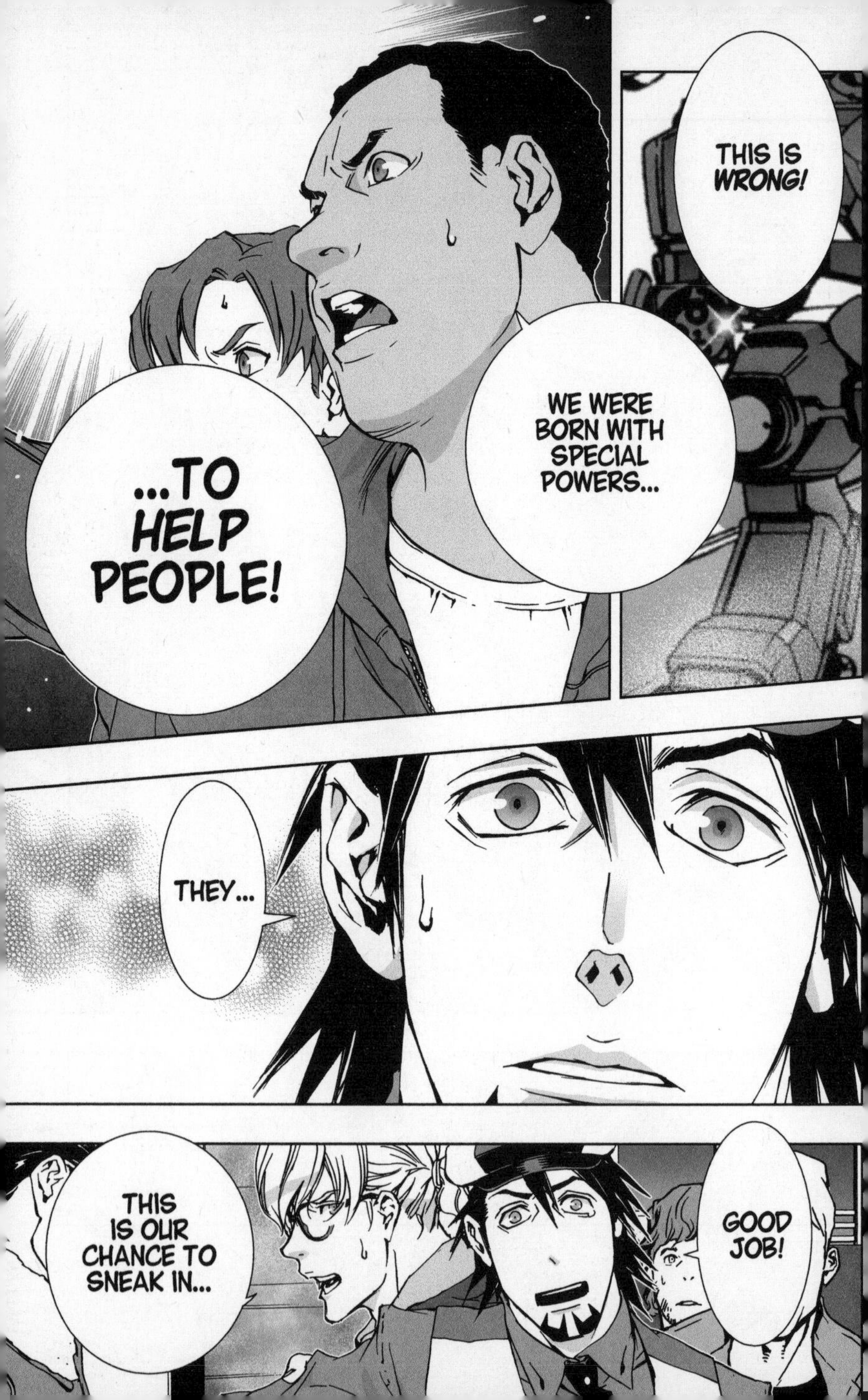
THIS IS WRONG!
WE WERE BORN WITH SPECIAL POWERS...
...TO HELP PEOPLE!
THEY...
GOOD JOB!
THIS IS OUR CHANCE TO SNEAK IN...

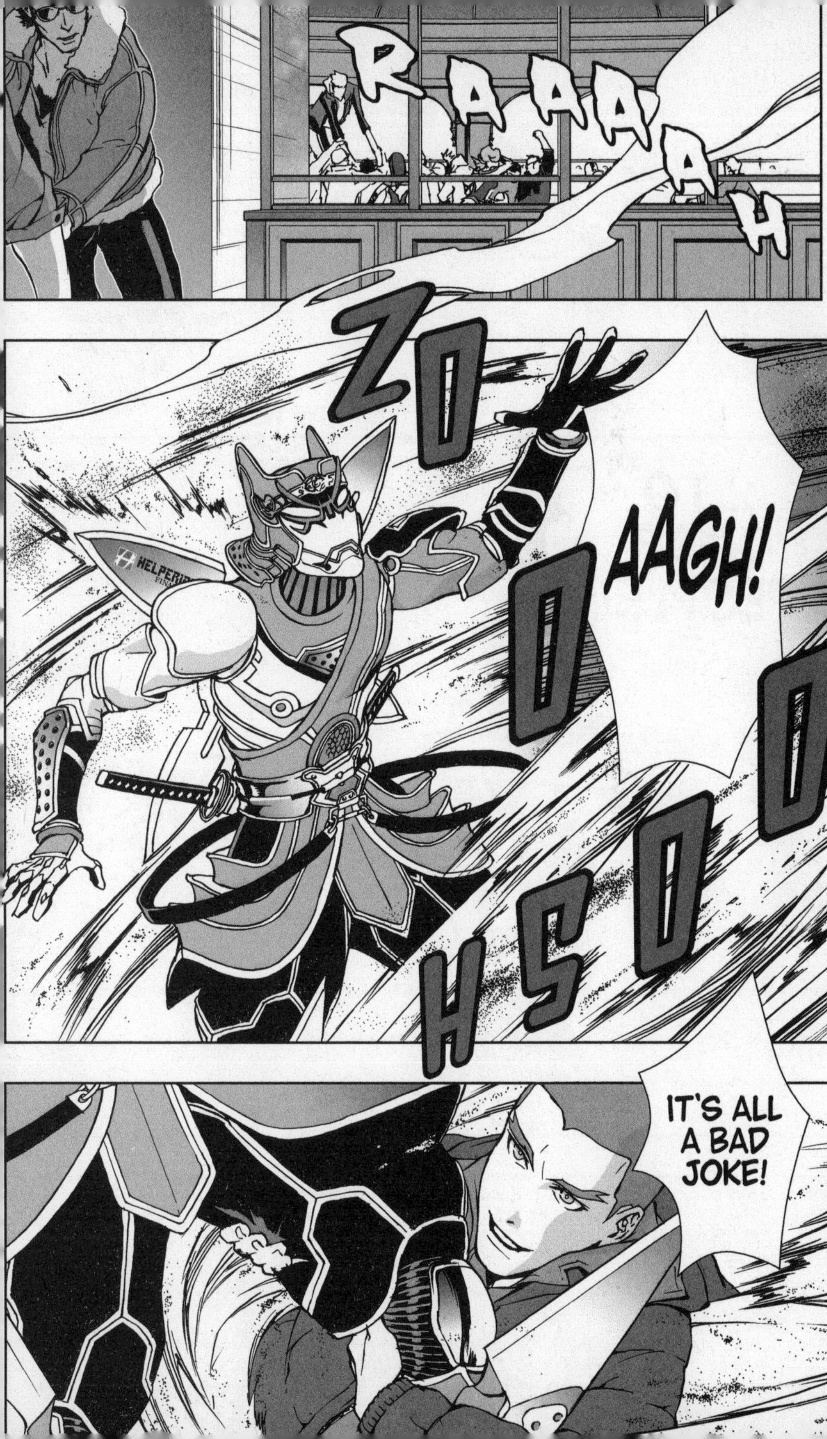
RAAAAAH
ZOOOOOSH
AAGH!
IT'S ALL A BAD JOKE!

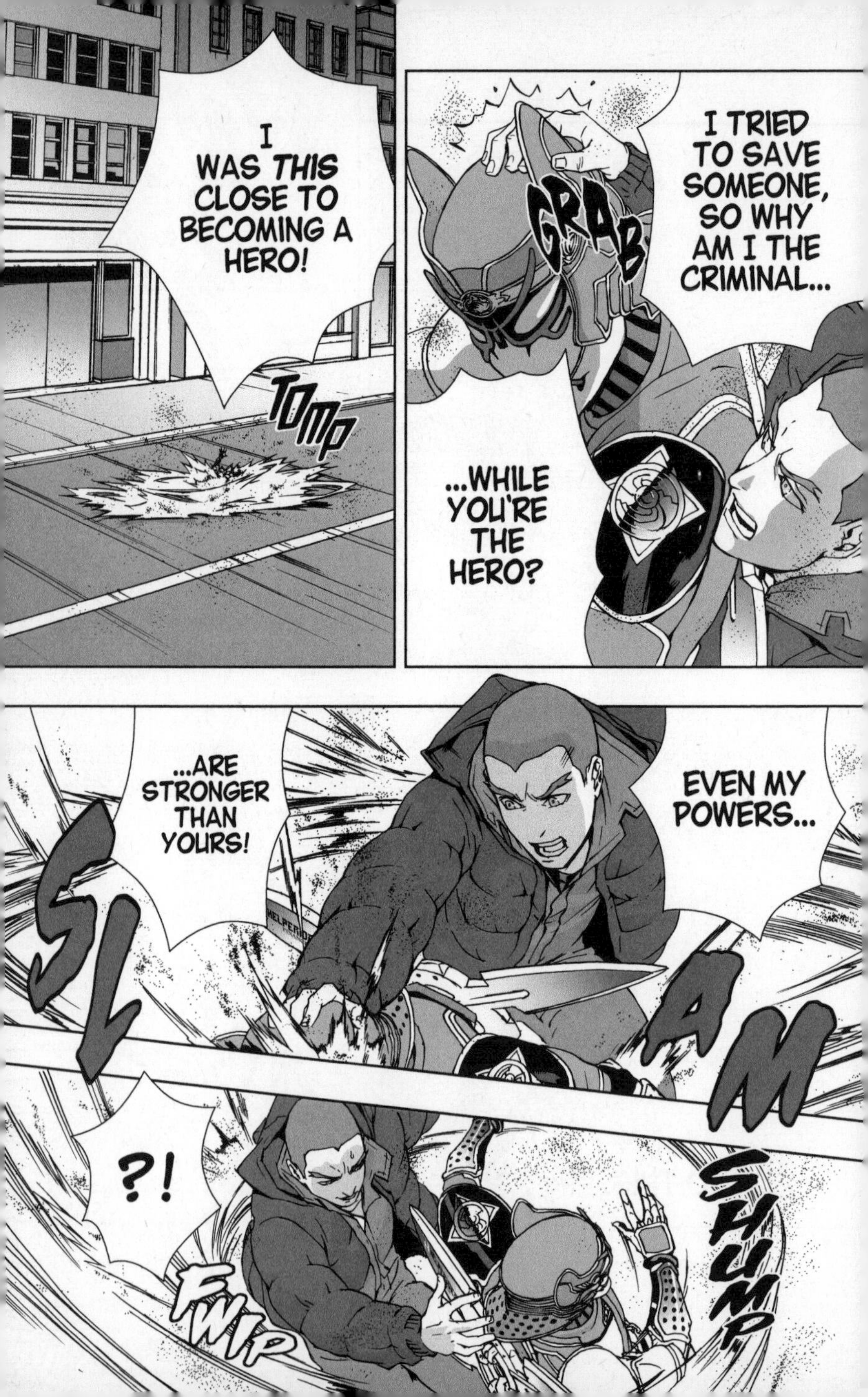
I TRIED TO SAVE SOMEONE, SO WHY AM I THE CRIMINAL...
GRAB
...WHILE YOU'RE THE HERO?
I WAS THIS CLOSE TO BECOMING A HERO!
TOMP
EVEN MY POWERS...
...ARE STRONGER THAN YOURS!
SLAM
?!
SHUMP
FWIP

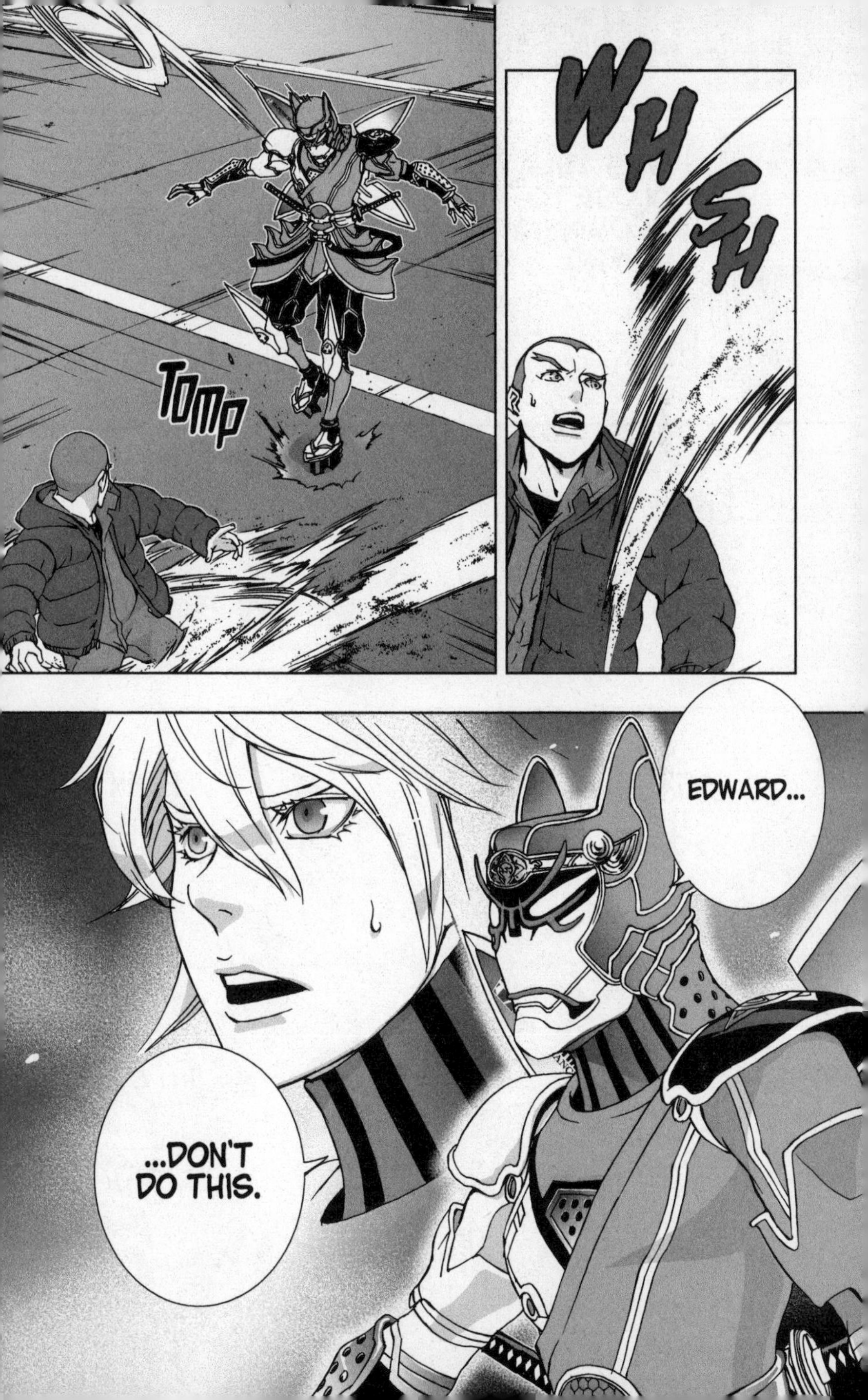
WHSH
TOMP
EDWARD...
...DON'T DO THIS.

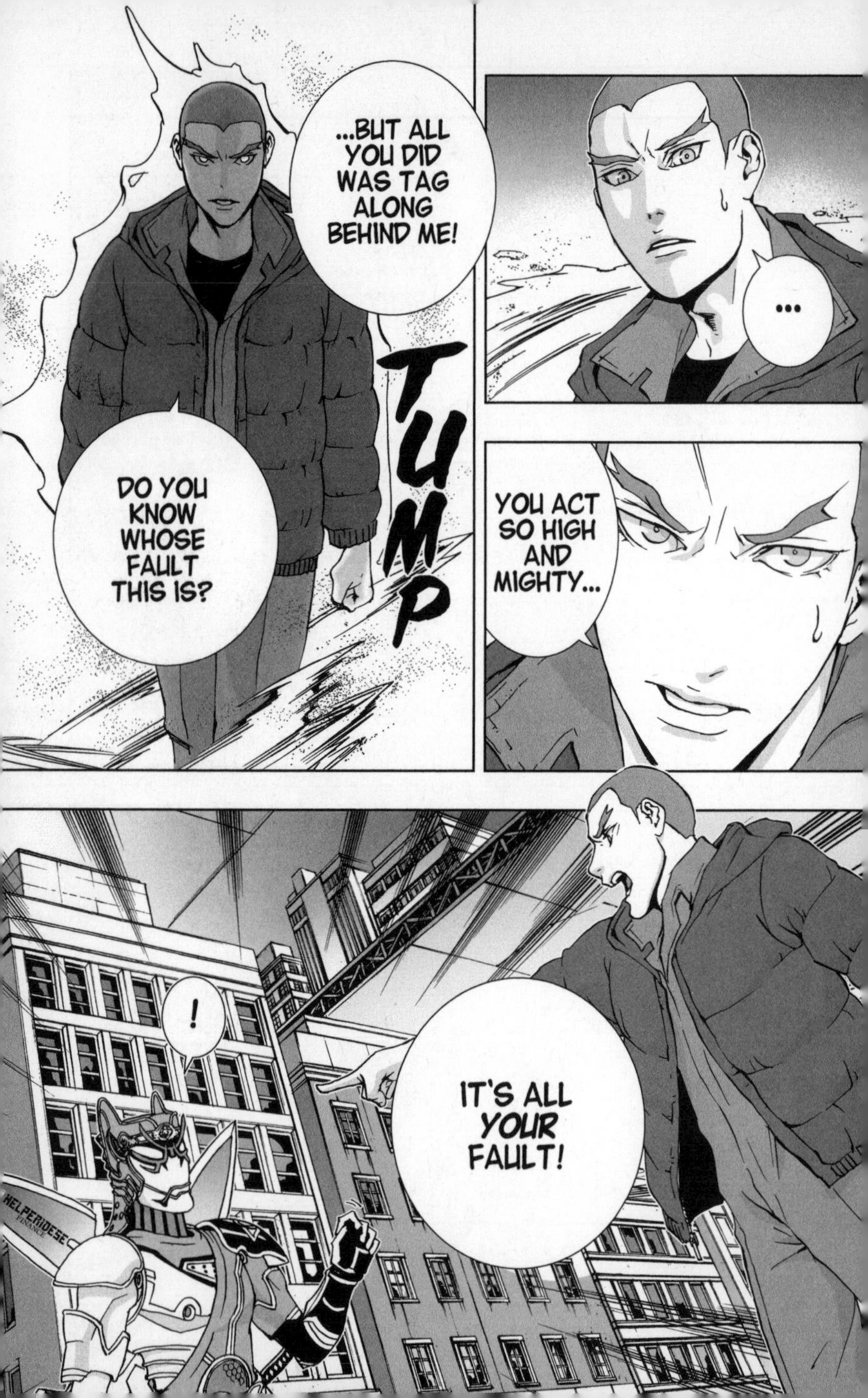
...
YOU ACT SO HIGH AND MIGHTY...
...BUT ALL YOU DID WAS TAG ALONG BEHIND ME!
TUMP
DO YOU KNOW WHOSE FAULT THIS IS?
IT'S ALL *YOUR* FAULT!
!
HELPERIDESE FINANCE

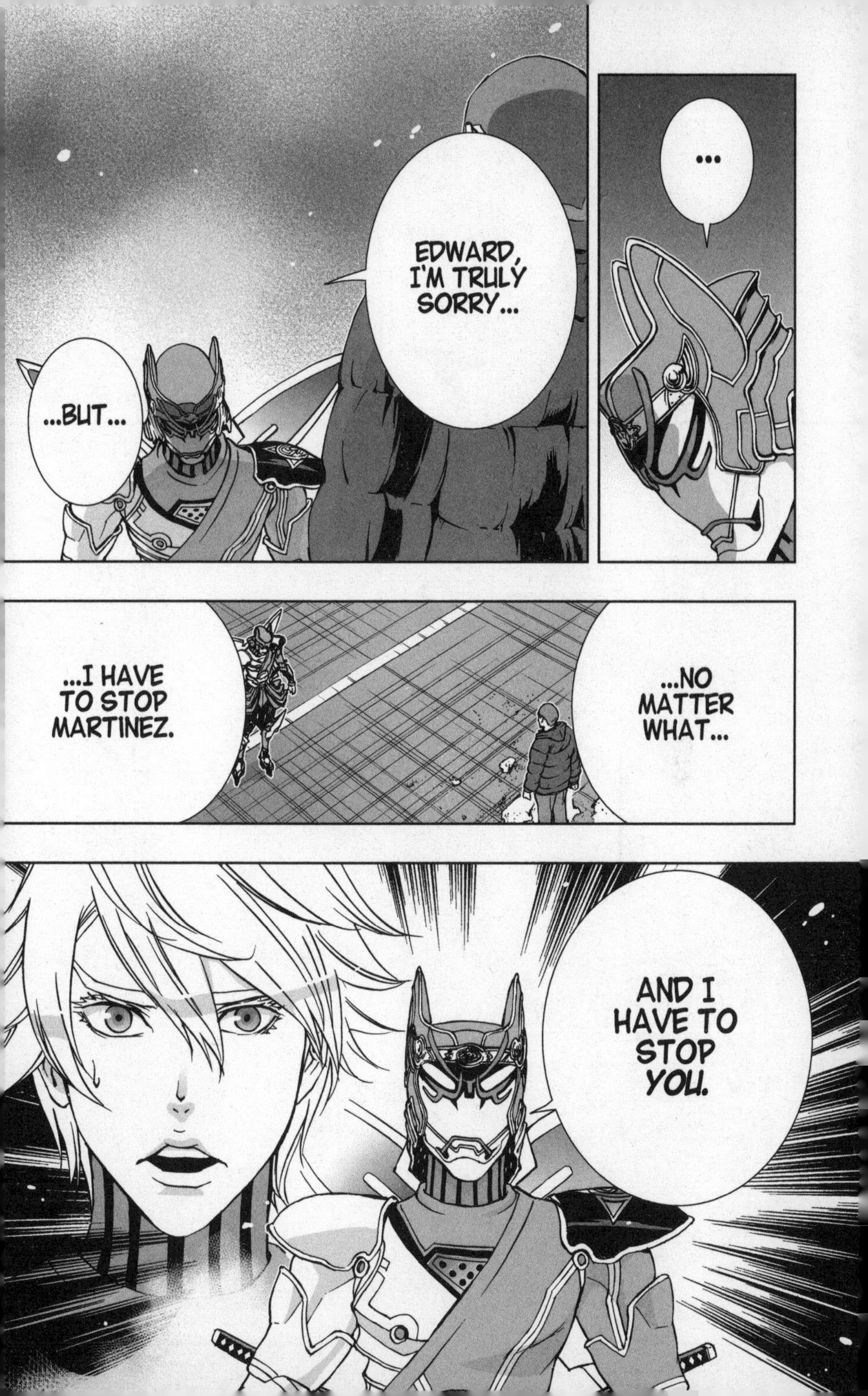
...
EDWARD, I'M TRULY SORRY...
...BUT...
...NO MATTER WHAT...
...I HAVE TO STOP MARTINEZ.
AND I HAVE TO STOP YOU.

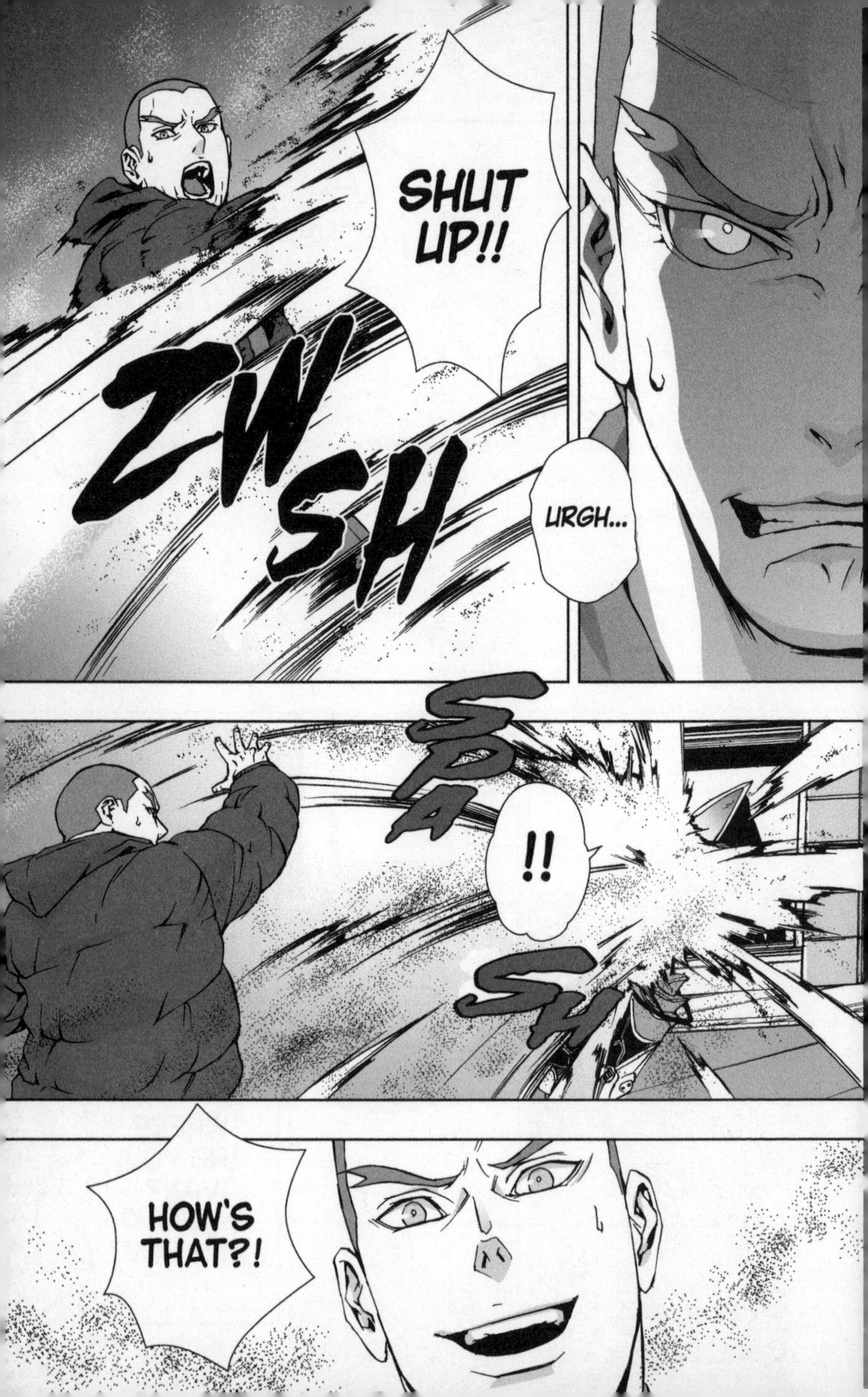
URGH...
SHUT UP!!
ZWSH
SPA
!!
SH
HOW'S THAT?!

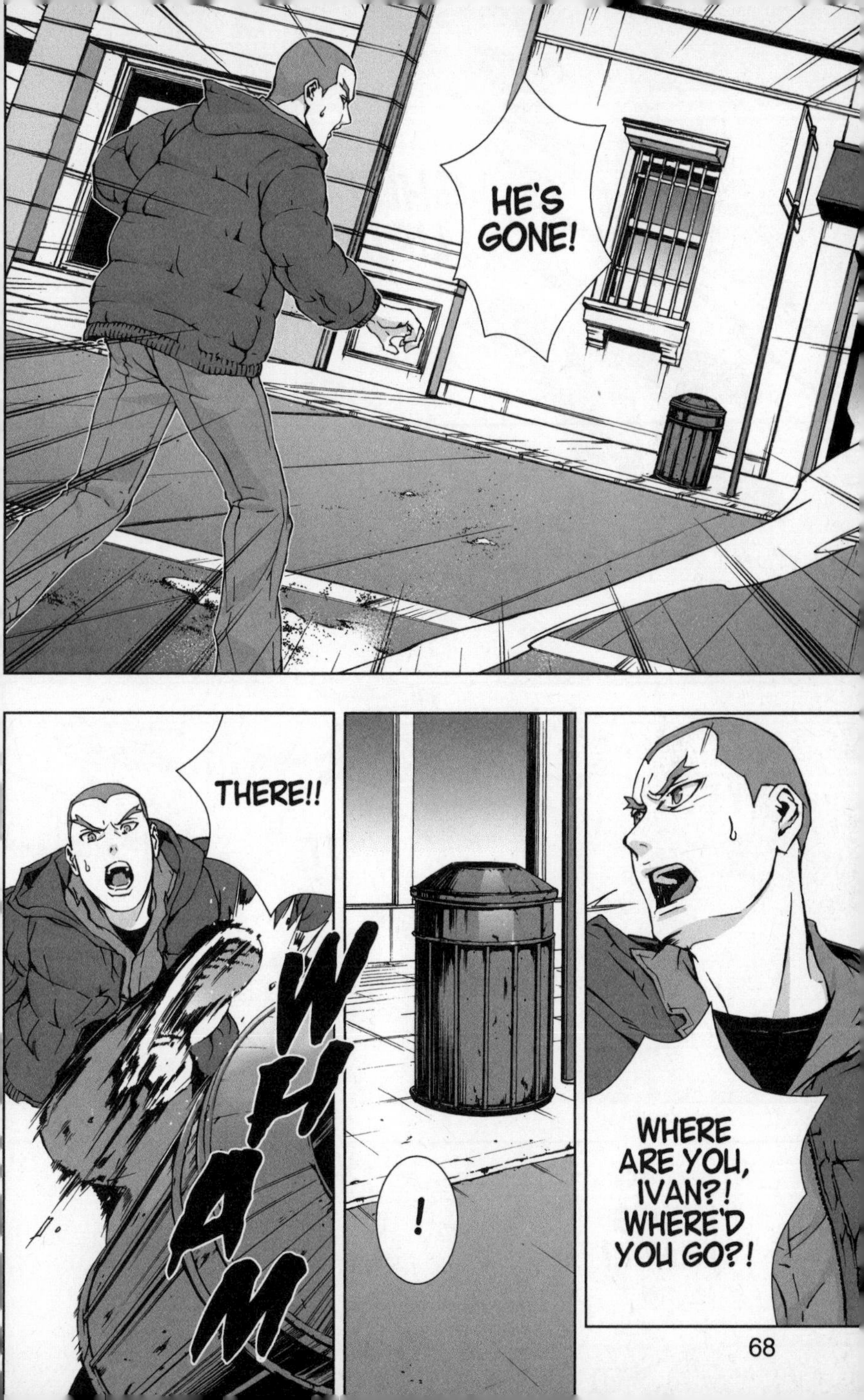
HE'S GONE!
WHERE ARE YOU, IVAN?! WHERE'D YOU GO?!
!
THERE!!
WHAM

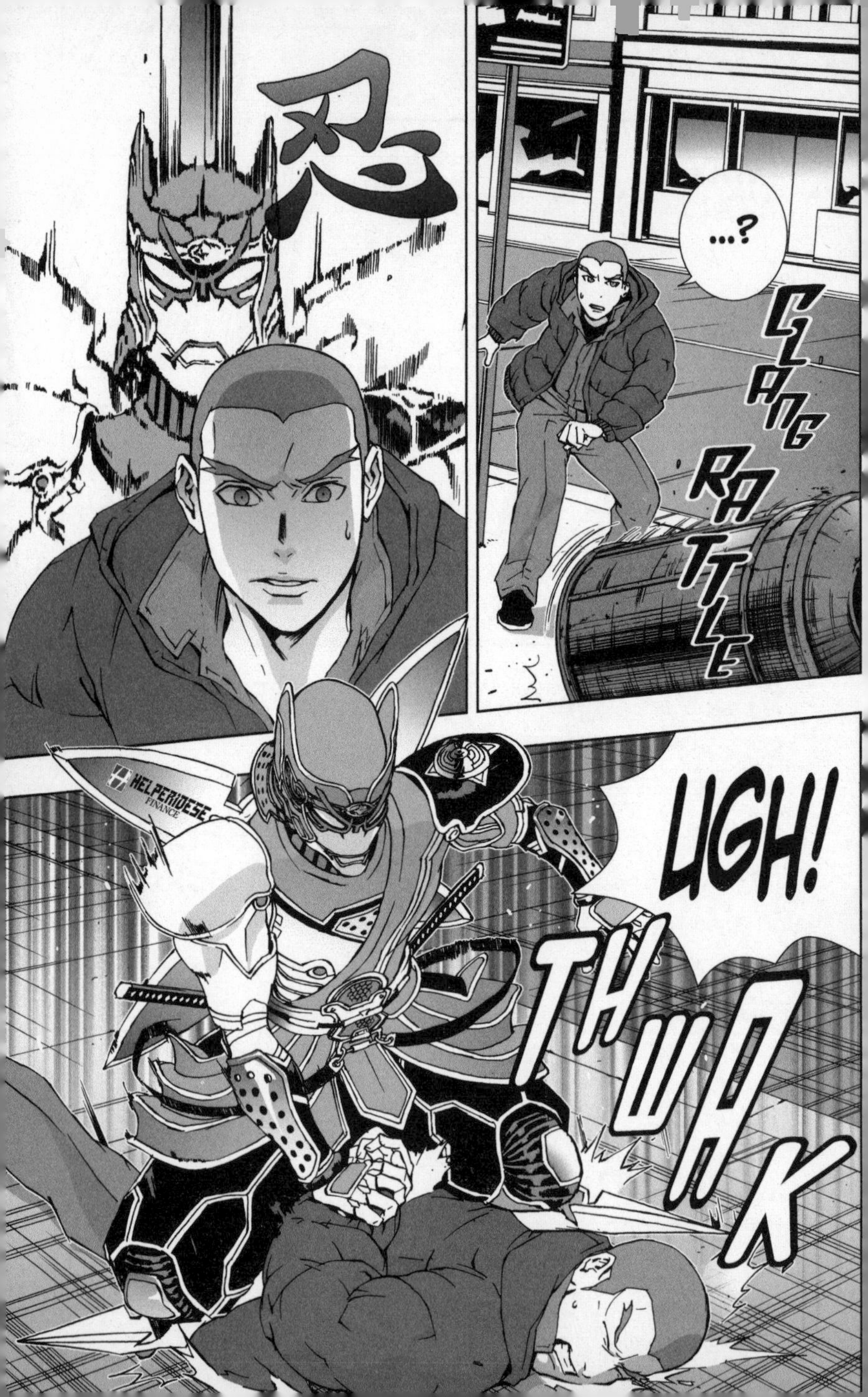
...?
CLANG
RATTLE
忍
HELPERIDESE
FINANCE
UGH!
THWAK

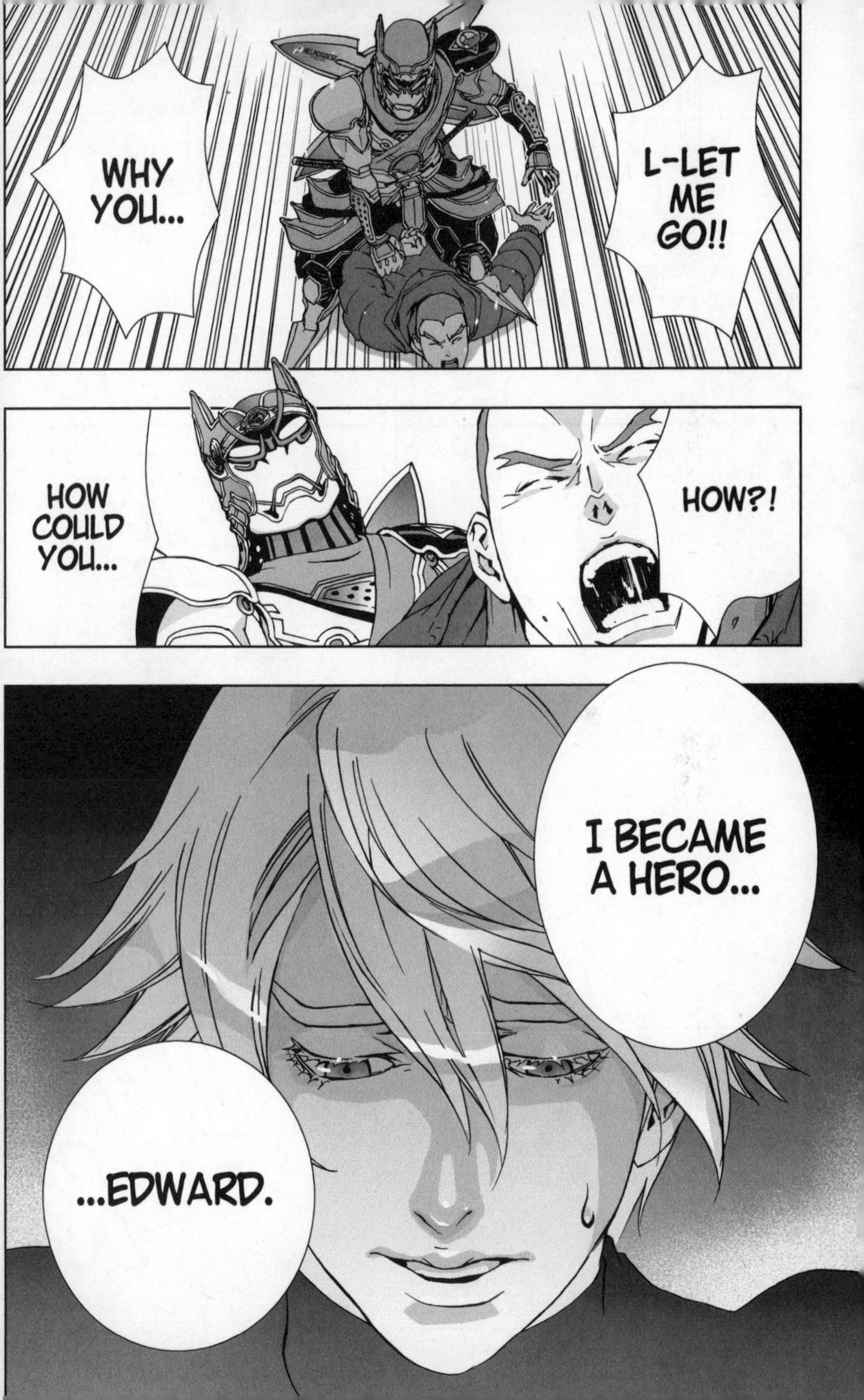
L-LET ME GO!!
WHY YOU...
HOW?!
HOW COULD YOU...
I BECAME A HERO...
...EDWARD.

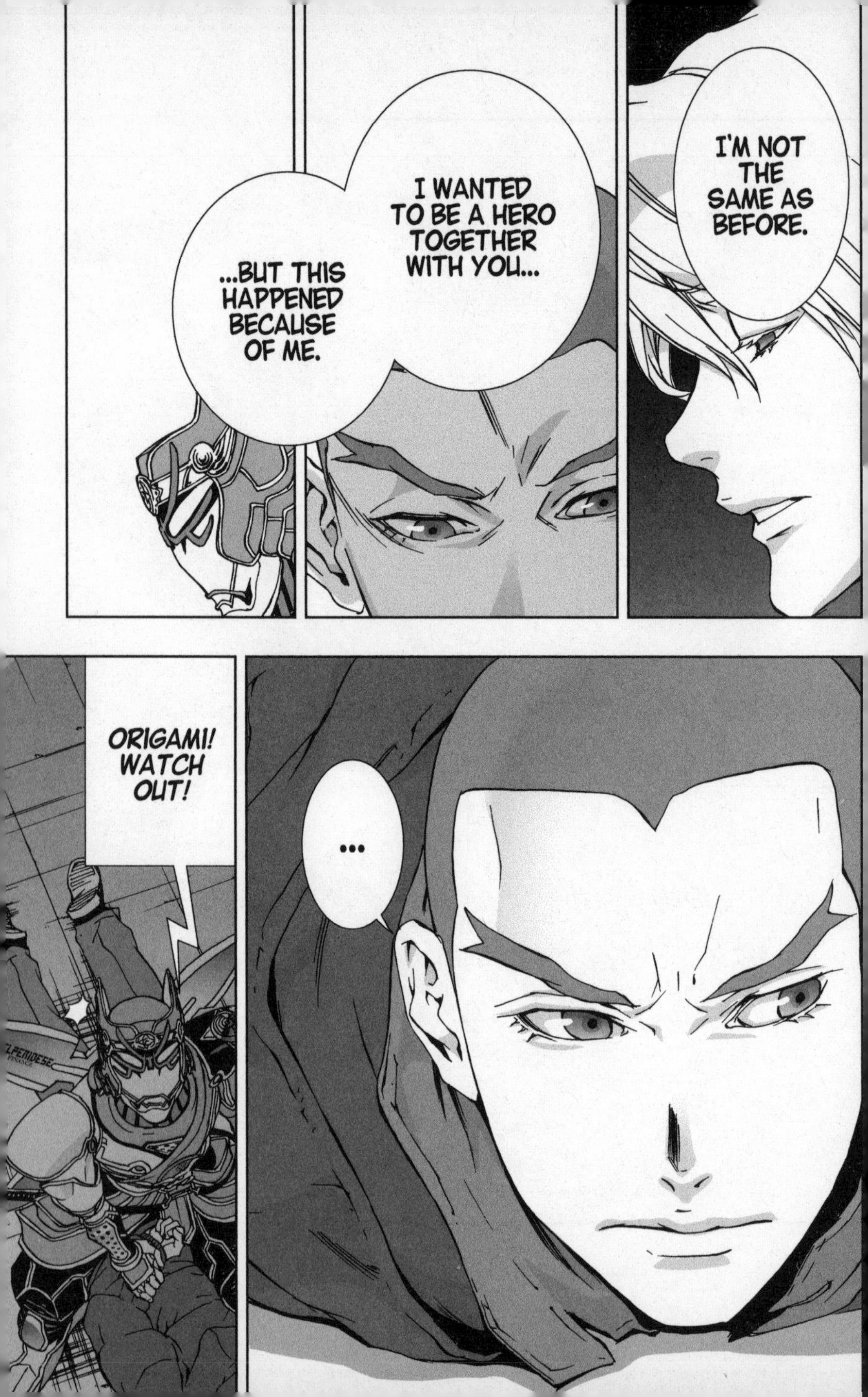
I'M NOT THE SAME AS BEFORE.
I WANTED TO BE A HERO TOGETHER WITH YOU...
...BUT THIS HAPPENED BECAUSE OF ME.
...
ORIGAMI! WATCH OUT!

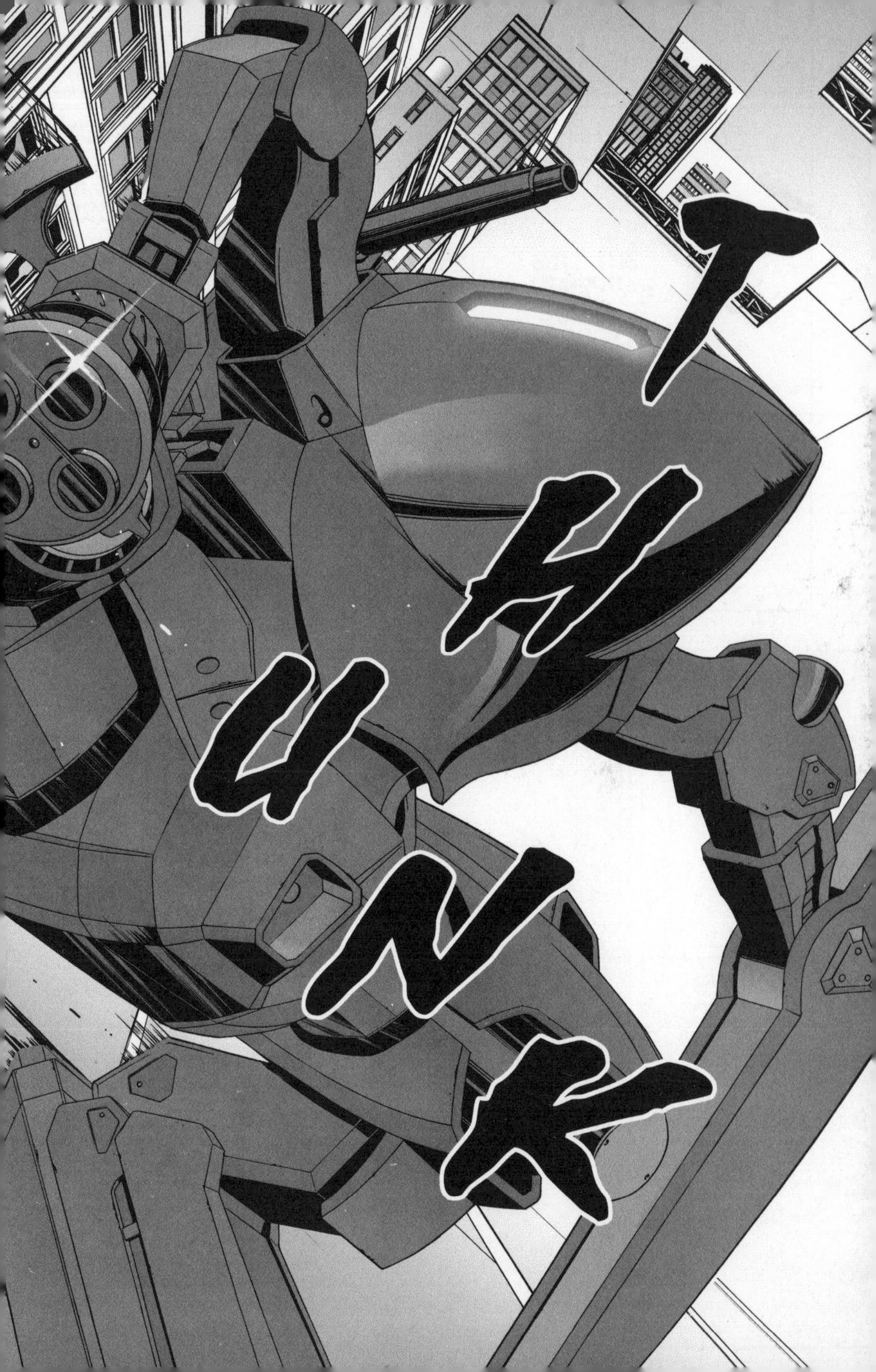
THUNK

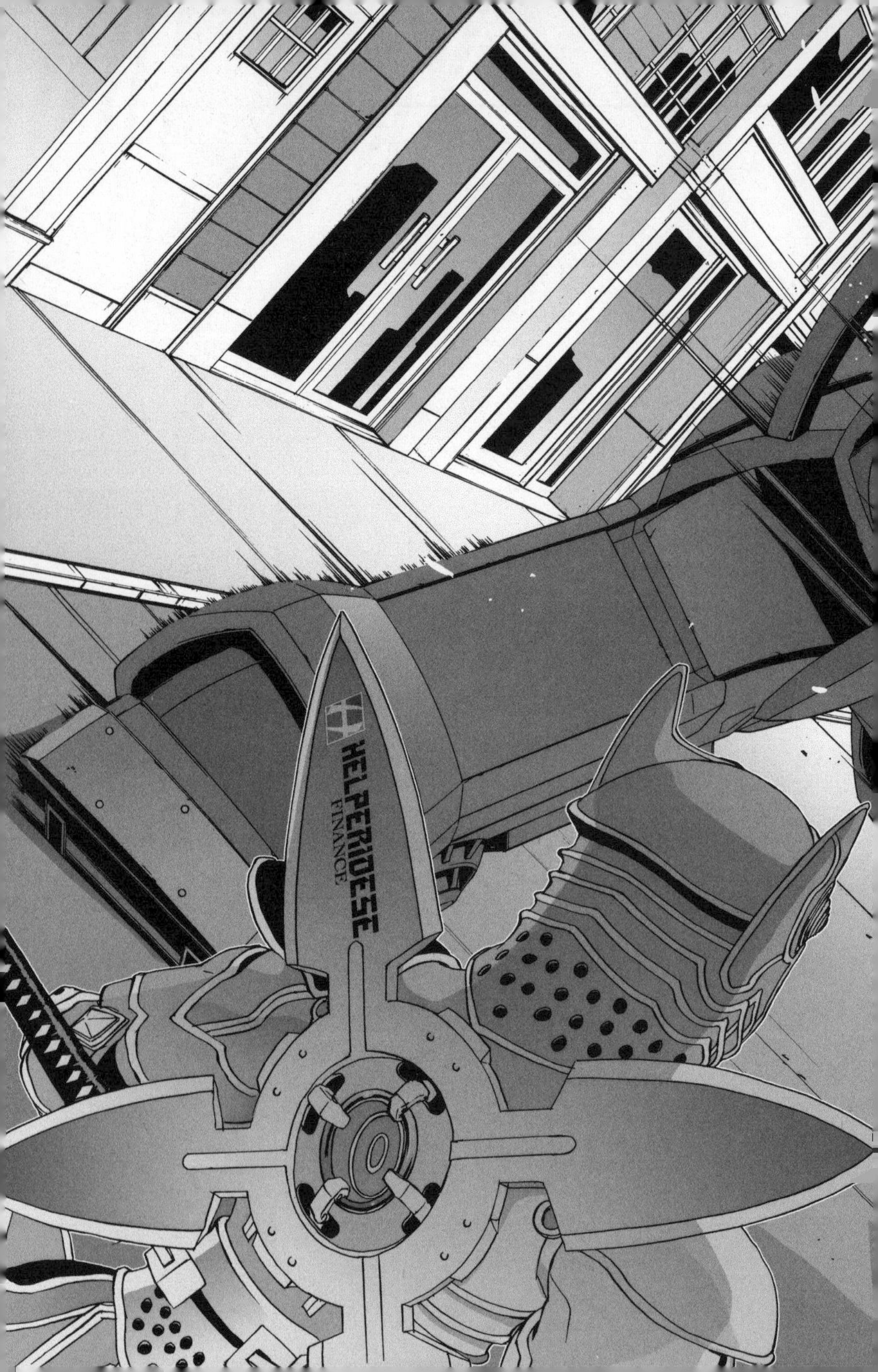
HELPERIDESE
FINANCE

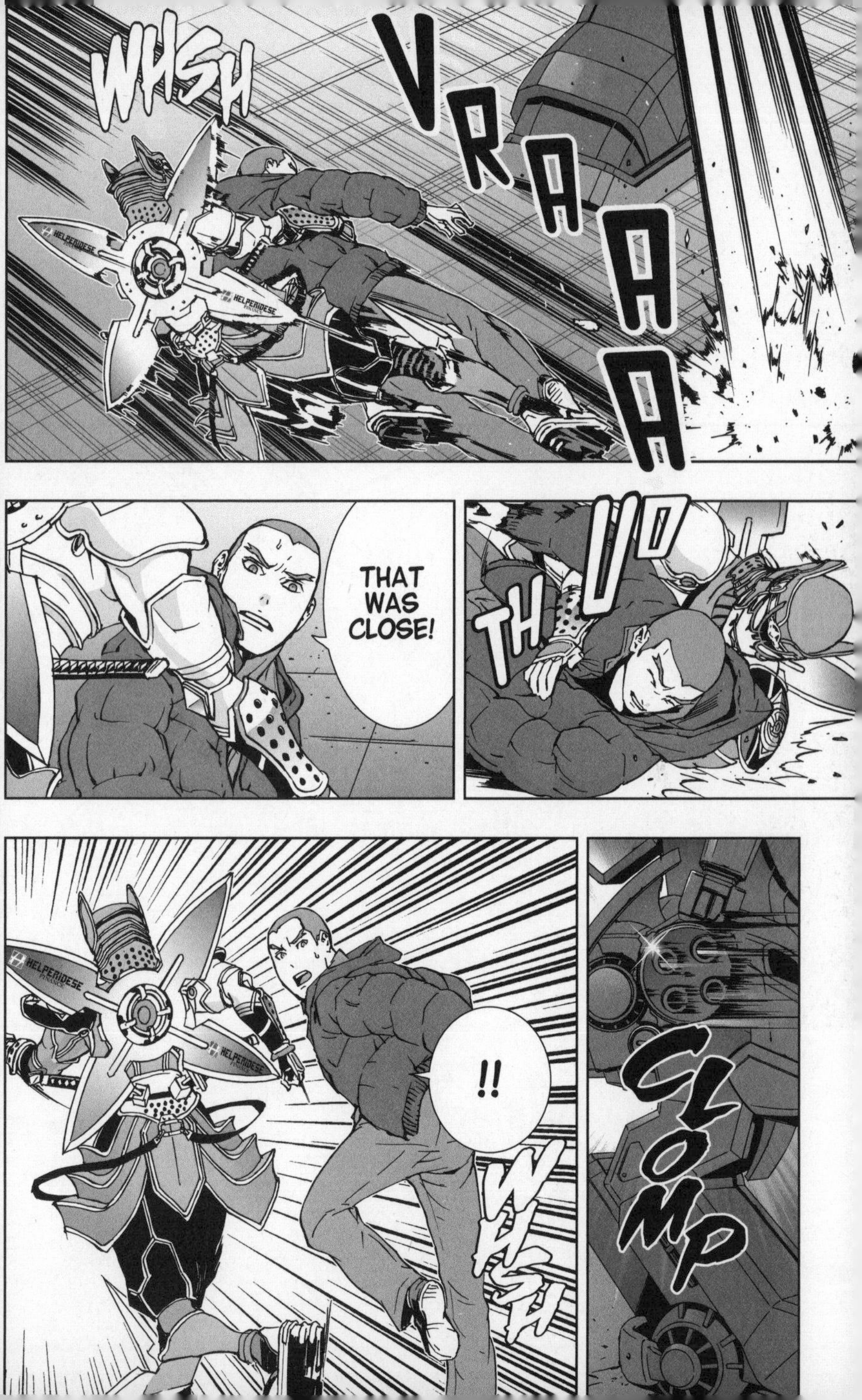
VRAAAA
WHSH
THUD
THAT WAS CLOSE!
CLOMP
!!
WHSH

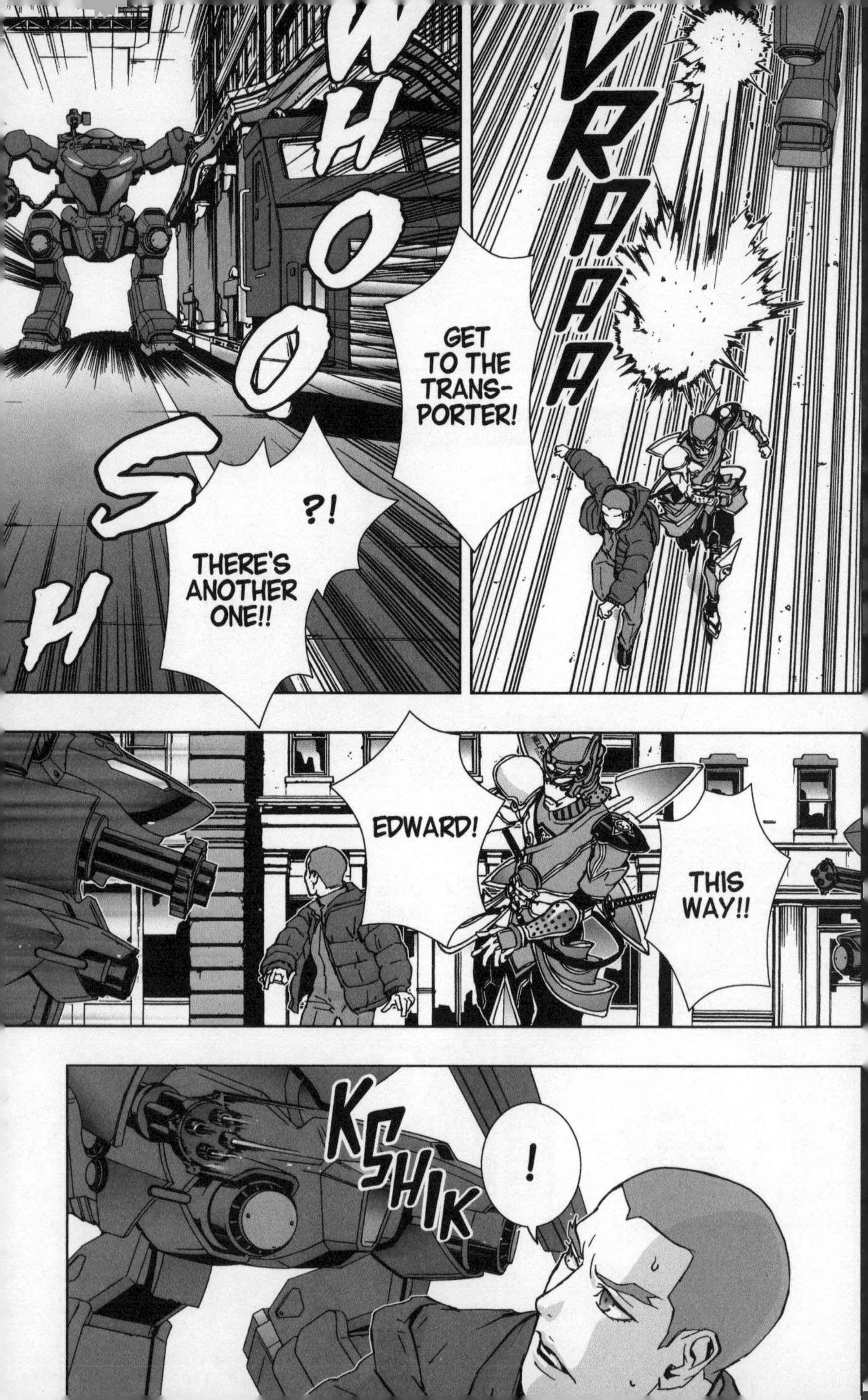
VRAAAA
GET TO THE TRANS-PORTER!
WHOOOSH
?!
THERE'S ANOTHER ONE!!
EDWARD!
THIS WAY!!
KSHIK
!

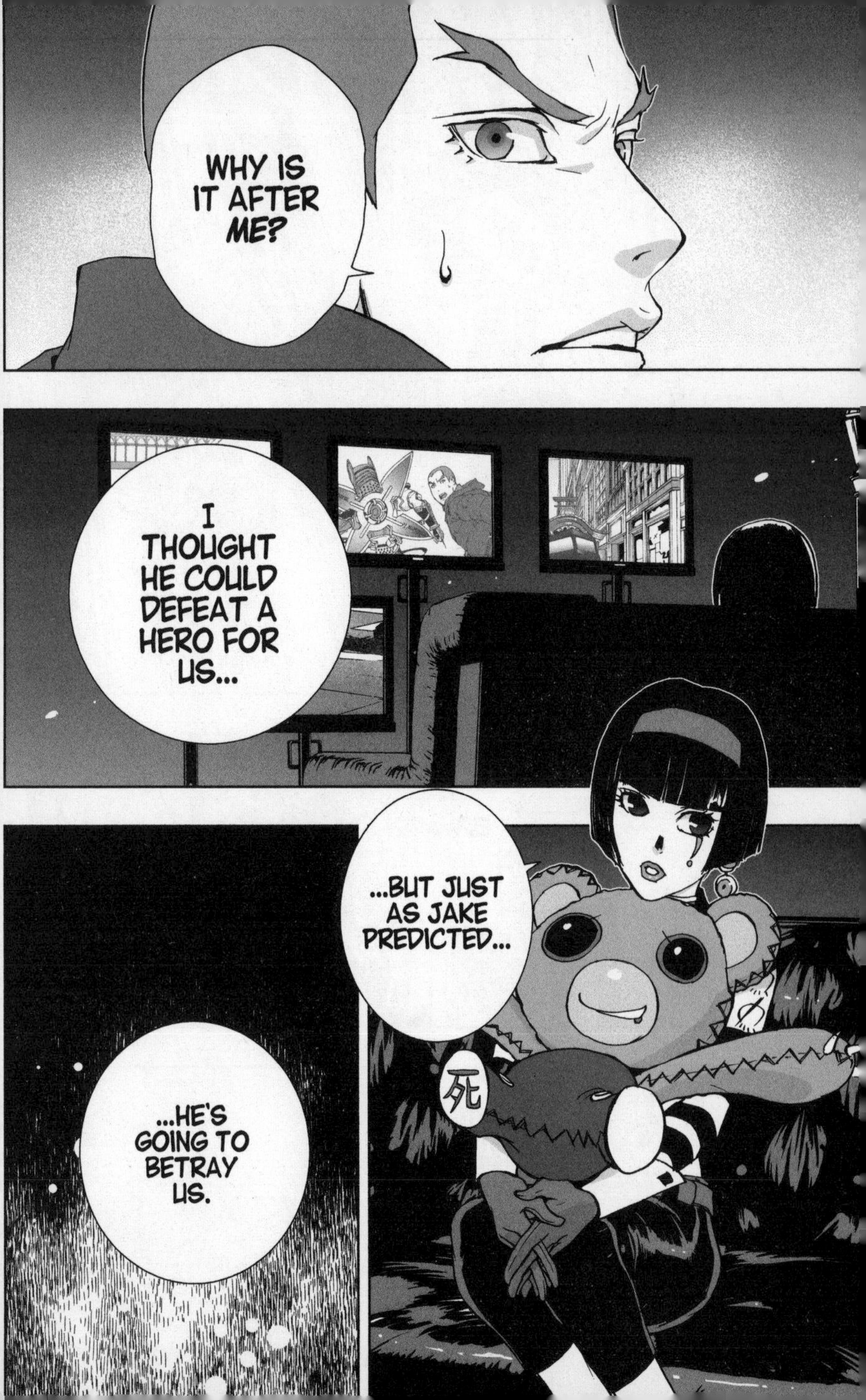
WHY IS IT AFTER ME?
I THOUGHT HE COULD DEFEAT A HERO FOR US...
...BUT JUST AS JAKE PREDICTED...
...HE'S GOING TO BETRAY US.
死

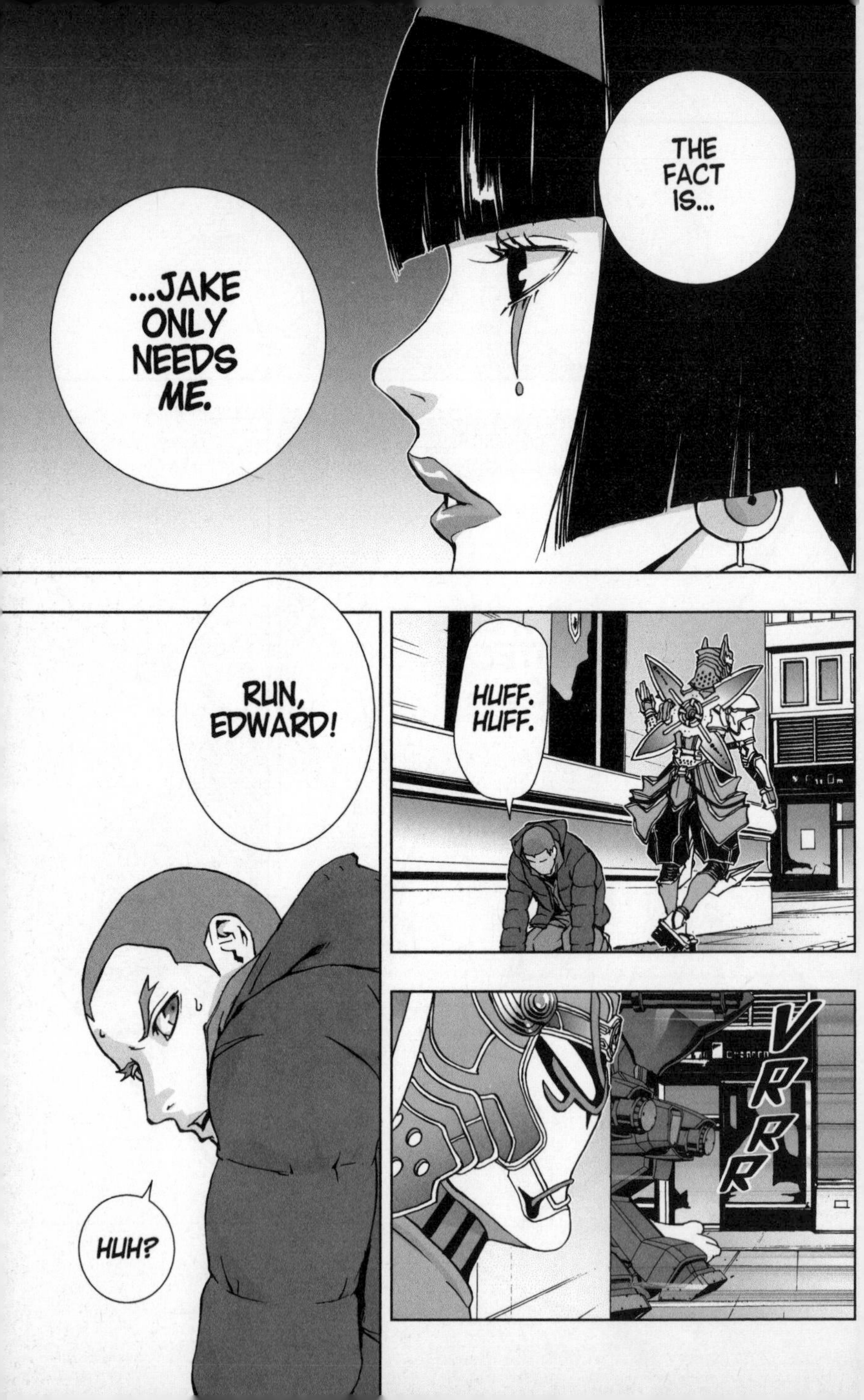
THE FACT IS...
...JAKE ONLY NEEDS ME.
HUFF. HUFF.
VRRR
RUN, EDWARD!
HUH?

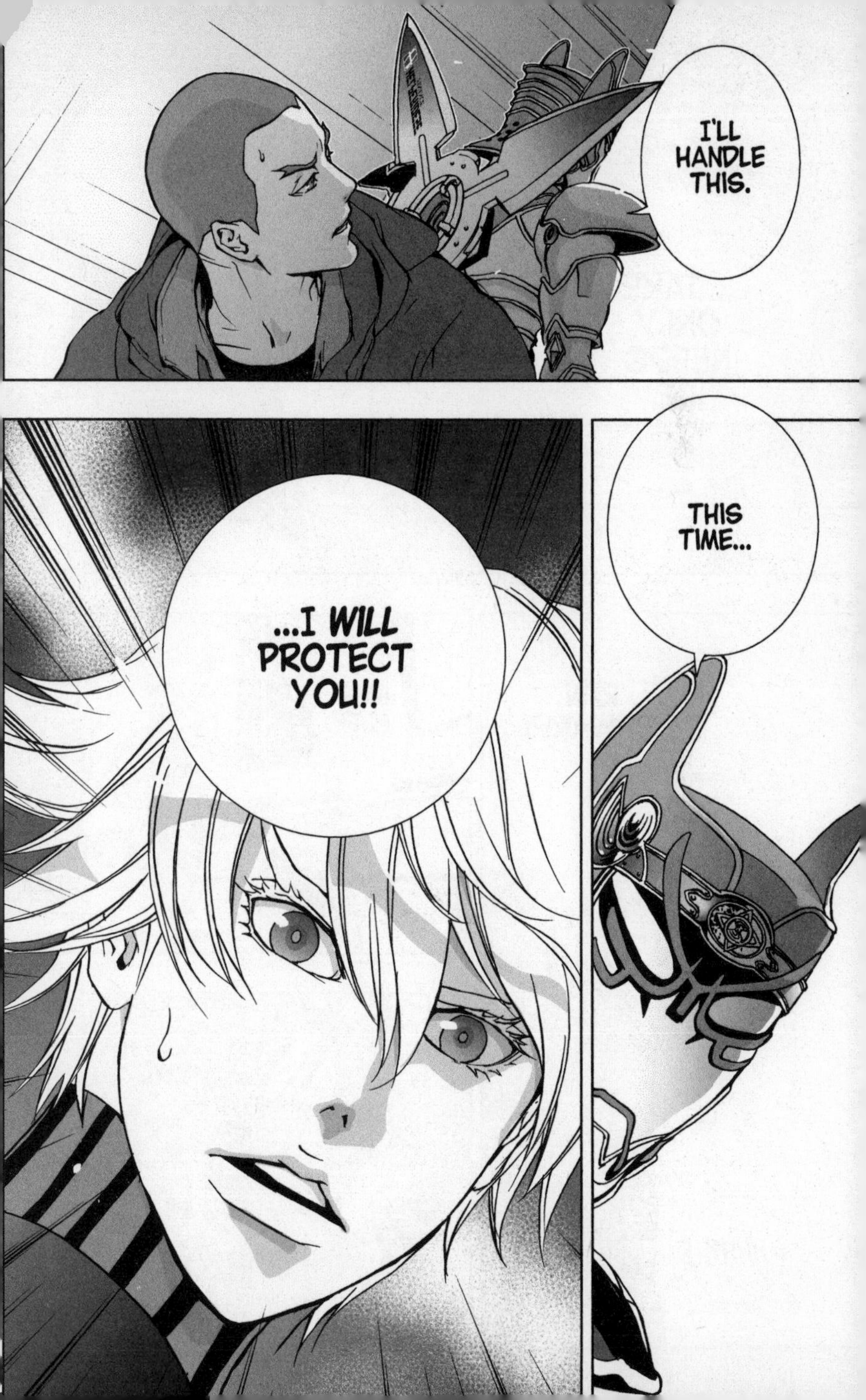
I'LL HANDLE THIS.
THIS TIME...
...I WILL PROTECT YOU!!

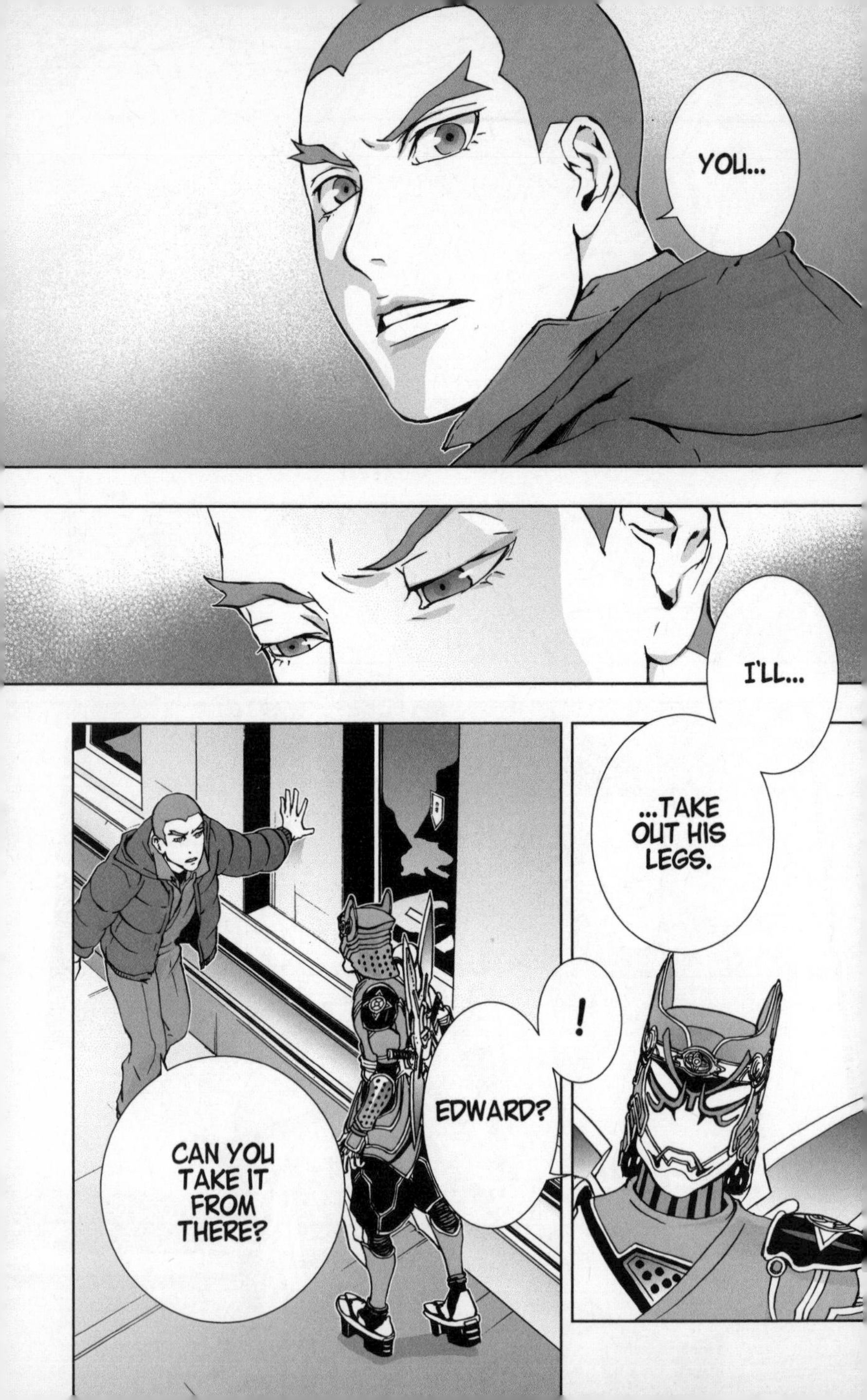
YOU...
I'LL...
...TAKE OUT HIS LEGS.
!
EDWARD?
CAN YOU TAKE IT FROM THERE?

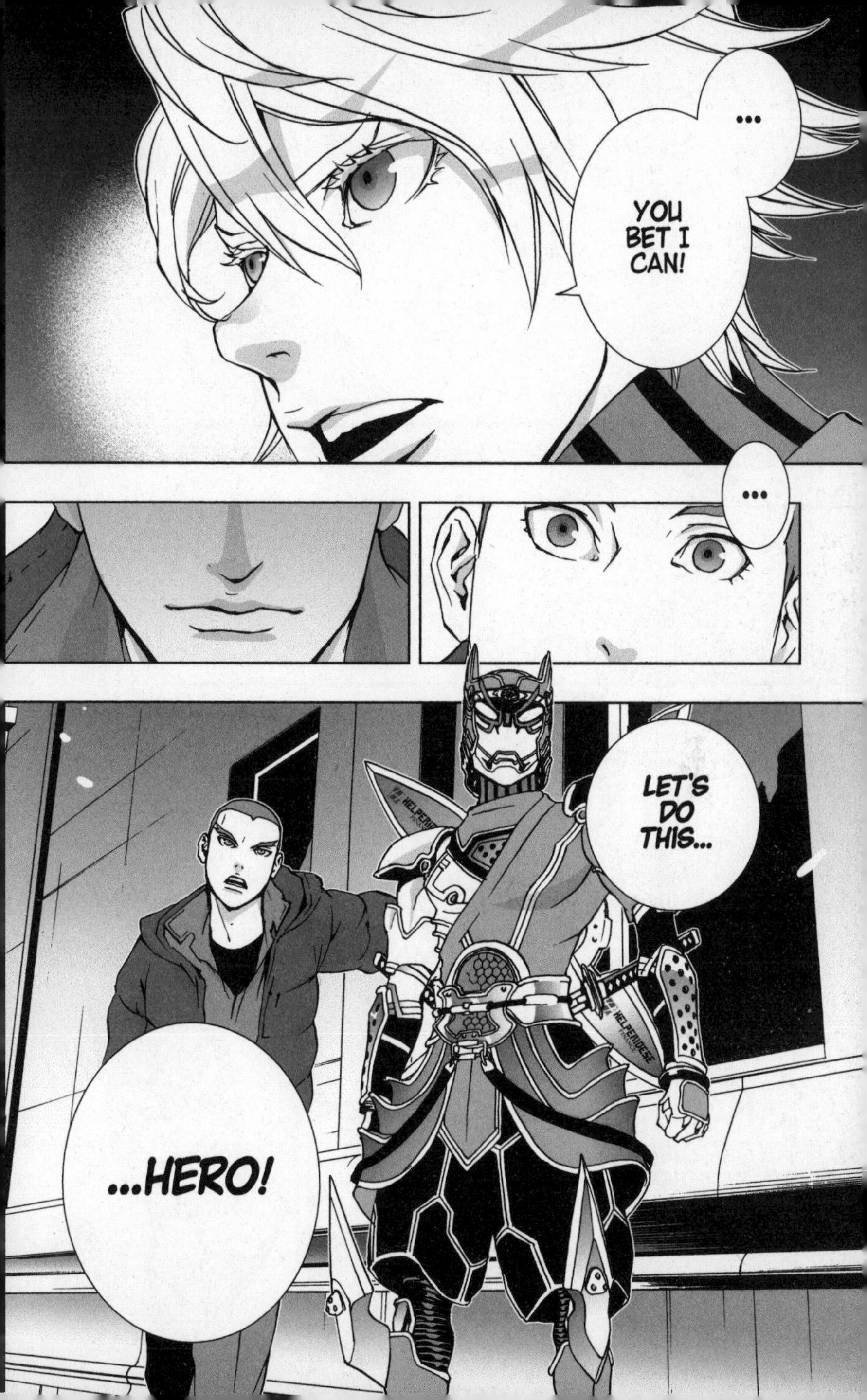
...
YOU BET I CAN!
...
LET'S DO THIS...
...HERO!

TIGER&BUNNY

TIGER&BUNNY

# #24 Confidence Is a Plant of Slow Growth

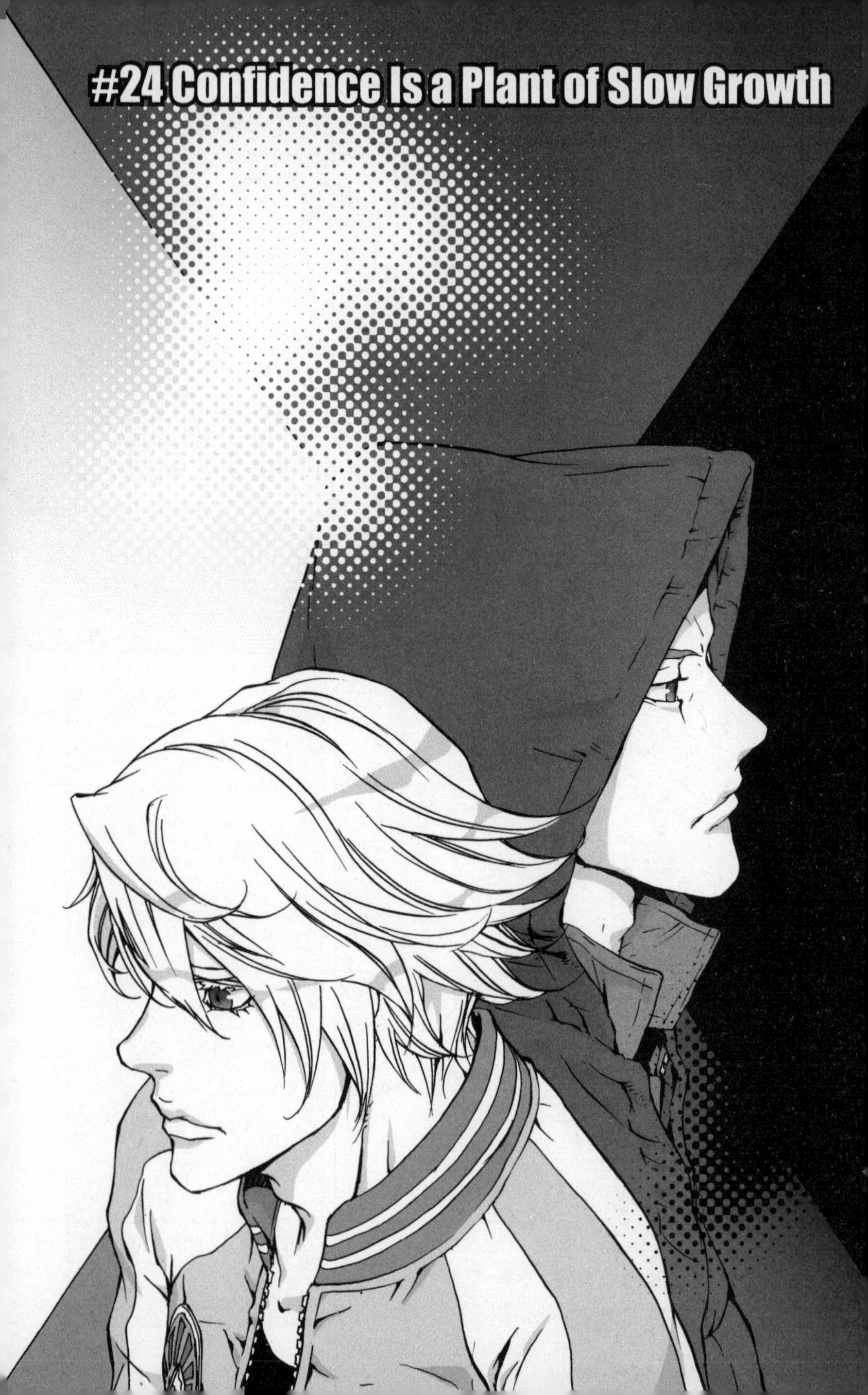

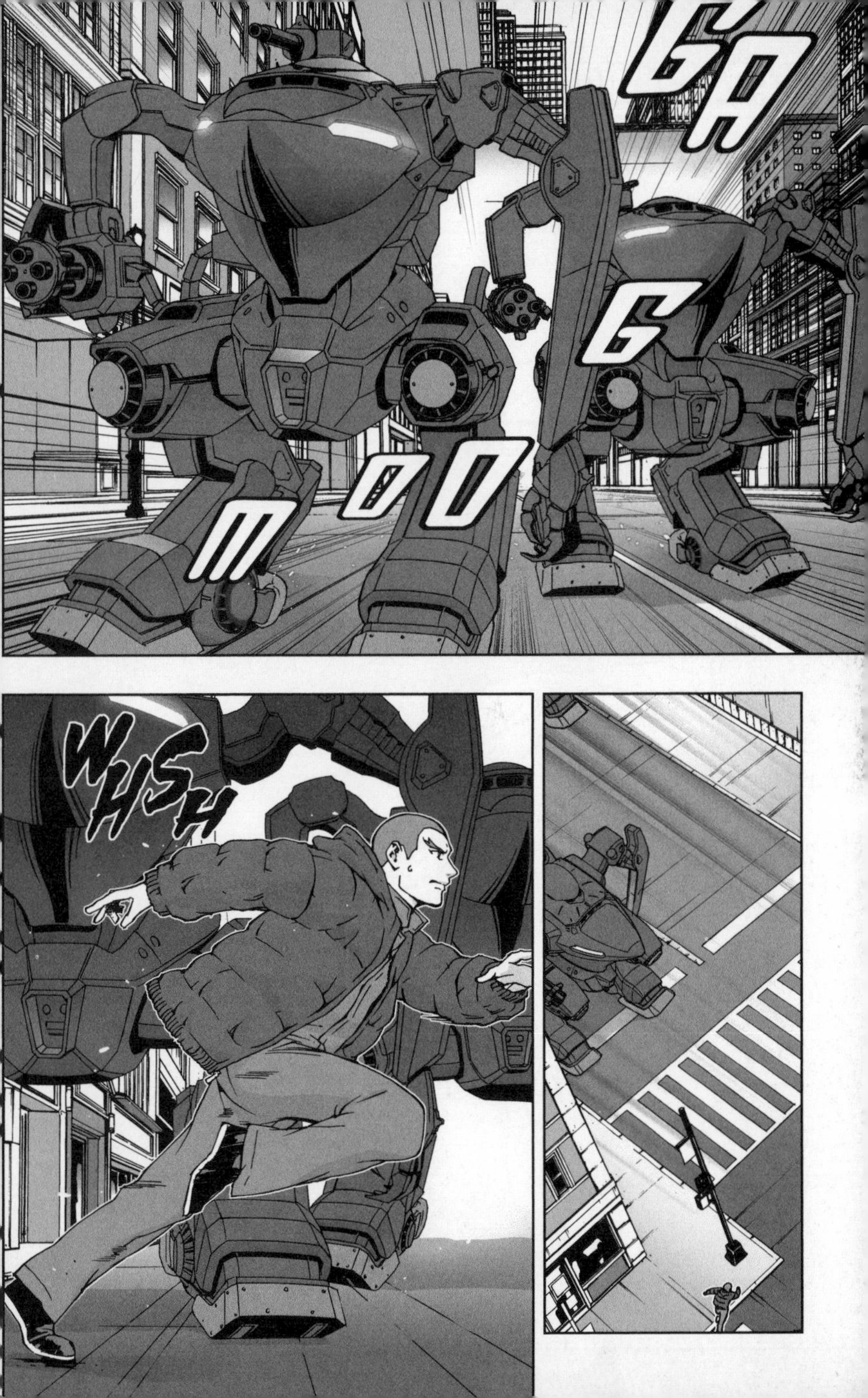
GAGOOM
WHSH

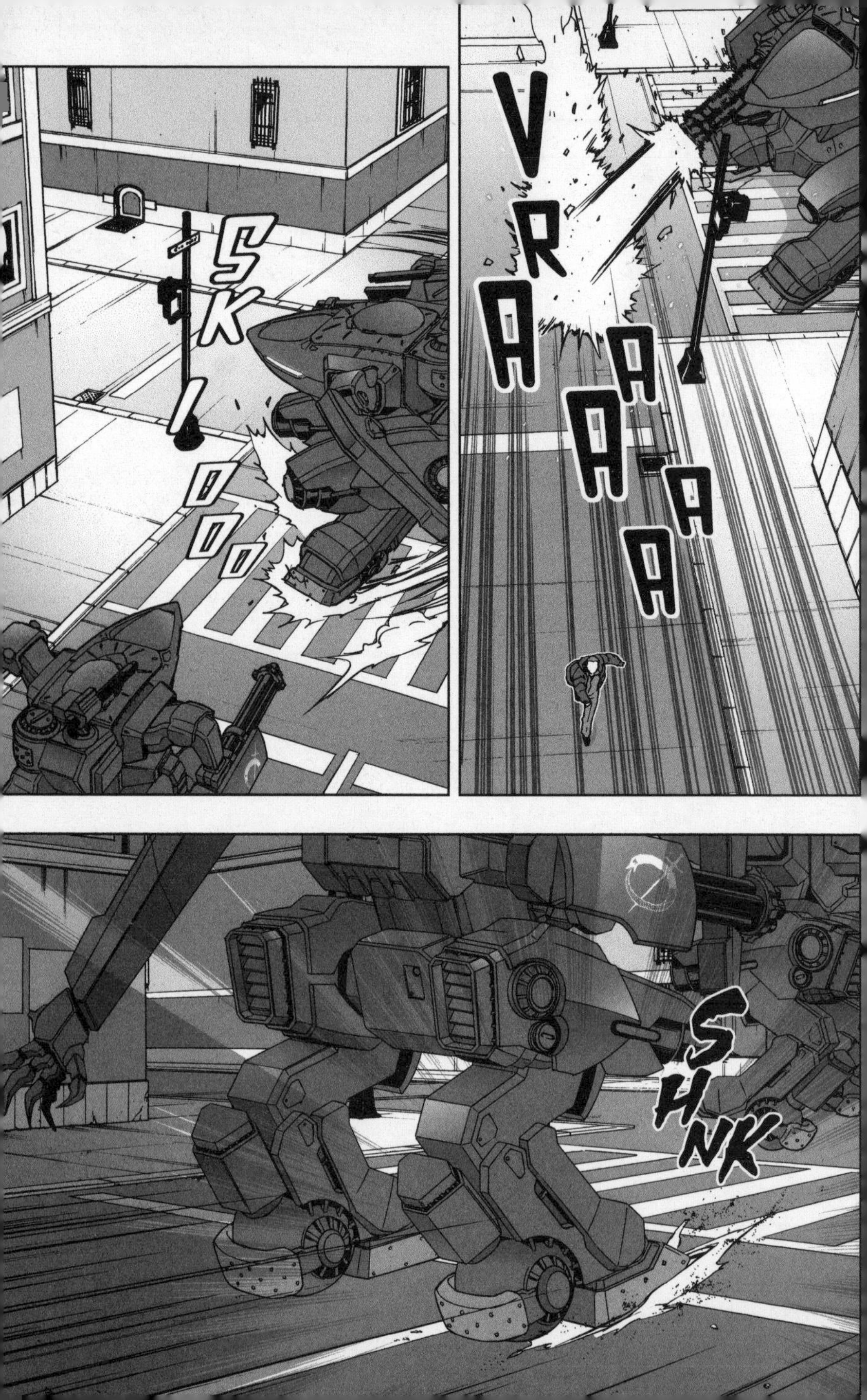
VRAAA-AA
SKIDDD
SHNK

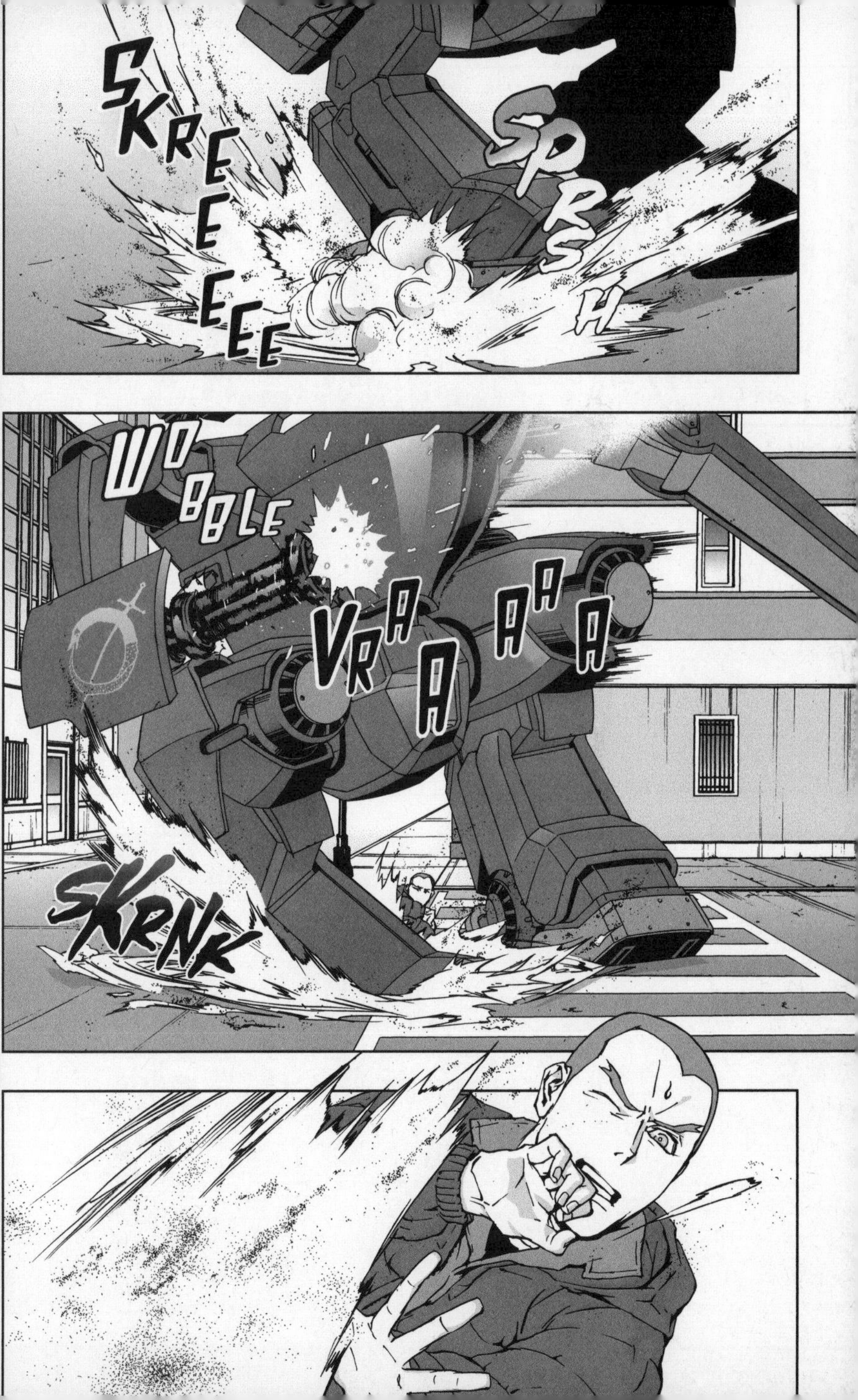
SPRSH
SKREEEEEE
WOBBLE
VRAAAAA
SKRNK

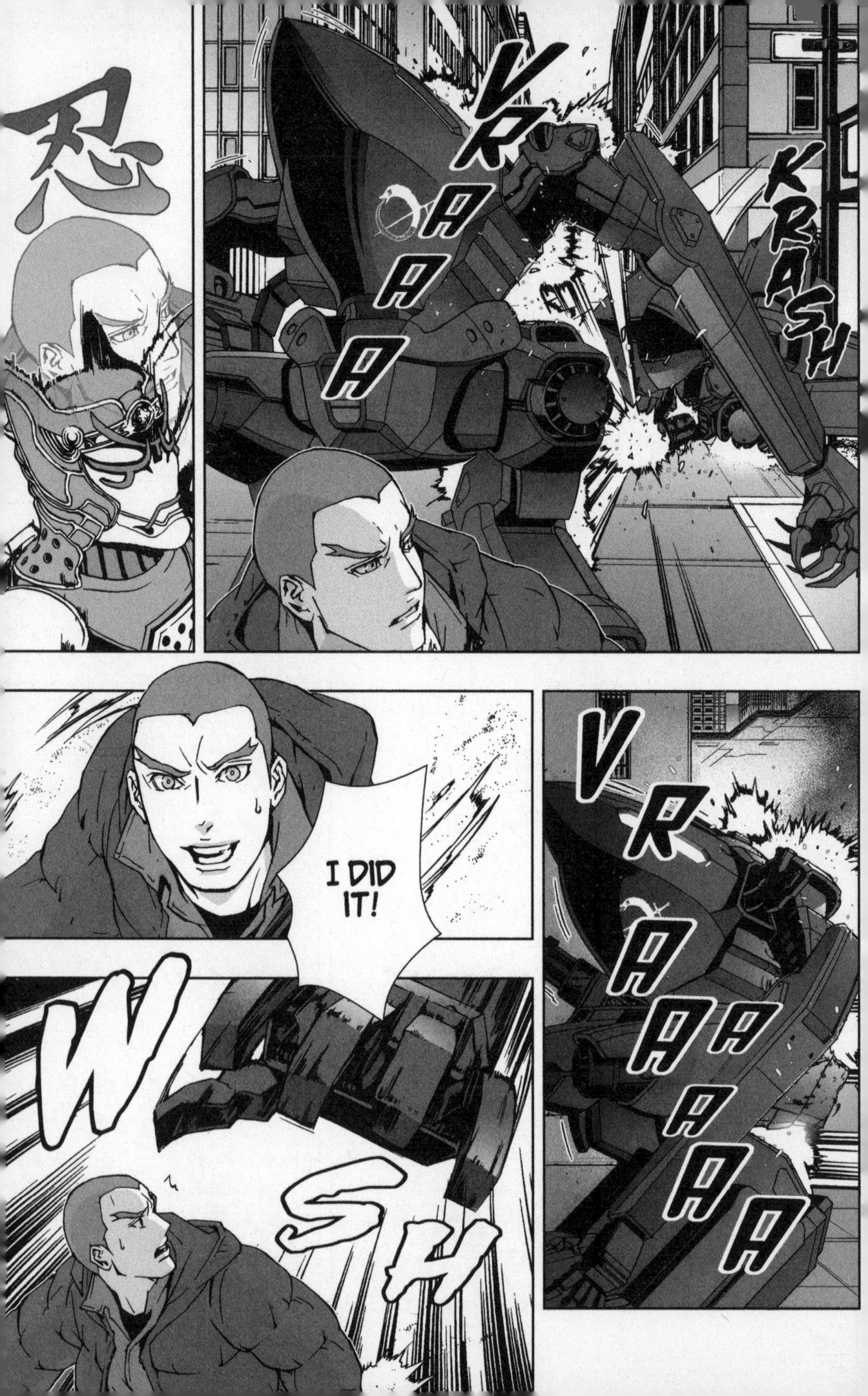
KRASH
VRAAA
忍
VRAAAAAAAAAA
I DID IT!
W
SH

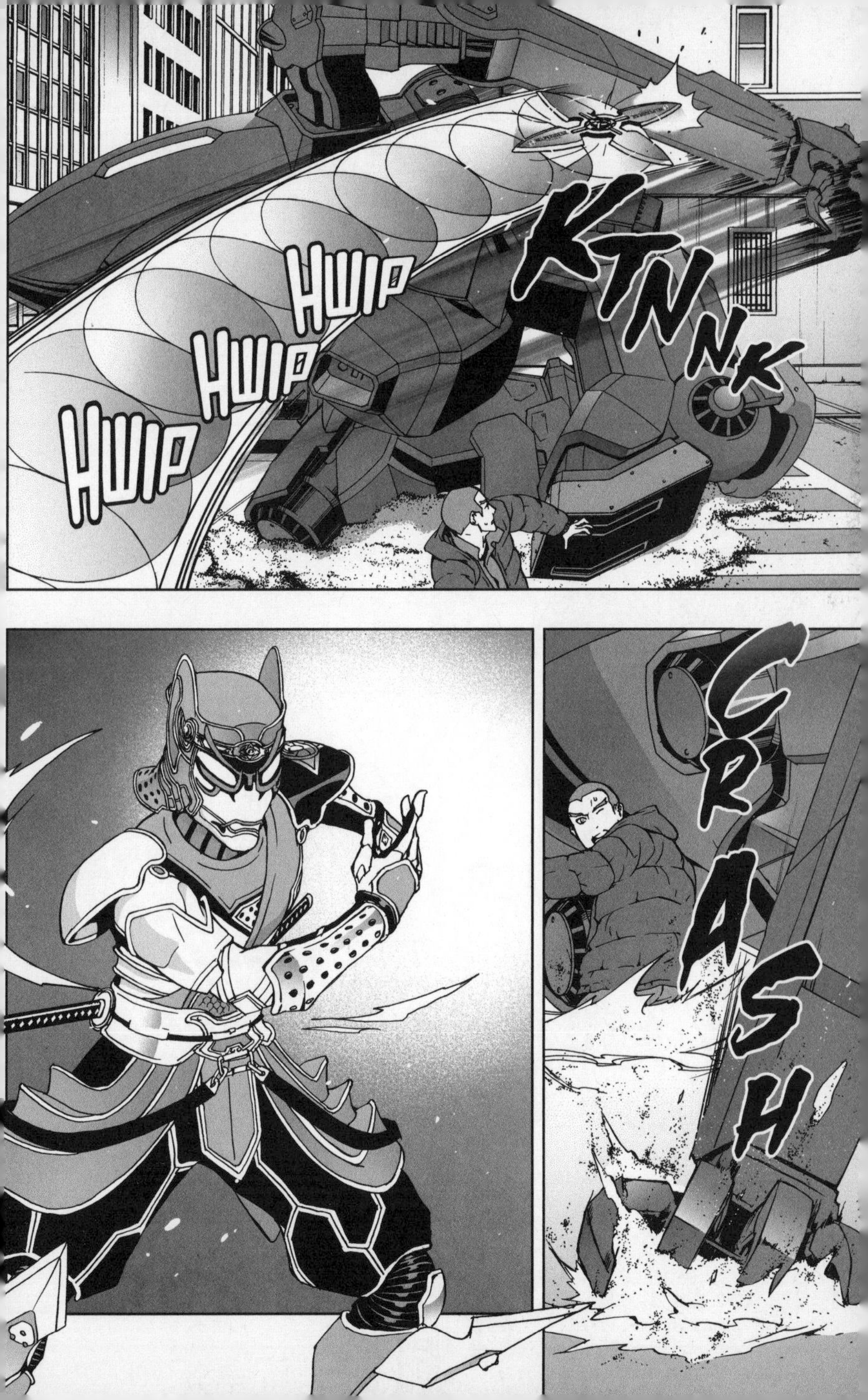
KTNNNK
HWIP
HWIP
HWIP
CRASH

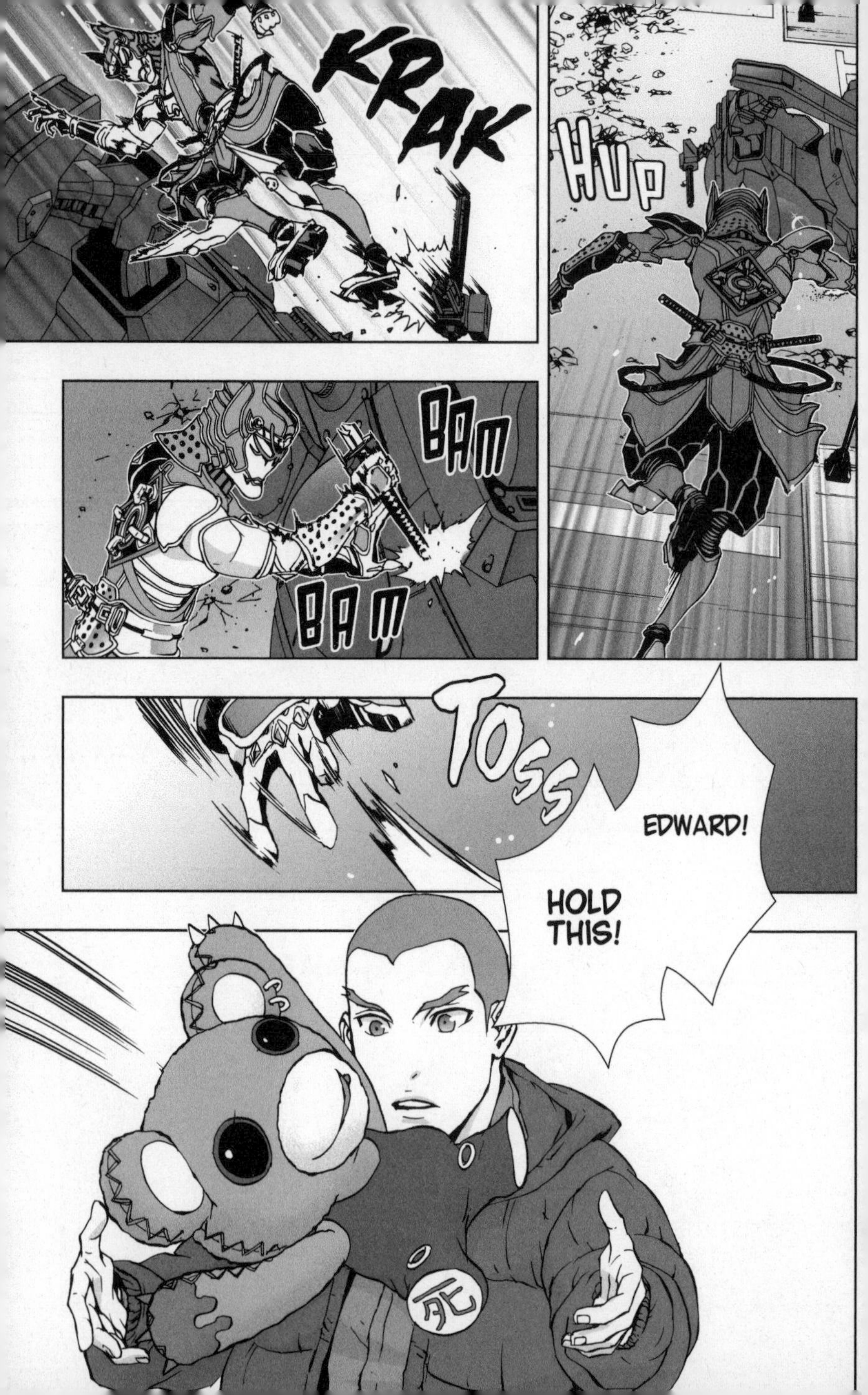
HUP
KRAK
BAM
BAM
TOSS
EDWARD!
HOLD THIS!

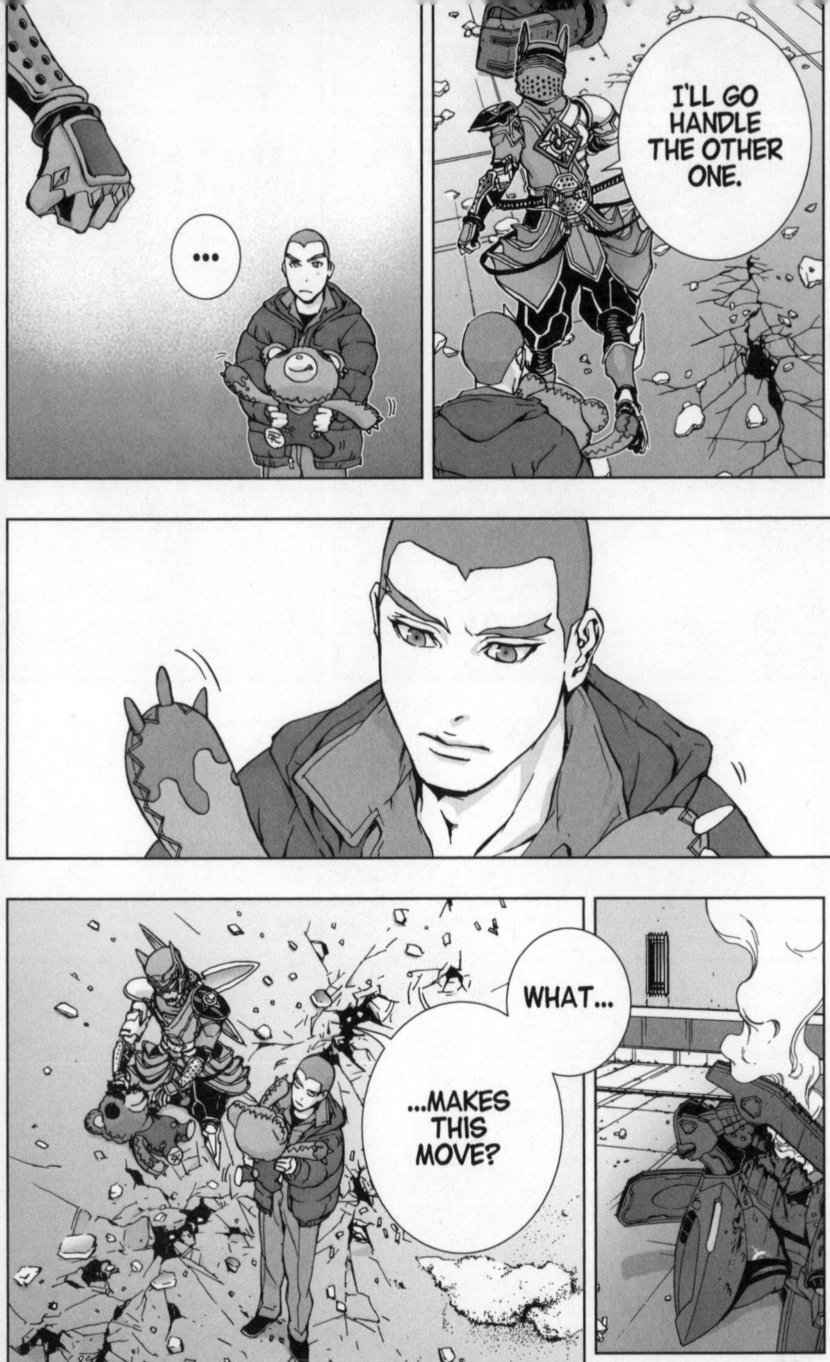
I'LL GO HANDLE THE OTHER ONE.
...
WHAT...
...MAKES THIS MOVE?

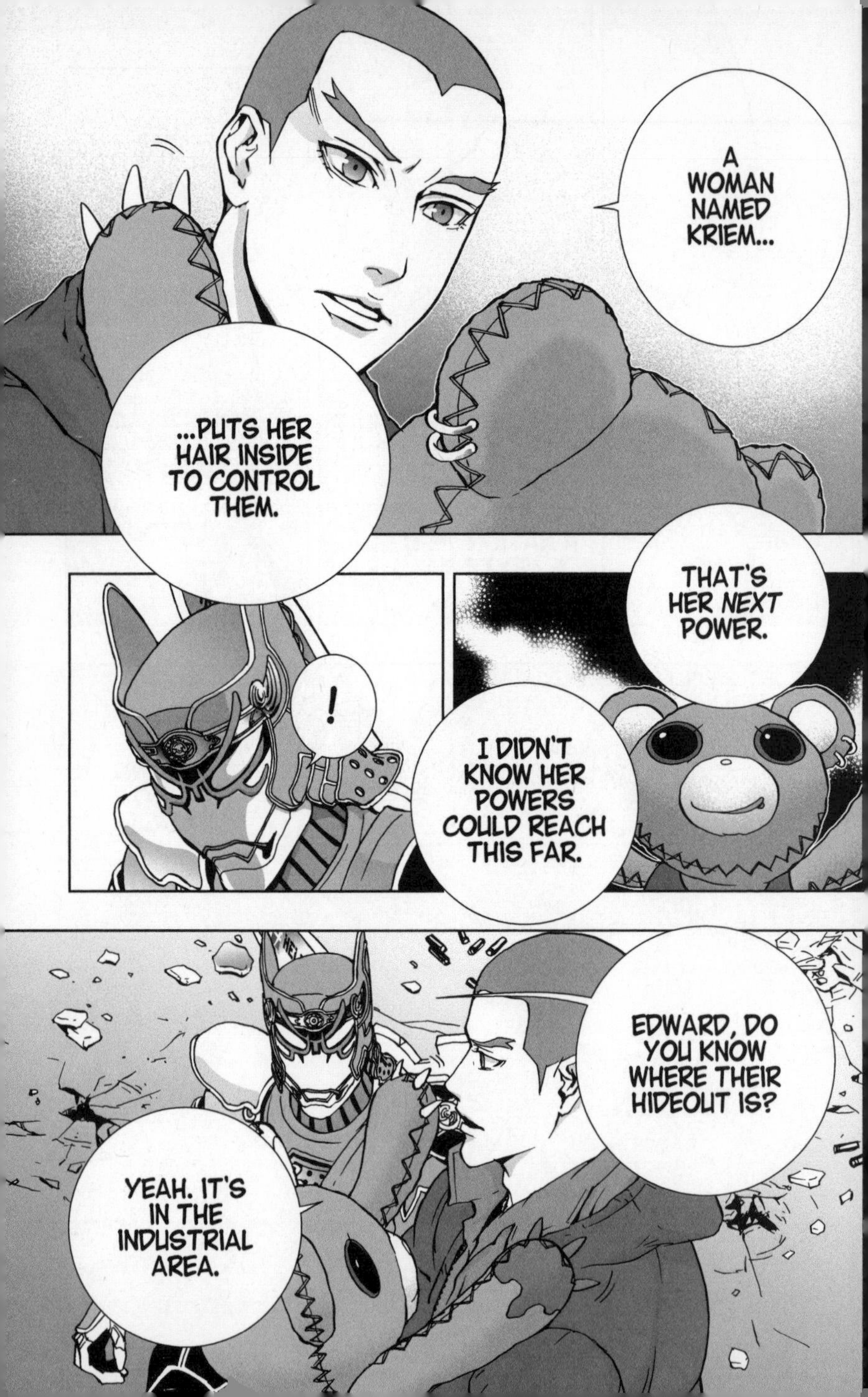
A WOMAN NAMED KRIEM...
...PUTS HER HAIR INSIDE TO CONTROL THEM.
THAT'S HER NEXT POWER.
I DIDN'T KNOW HER POWERS COULD REACH THIS FAR.
!
EDWARD, DO YOU KNOW WHERE THEIR HIDEOUT IS?
YEAH. IT'S IN THE INDUSTRIAL AREA.

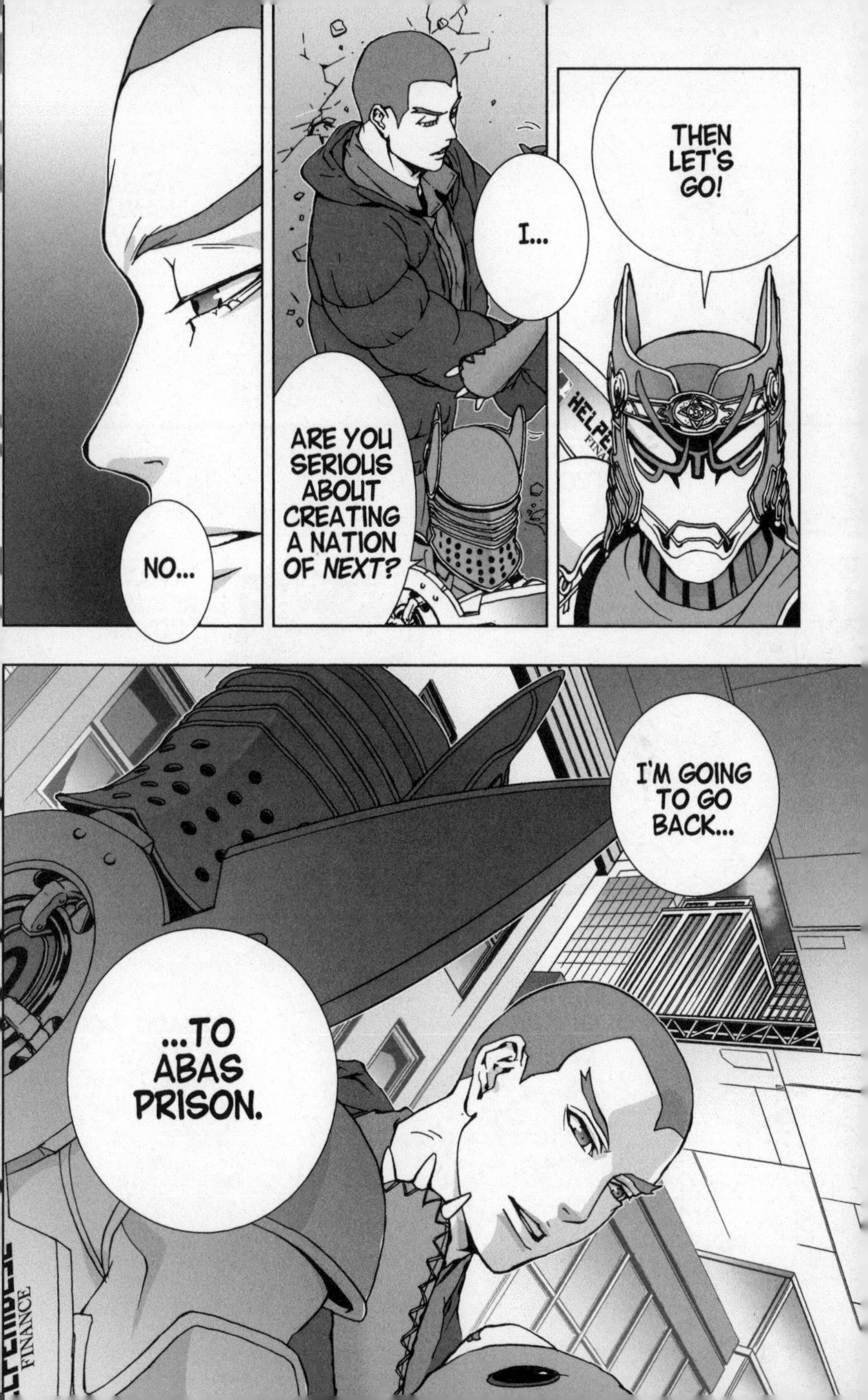
THEN LET'S GO!
I...
ARE YOU SERIOUS ABOUT CREATING A NATION OF NEXT?
NO...
I'M GOING TO GO BACK...
...TO ABAS PRISON.
FINANCE

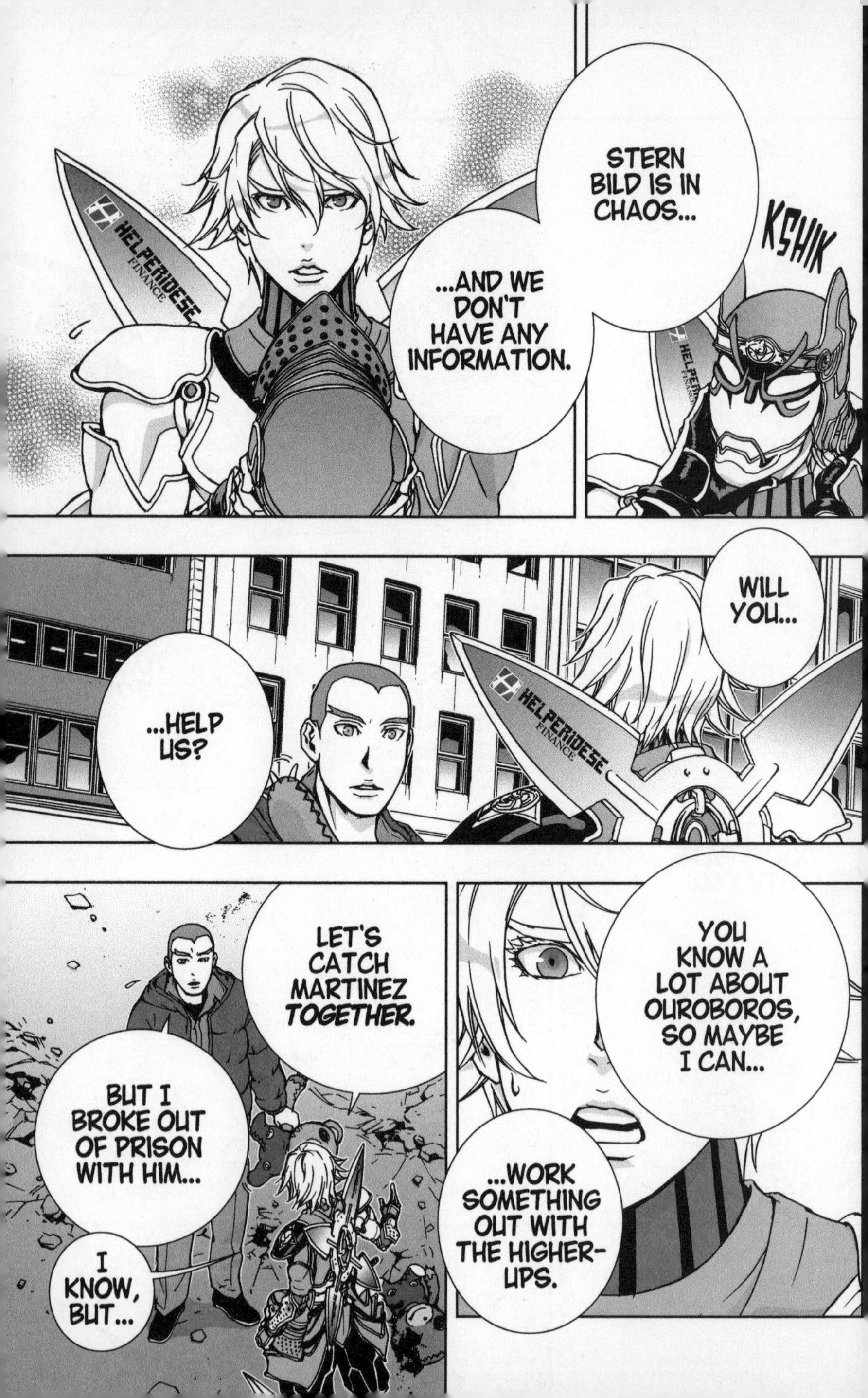
STERN BILD IS IN CHAOS...
KSHIK
...AND WE DON'T HAVE ANY INFORMATION.
WILL YOU...
...HELP US?
YOU KNOW A LOT ABOUT OUROBOROS, SO MAYBE I CAN...
...WORK SOMETHING OUT WITH THE HIGHER-UPS.
LET'S CATCH MARTINEZ *TOGETHER.*
BUT I BROKE OUT OF PRISON WITH HIM...
I KNOW, BUT...

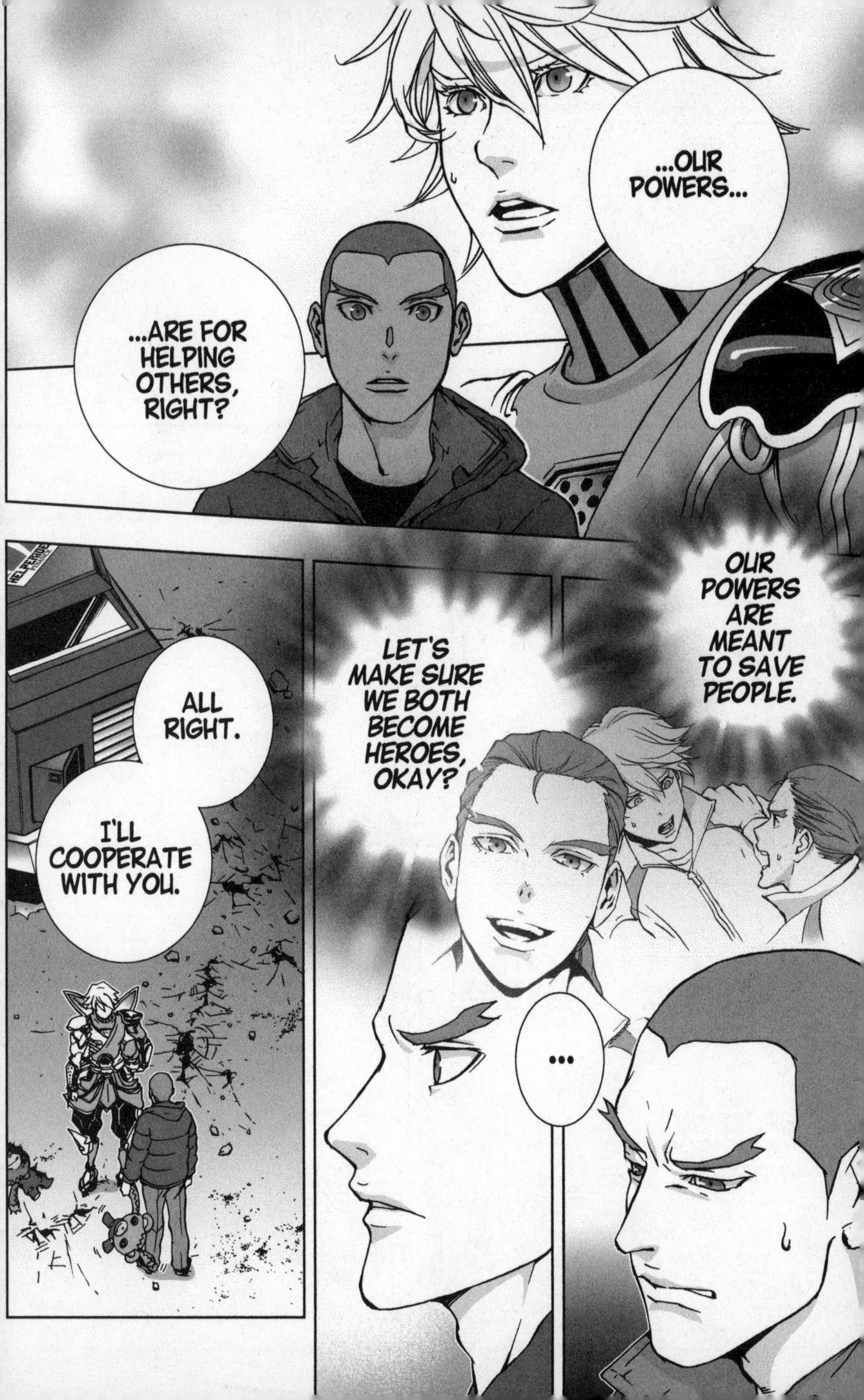
...OUR POWERS...
...ARE FOR HELPING OTHERS, RIGHT?
OUR POWERS ARE MEANT TO SAVE PEOPLE.
LET'S MAKE SURE WE BOTH BECOME HEROES, OKAY?
...
ALL RIGHT.
I'LL COOPERATE WITH YOU.

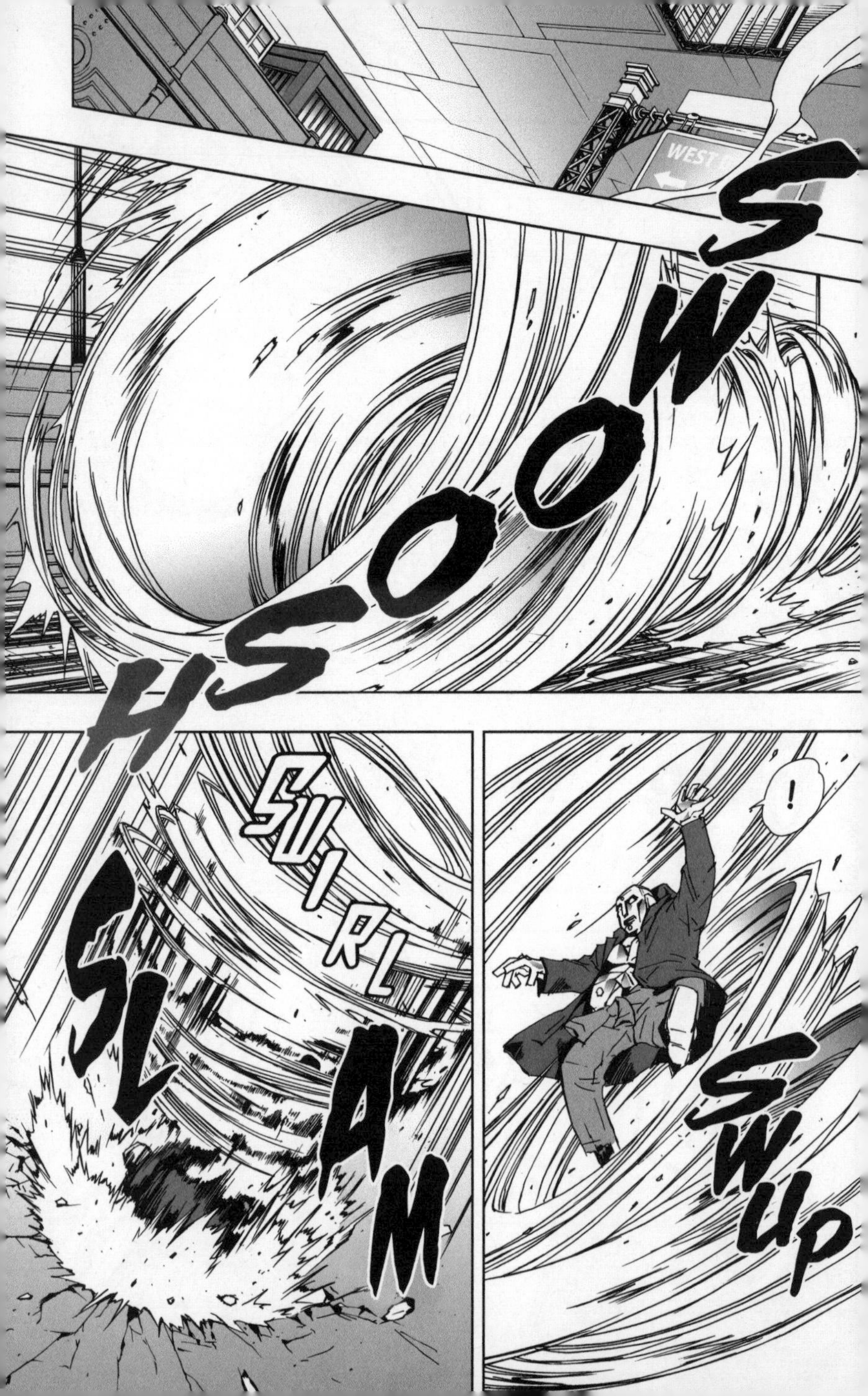

WEST
SWOOOSH
!
SWUP
SWIRL
SLAM

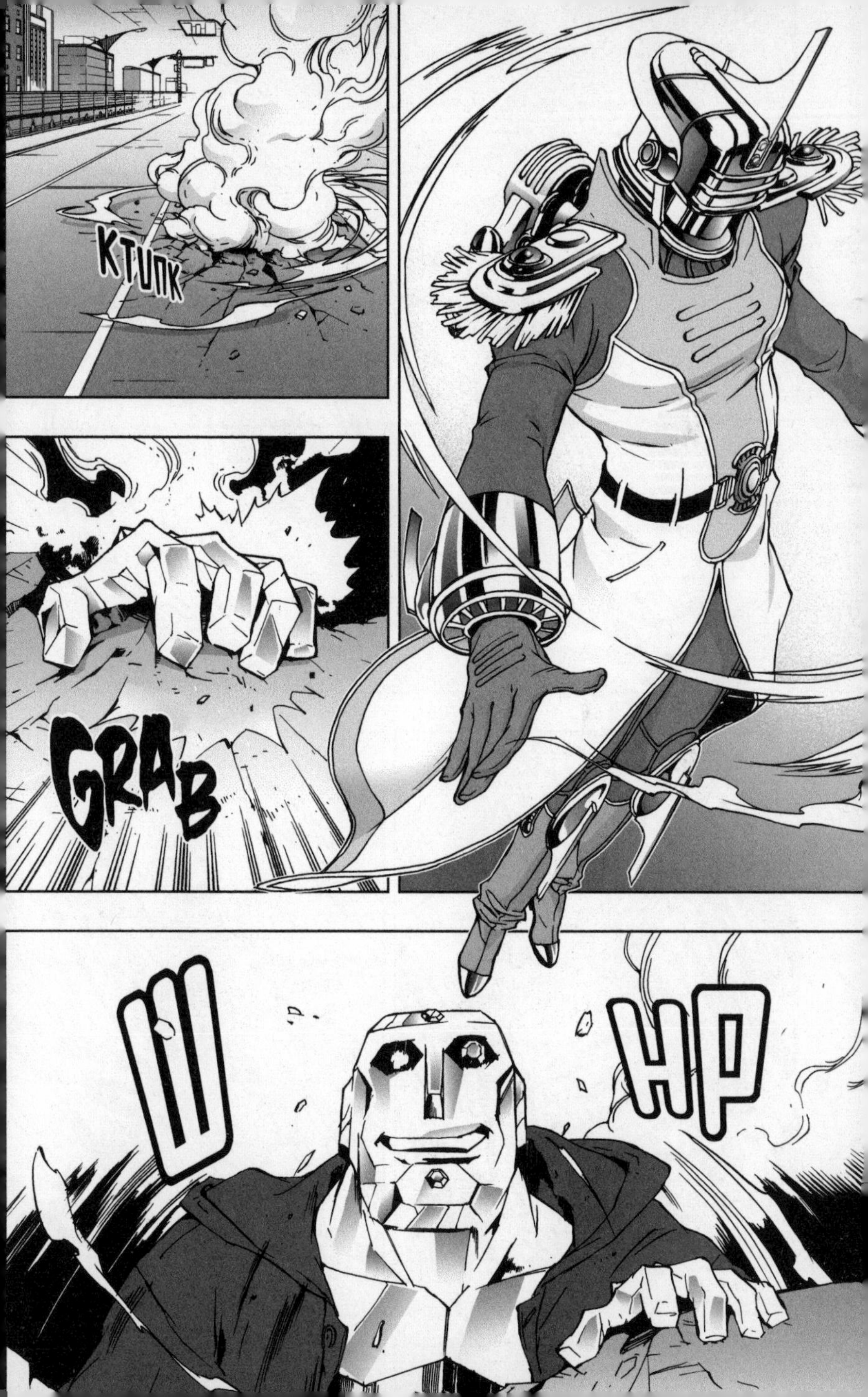
KTUNK
GRAB
HP

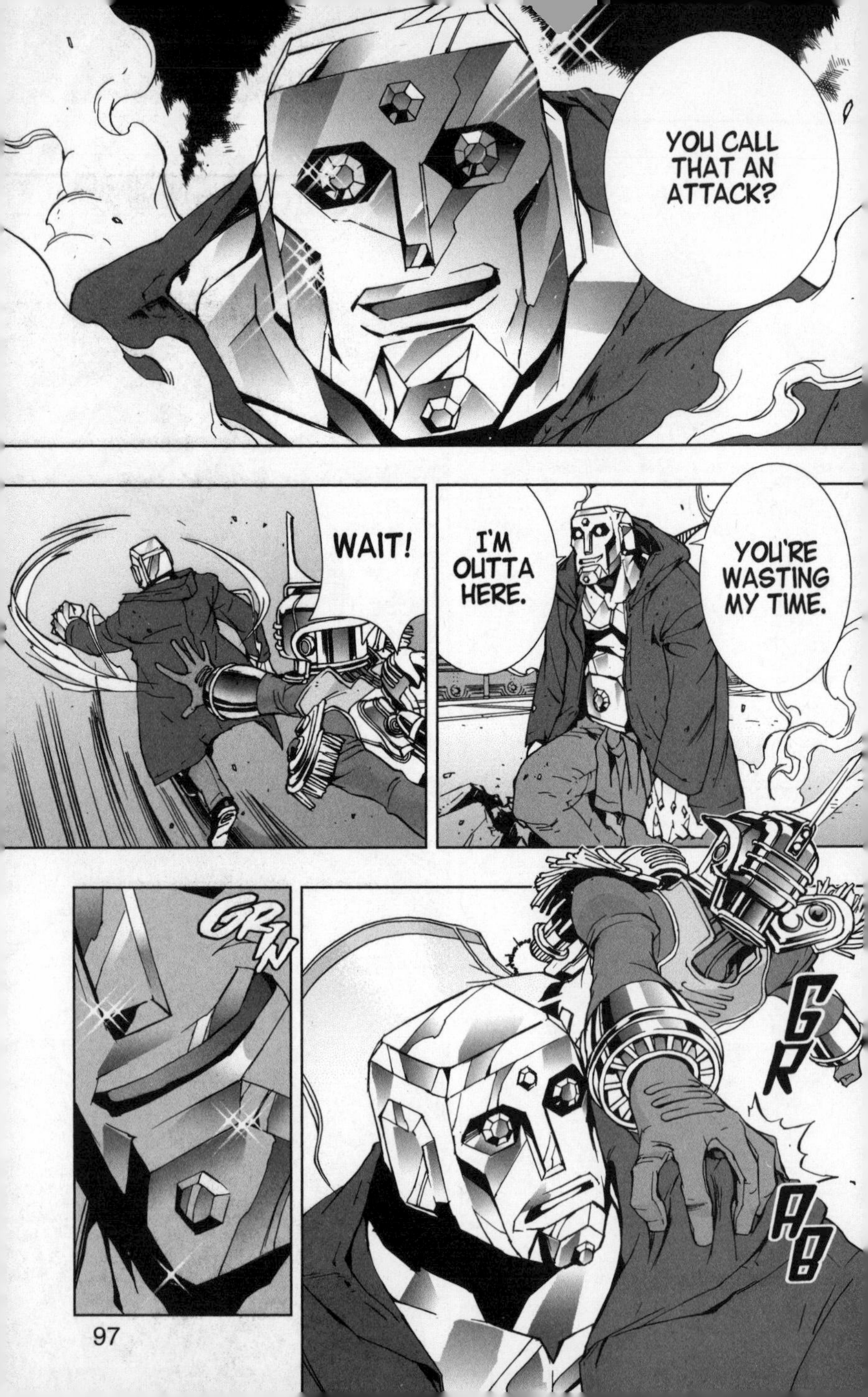

YOU CALL THAT AN ATTACK?
YOU'RE WASTING MY TIME.
I'M OUTTA HERE.
WAIT!
GRAB!
GRN

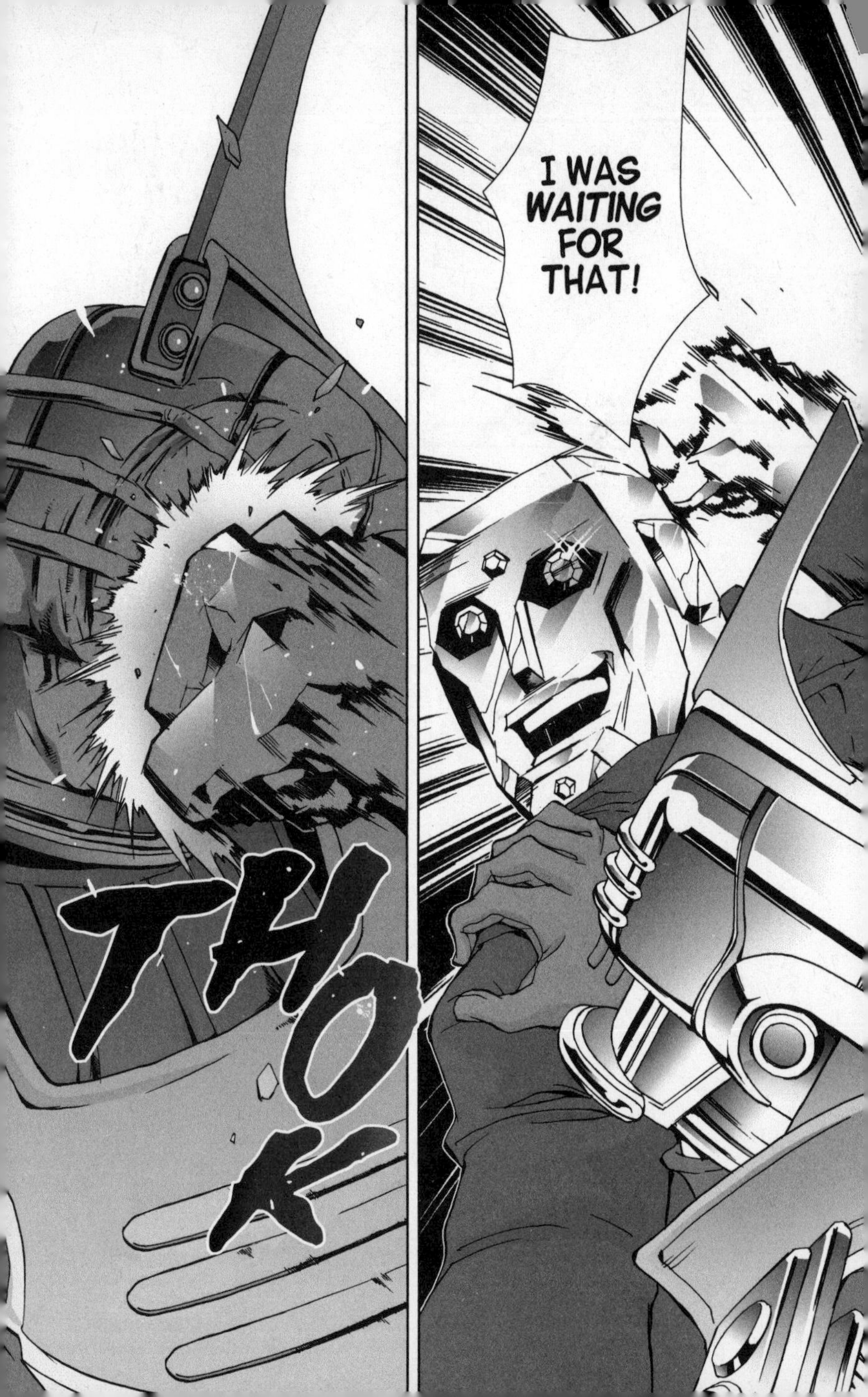
I WAS WAITING FOR THAT!
THOK

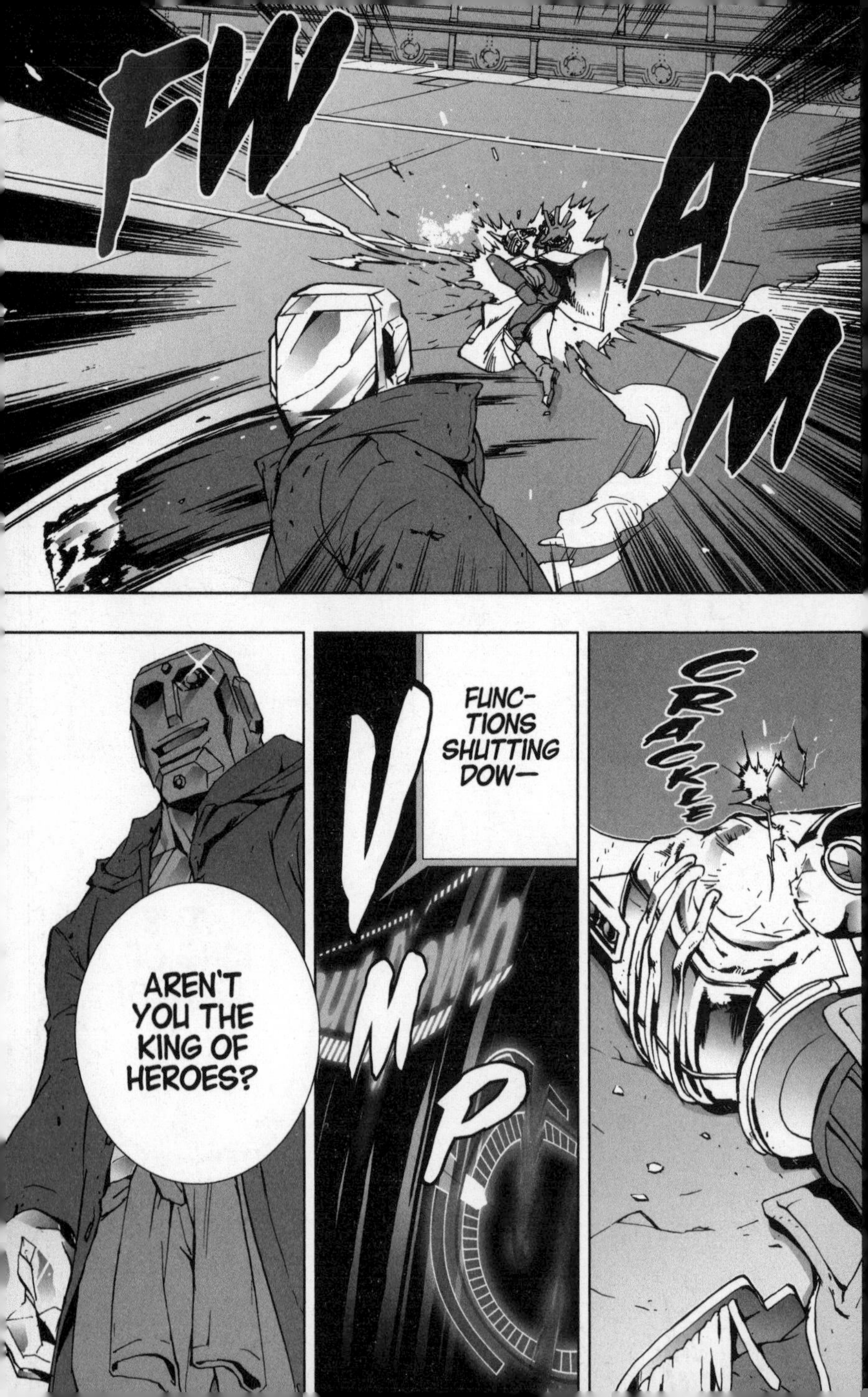
FWAM
CRACKLE
FUNCTIONS SHUTTING DOW—
VMP
AREN'T YOU THE KING OF HEROES?

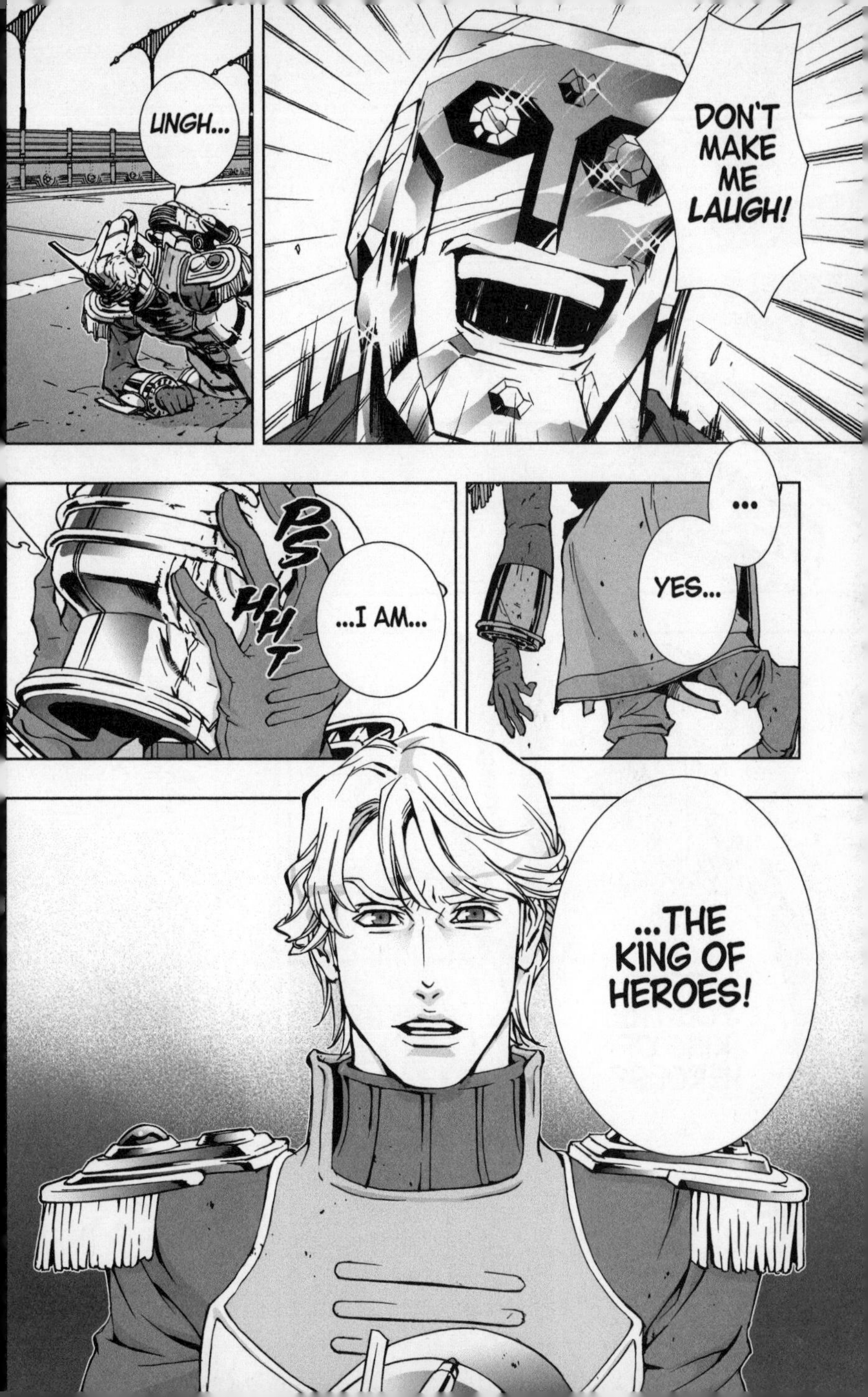
DON'T MAKE ME LAUGH!
UNGH...
...
YES...
...I AM...
PSHHT
...THE KING OF HEROES!

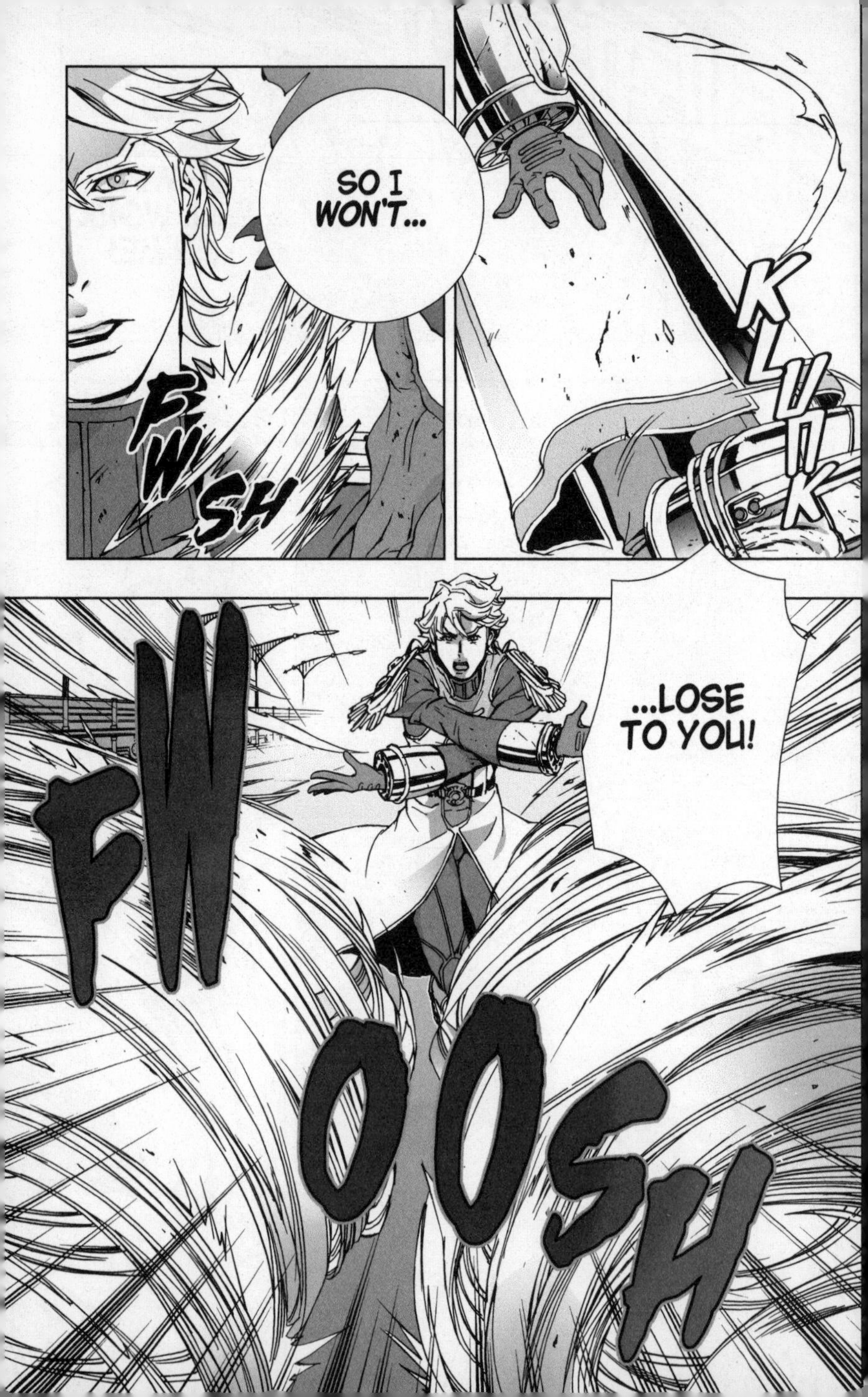
KLUNK
SO I WON'T...
FWSH
...LOSE TO YOU!
FWOOSH

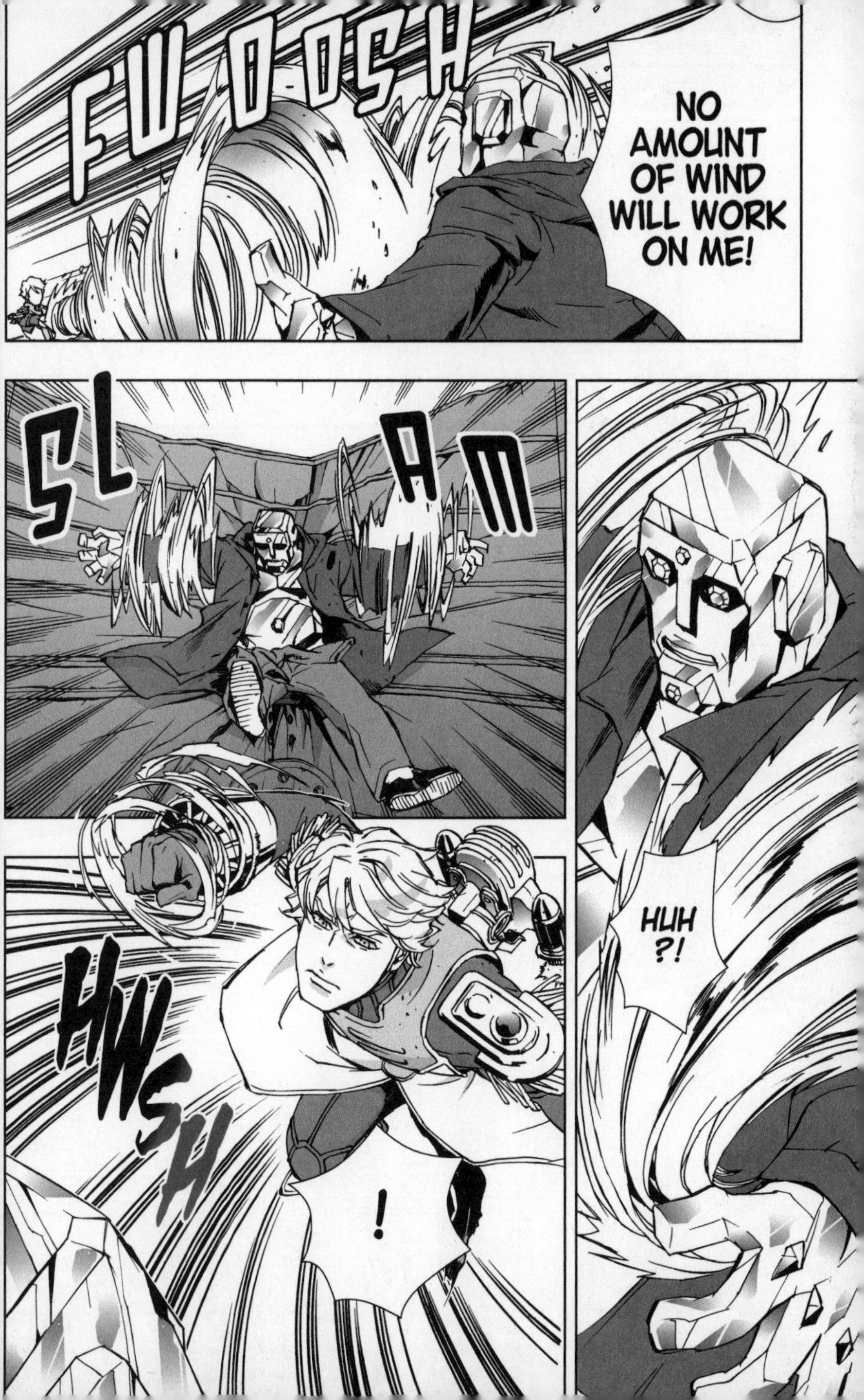
FWOOSH
NO AMOUNT OF WIND WILL WORK ON ME!
HUH ?!
SLAM
HWSH
!

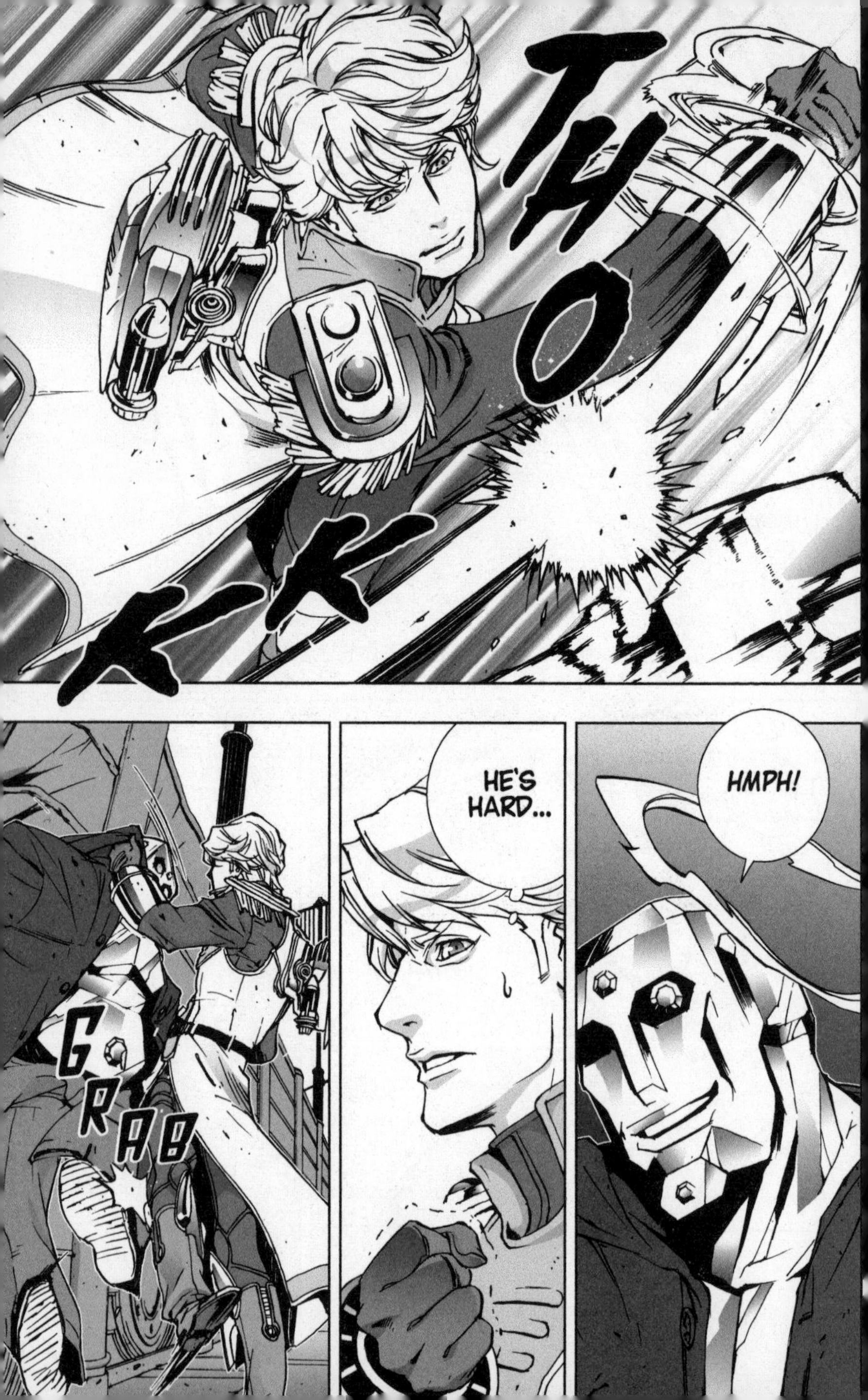
HMPH!
HE'S HARD...
GRAB

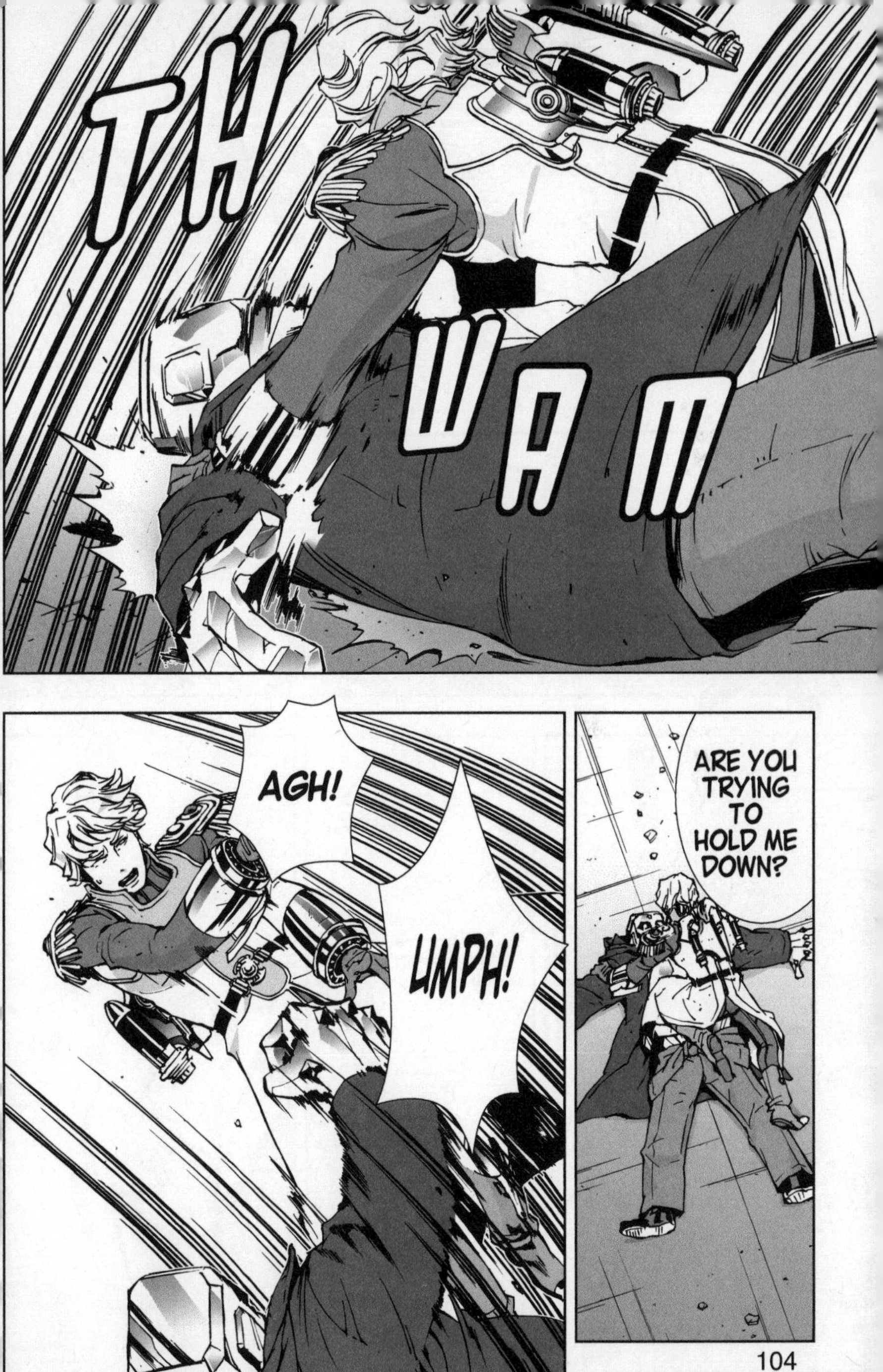
THWAM
ARE YOU TRYING TO HOLD ME DOWN?
AGH!
UMPH!

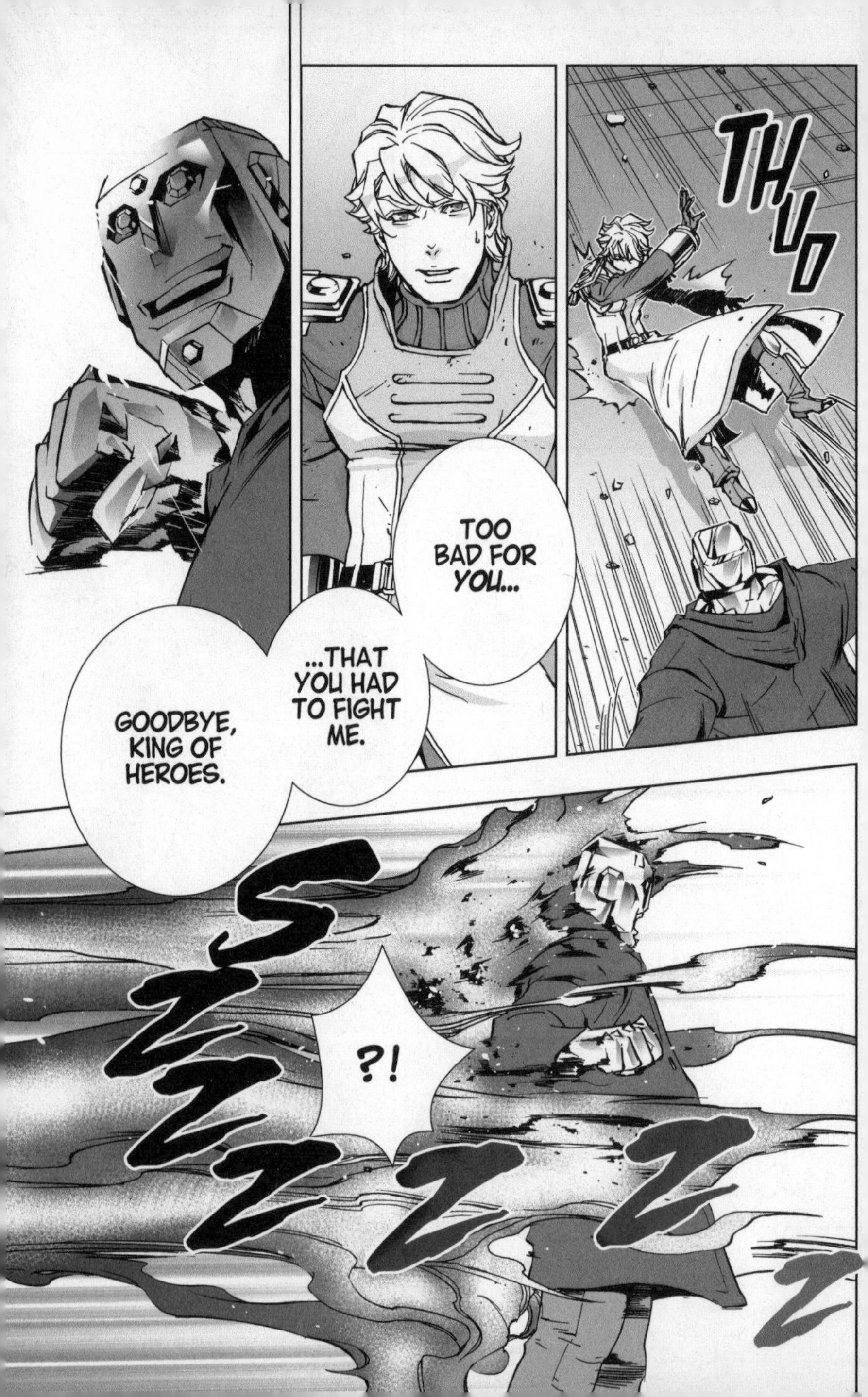
THUD
TOO BAD FOR YOU...
...THAT YOU HAD TO FIGHT ME.
GOODBYE, KING OF HEROES.
SZZZZZZZZ
?!

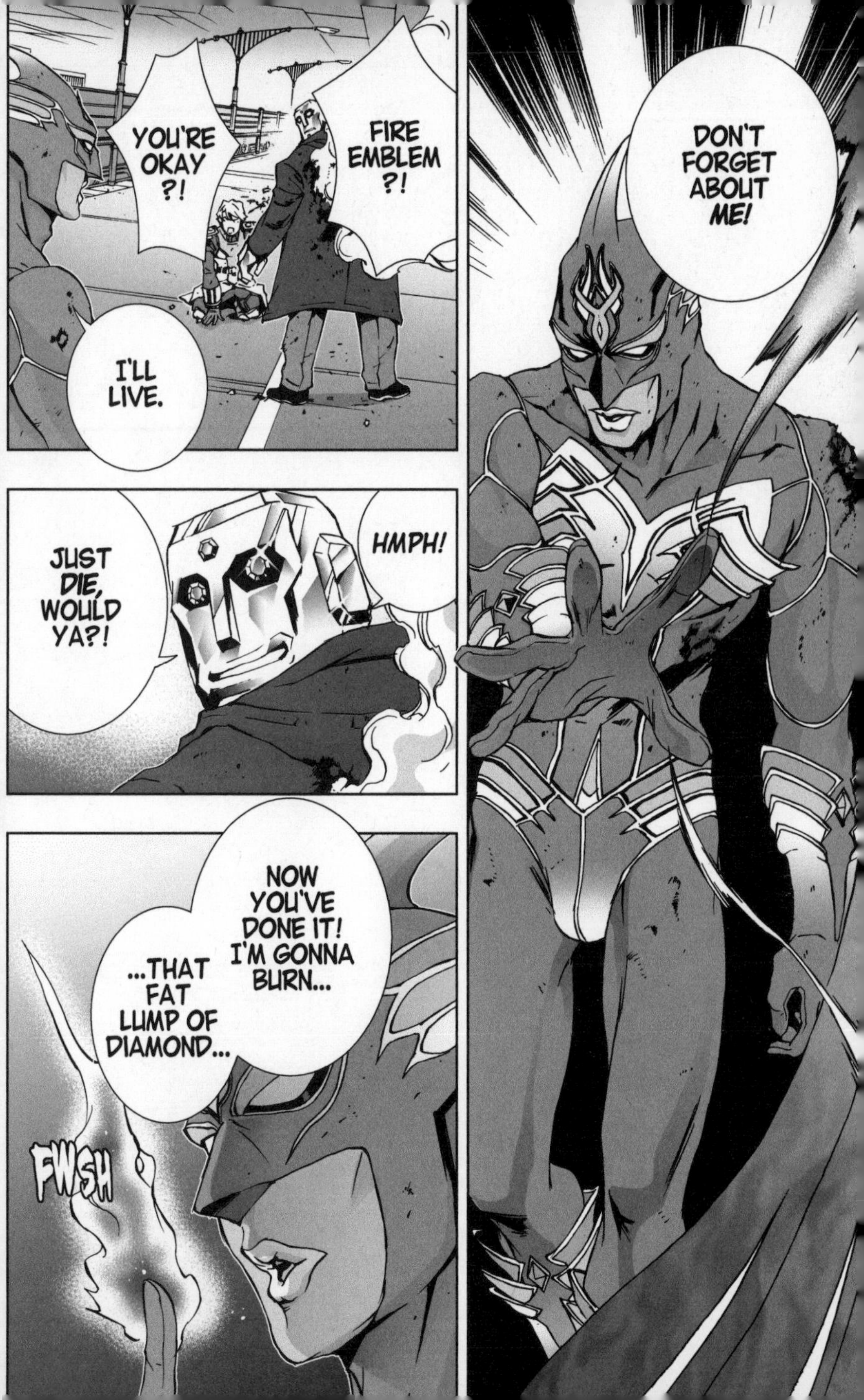
DON'T FORGET ABOUT ME!
FIRE EMBLEM?!
YOU'RE OKAY?!
I'LL LIVE.
HMPH!
JUST DIE, WOULD YA?!
NOW YOU'VE DONE IT! I'M GONNA BURN...
...THAT FAT LUMP OF DIAMOND...
FWSH

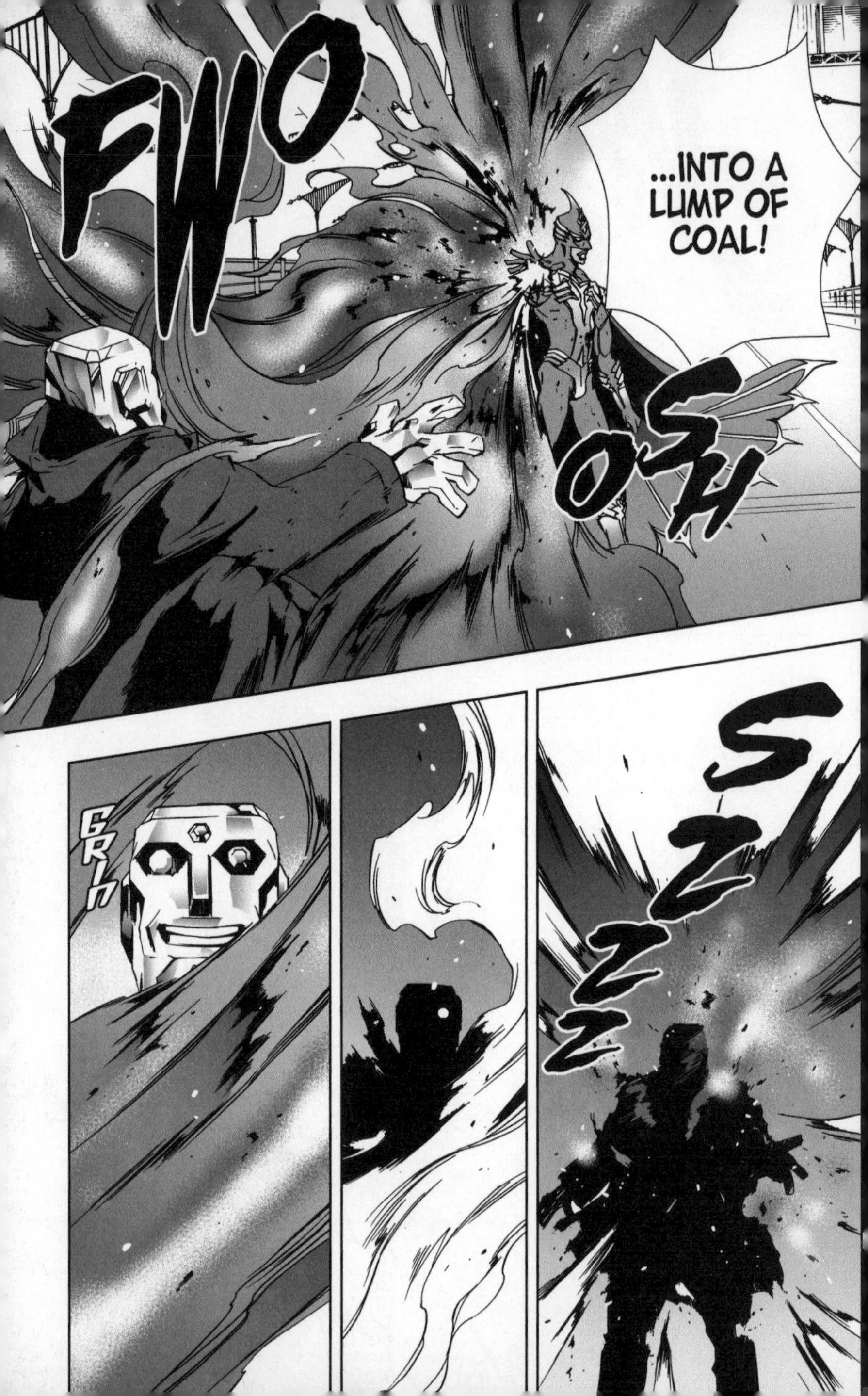
...INTO A LUMP OF COAL!
FWOOSH
SZZZZ
GRIN

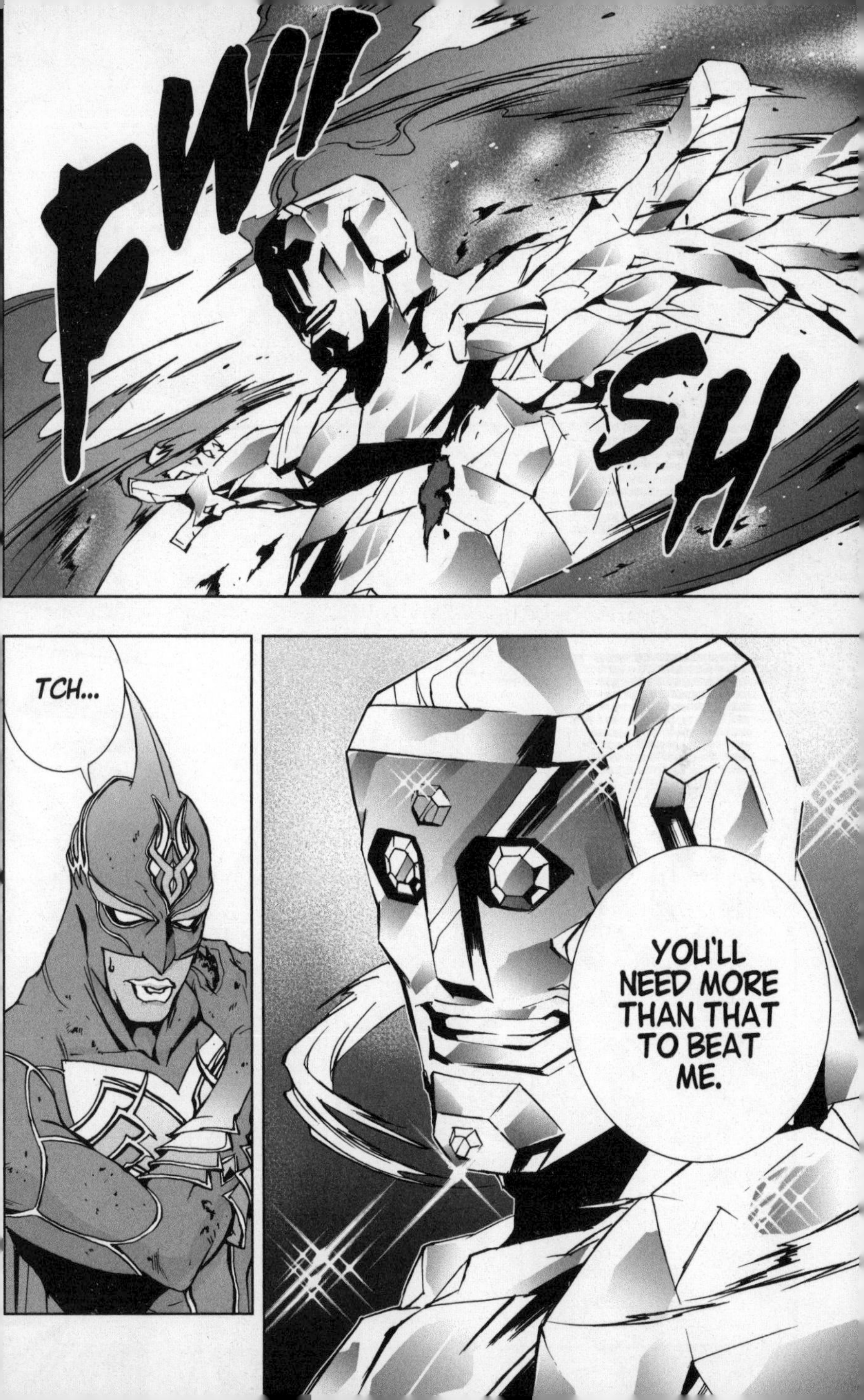
FWISH
YOU'LL NEED MORE THAN THAT TO BEAT ME.
TCH...

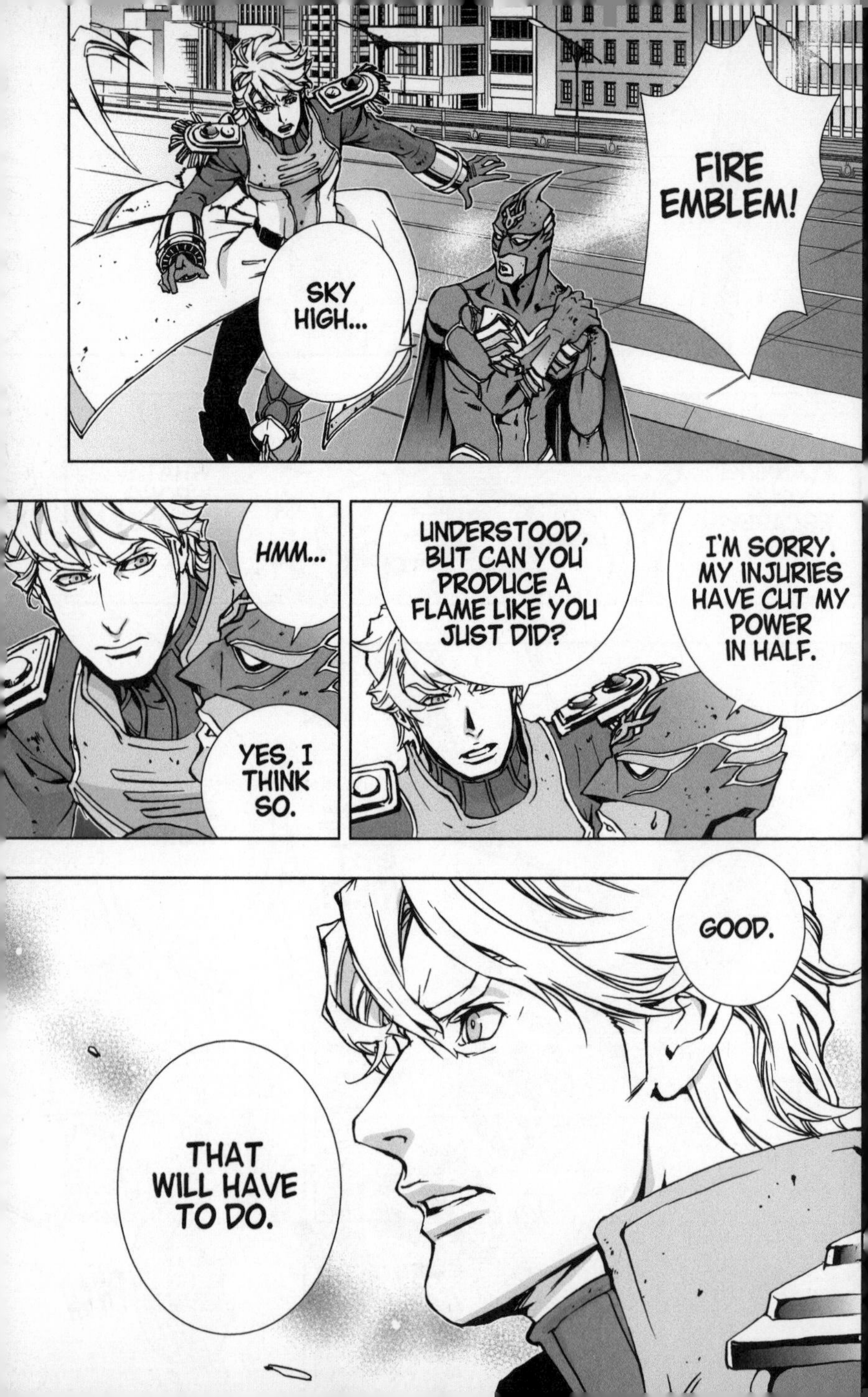
FIRE EMBLEM!
SKY HIGH...
I'M SORRY. MY INJURIES HAVE CUT MY POWER IN HALF.
UNDERSTOOD, BUT CAN YOU PRODUCE A FLAME LIKE YOU JUST DID?
HMM...
YES, I THINK SO.
GOOD.
THAT WILL HAVE TO DO.

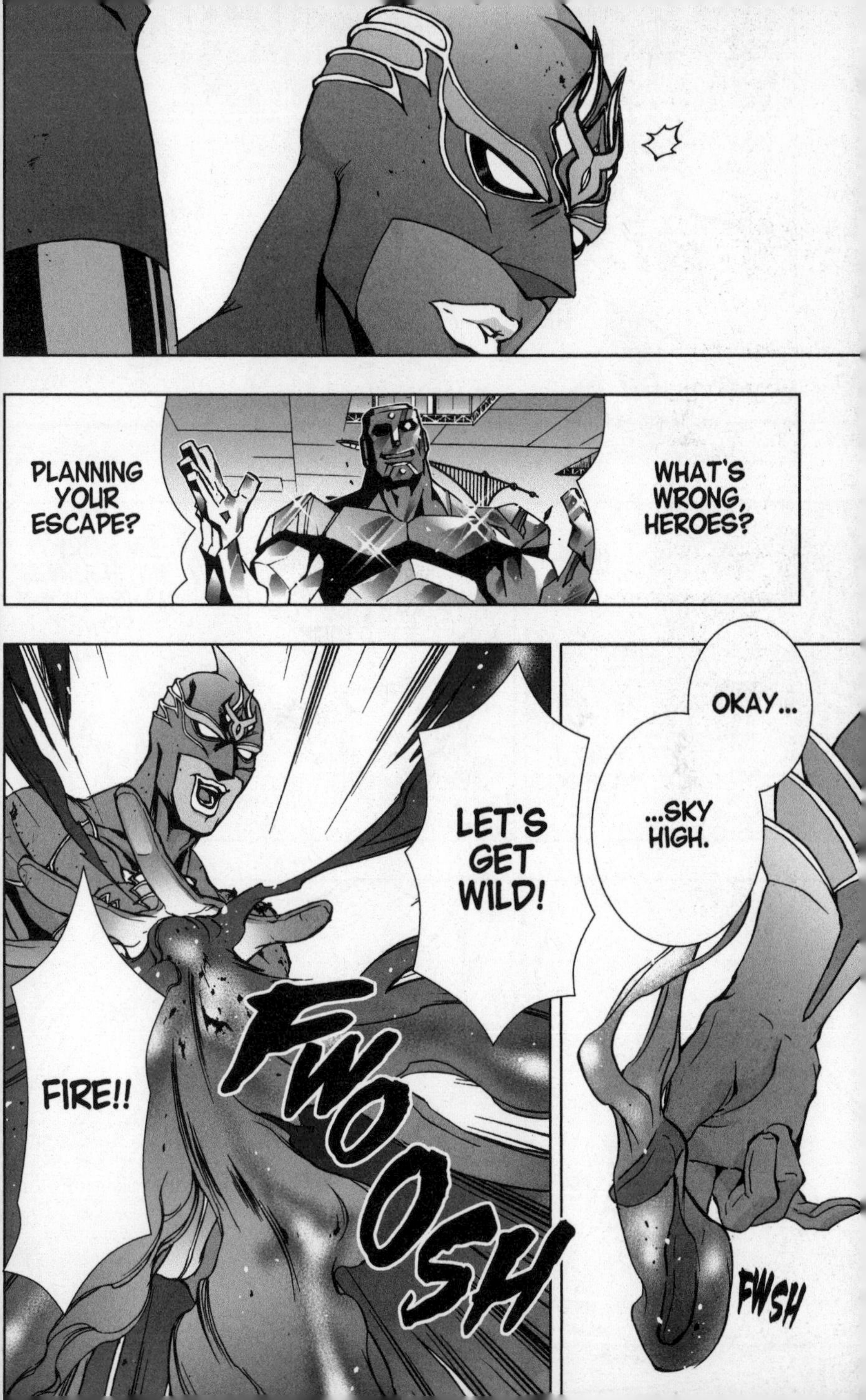
WHAT'S WRONG, HEROES?
PLANNING YOUR ESCAPE?
OKAY...
...SKY HIGH.
FWSH
LET'S GET WILD!
FIRE!!
FWOOSH

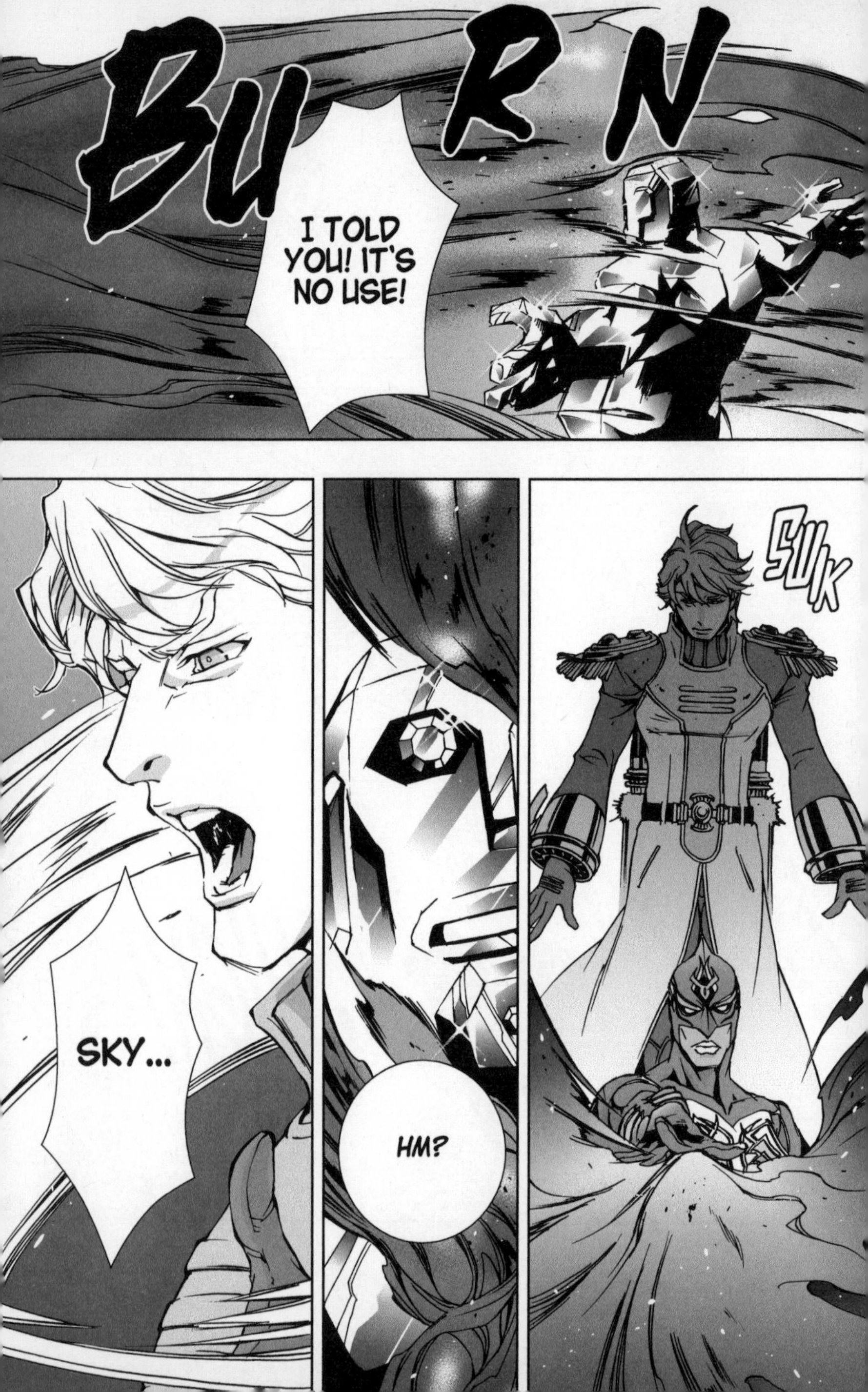
BURN
I TOLD YOU! IT'S NO USE!
SUK
HM?
SKY...

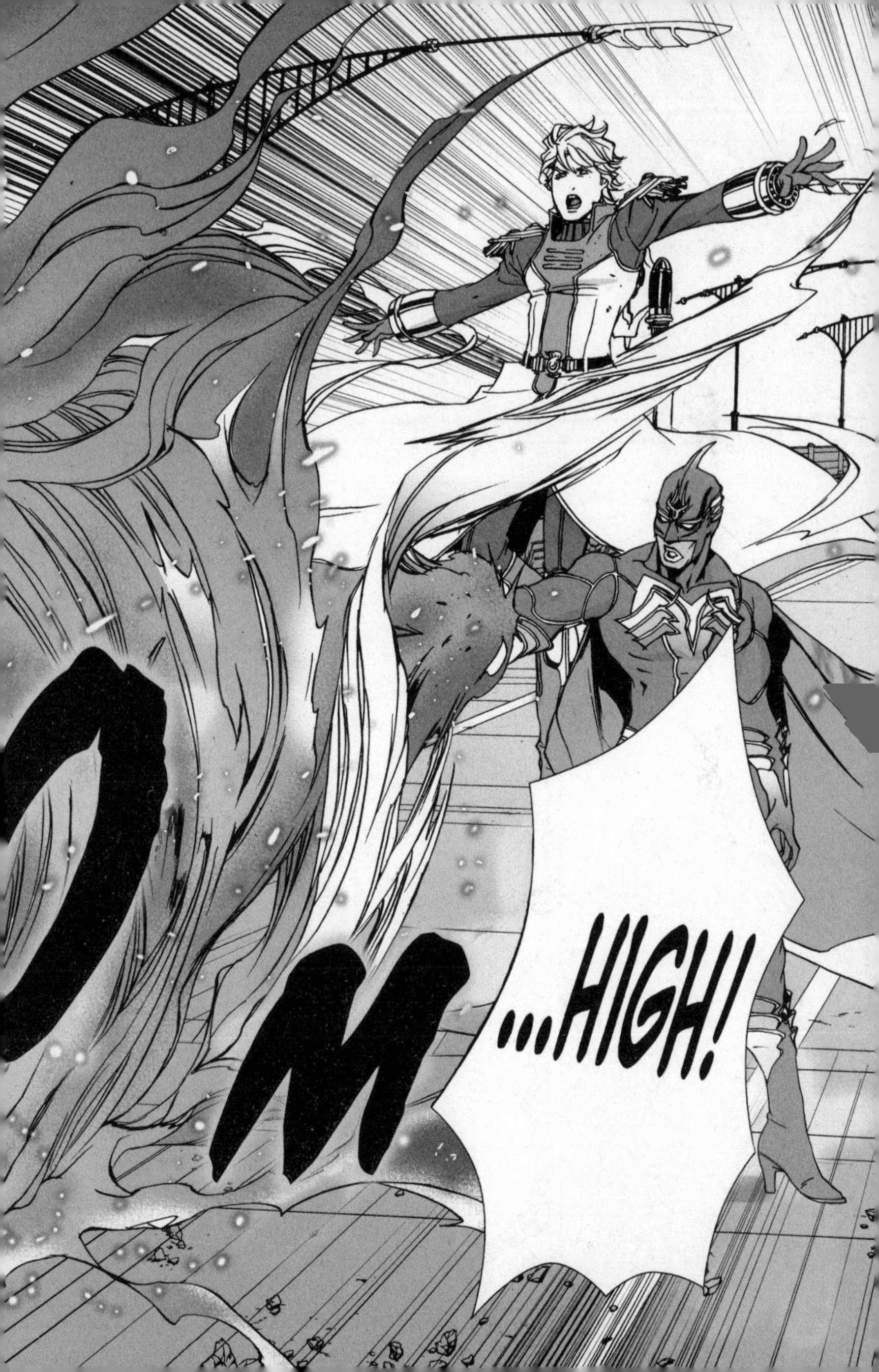

...HIGH!

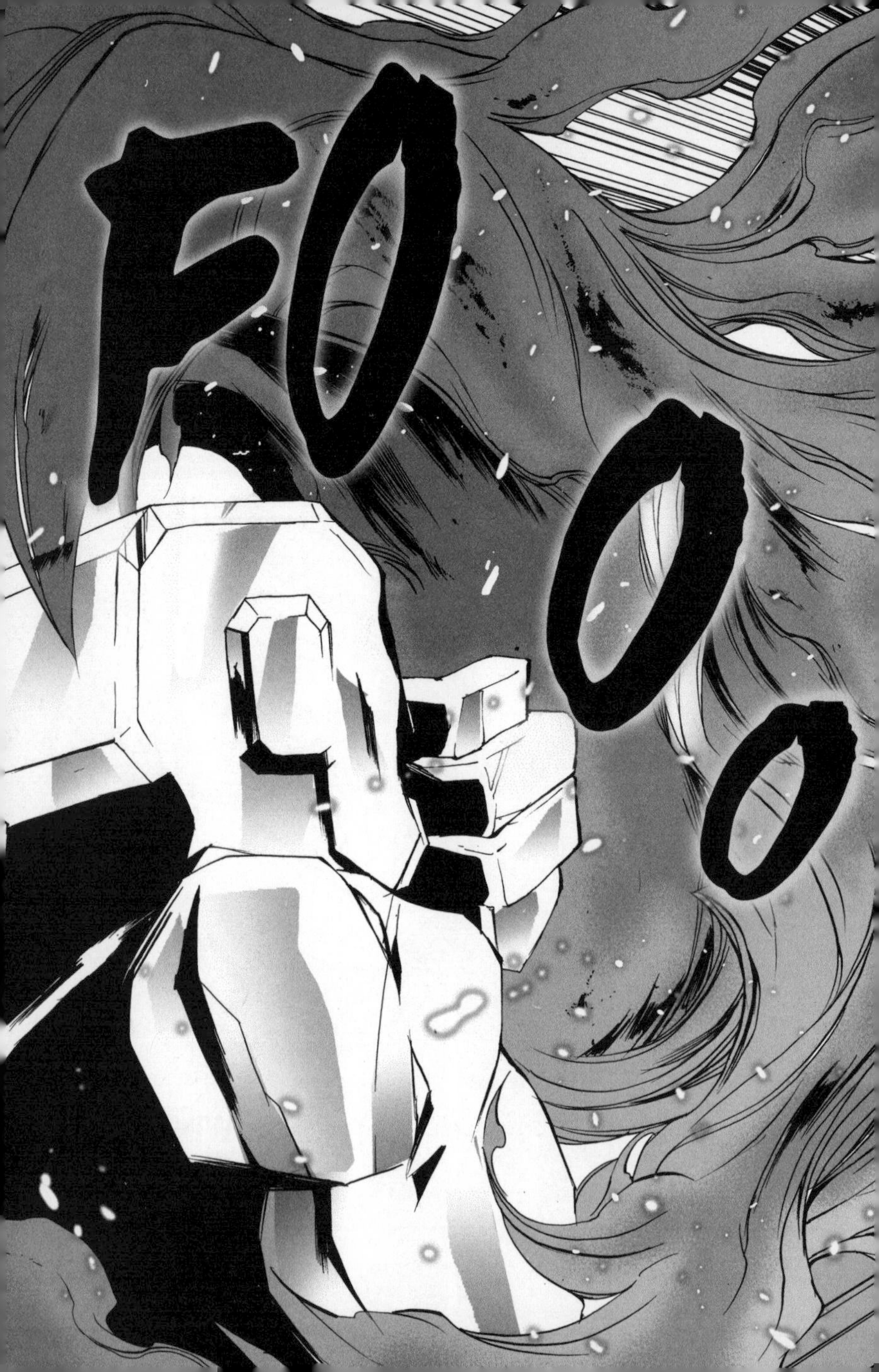
FOOOO

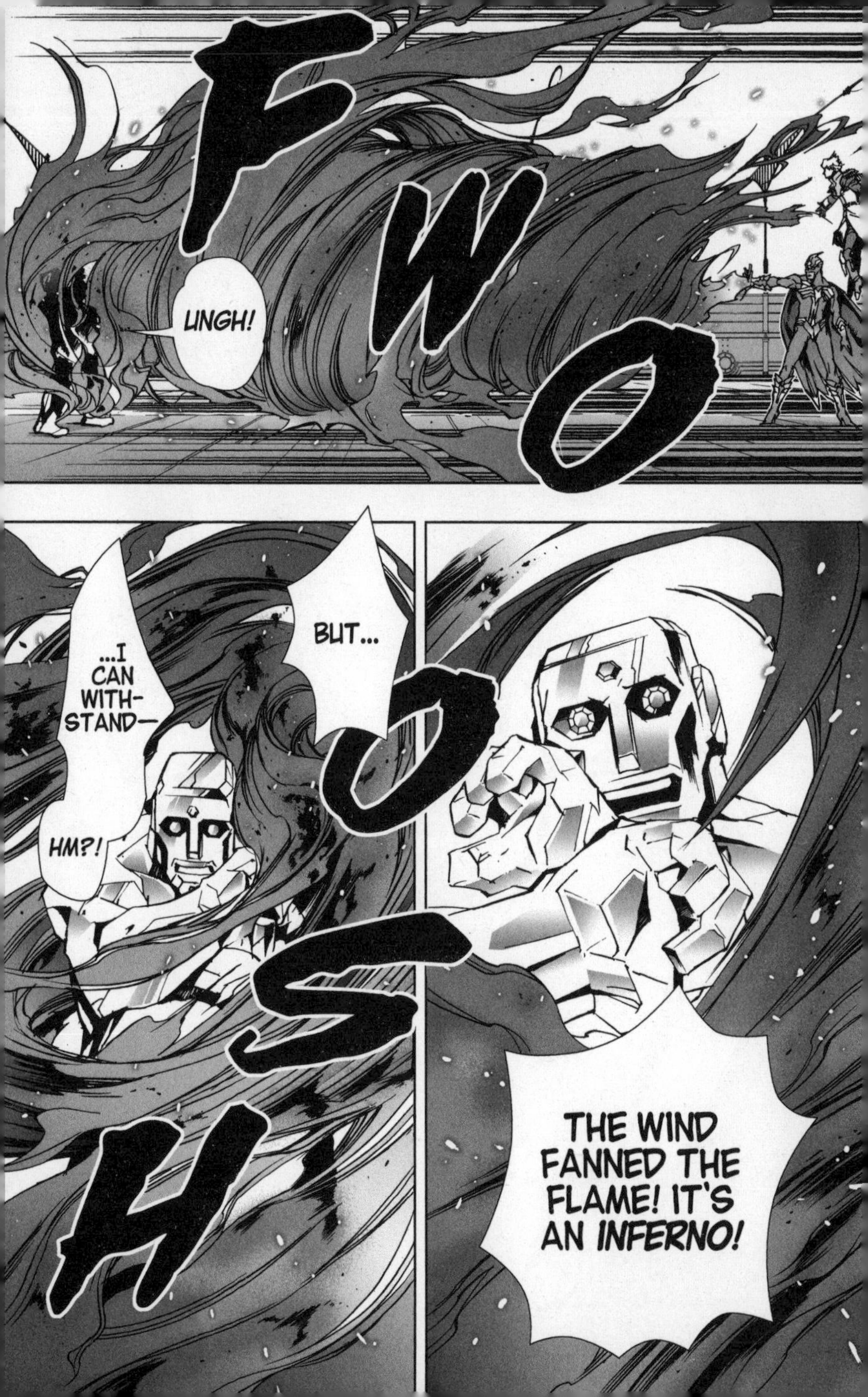
FWOOSH
UNGH!
THE WIND FANNED THE FLAME! IT'S AN INFERNO!
BUT...
...I CAN WITH-STAND—
HM?!

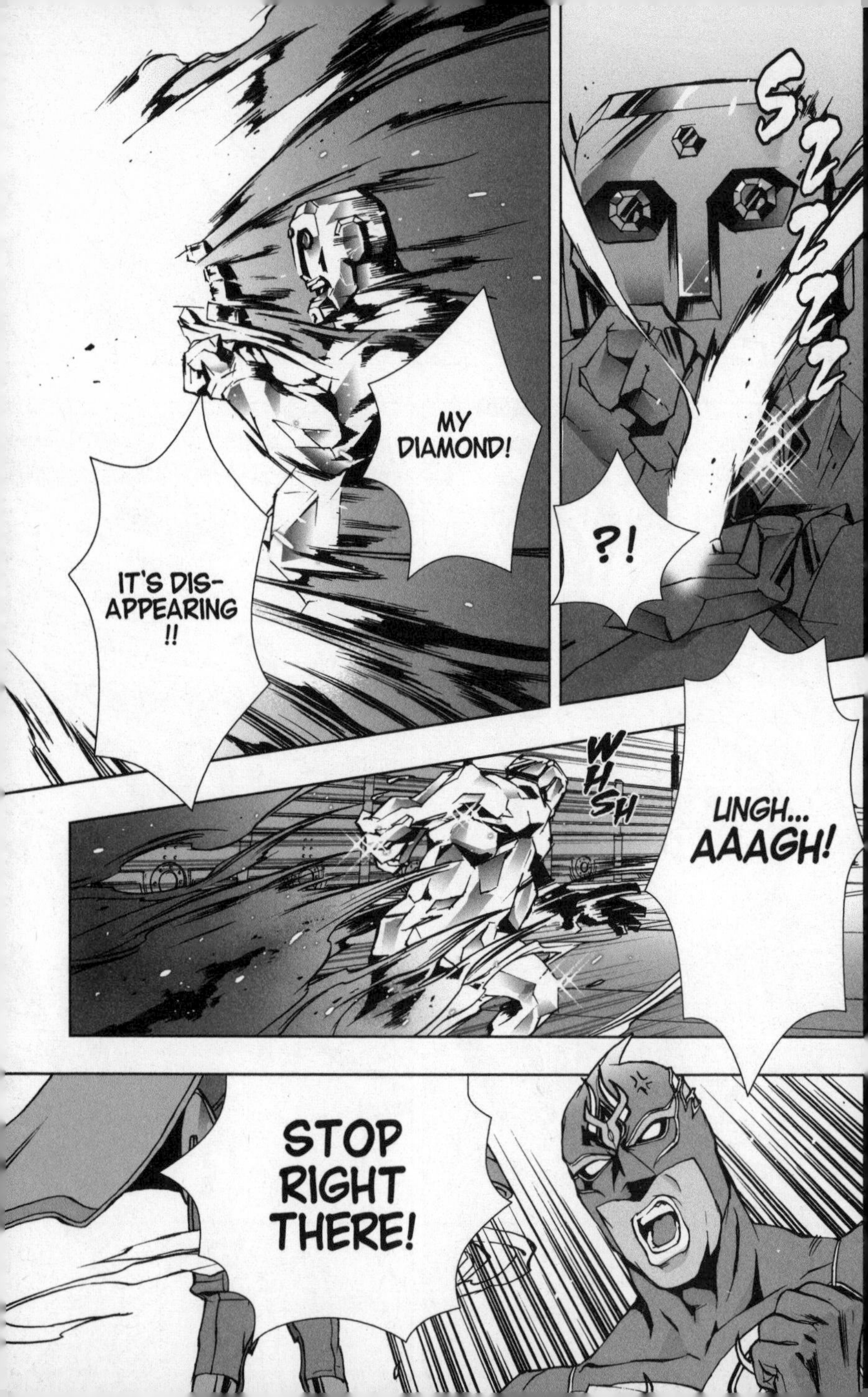
SZZZZZ
?!
MY DIAMOND!
IT'S DIS-APPEARING !!
WHSH
UNGH... AAAGH!
STOP RIGHT THERE!

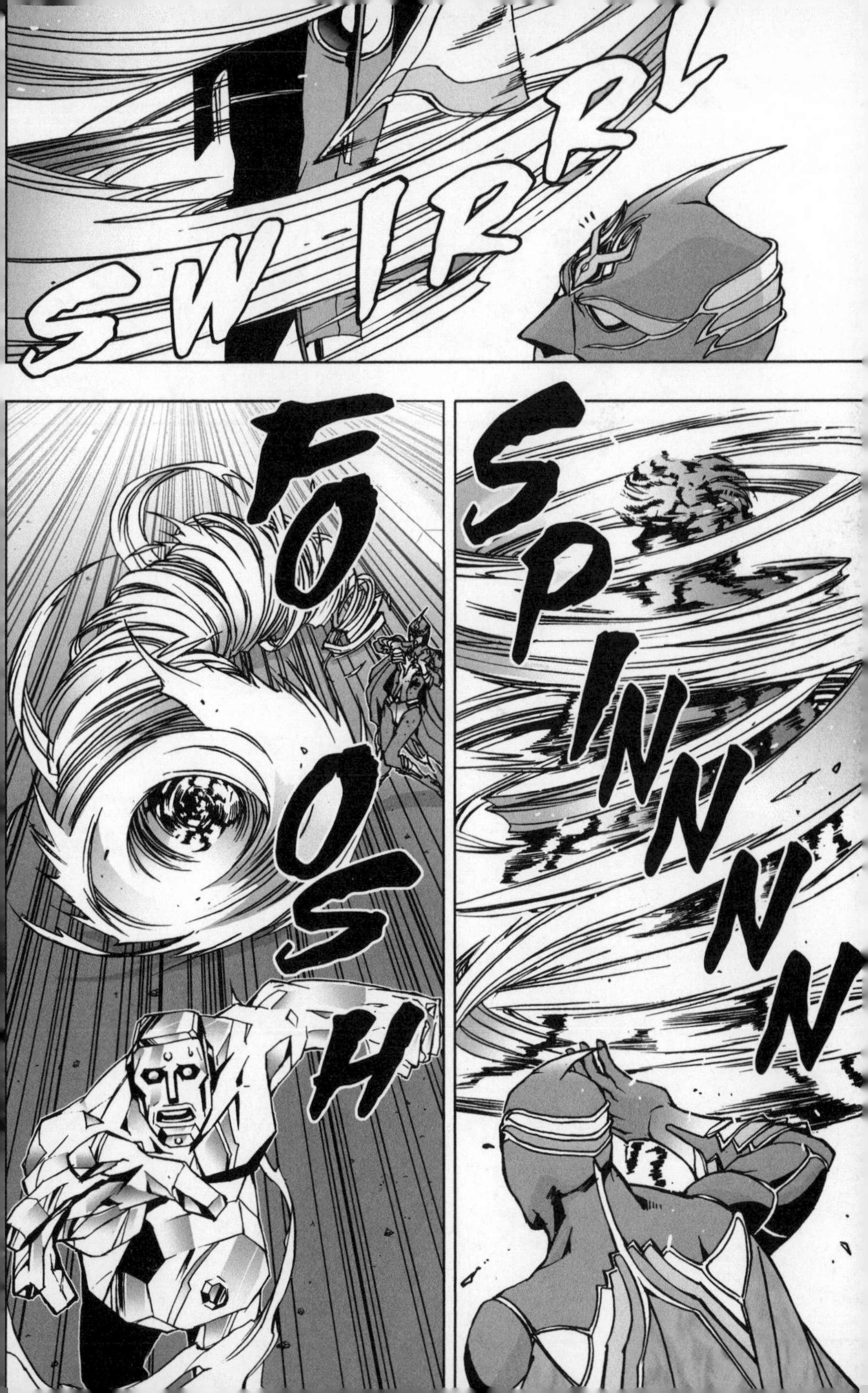
SWIRRL
SPINNNN
FOOOSH

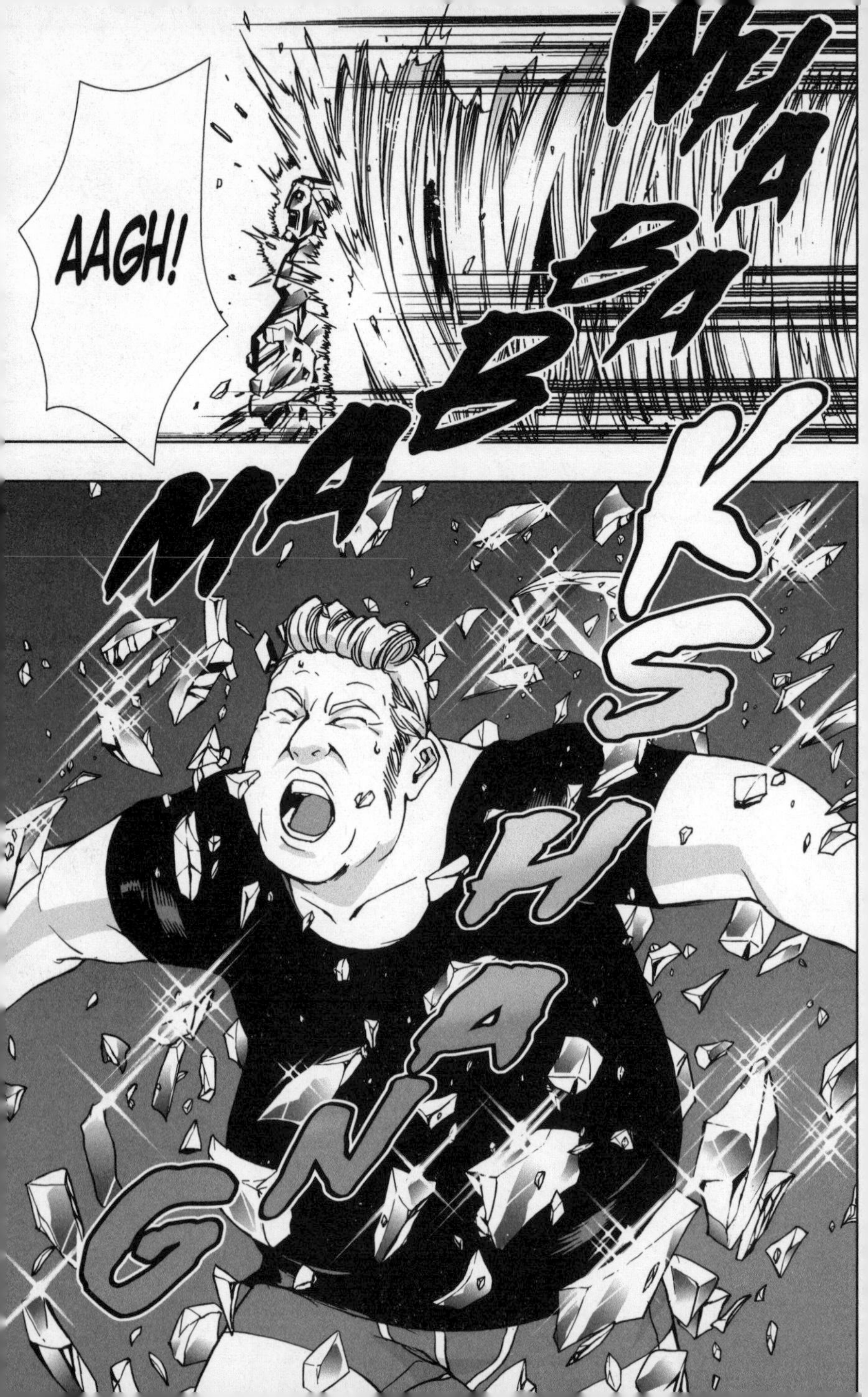
AAGH!
WHABABAM
KSHANG

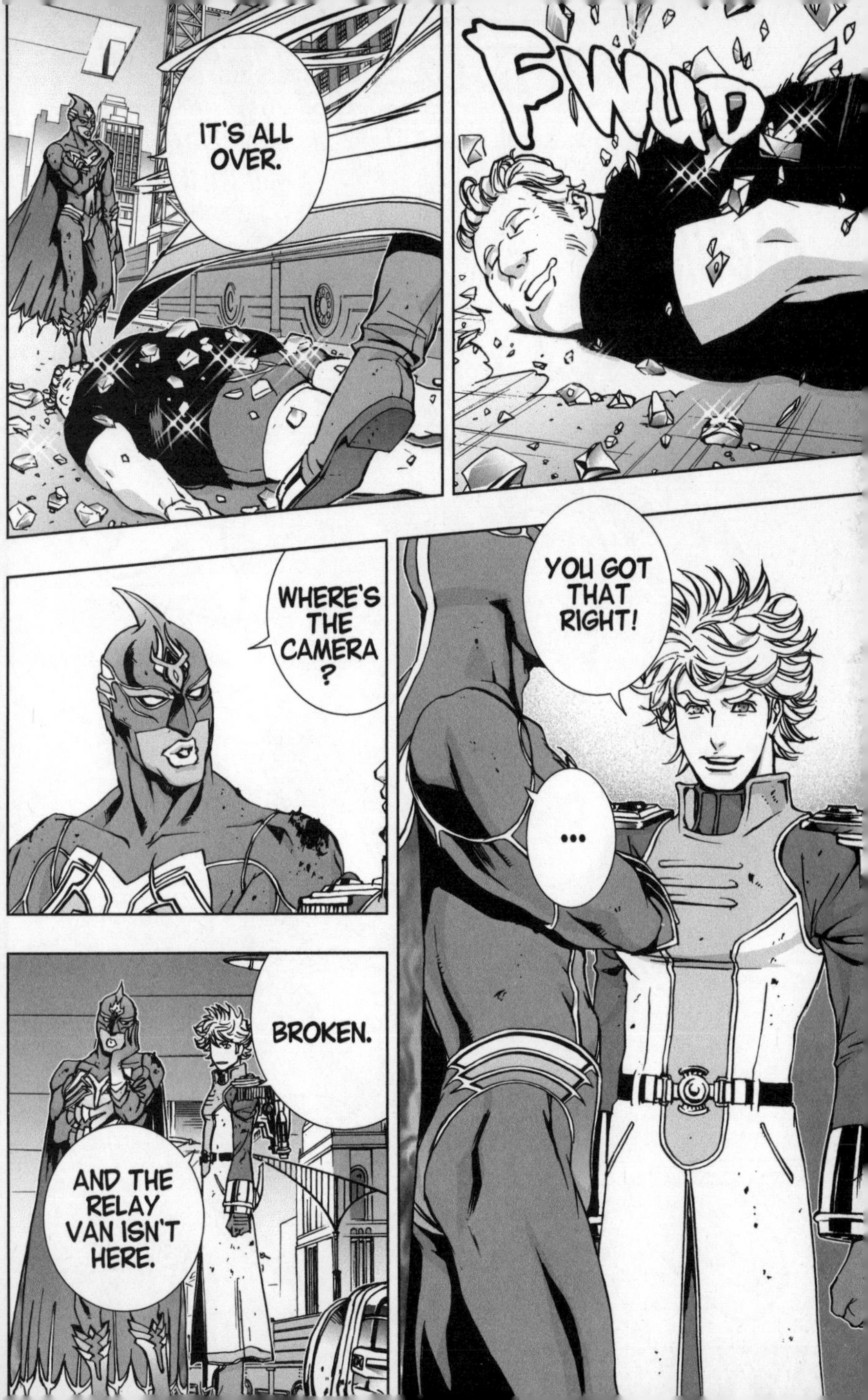
FWUD
IT'S ALL OVER.
YOU GOT THAT RIGHT!
...
WHERE'S THE CAMERA?
BROKEN.
AND THE RELAY VAN ISN'T HERE.

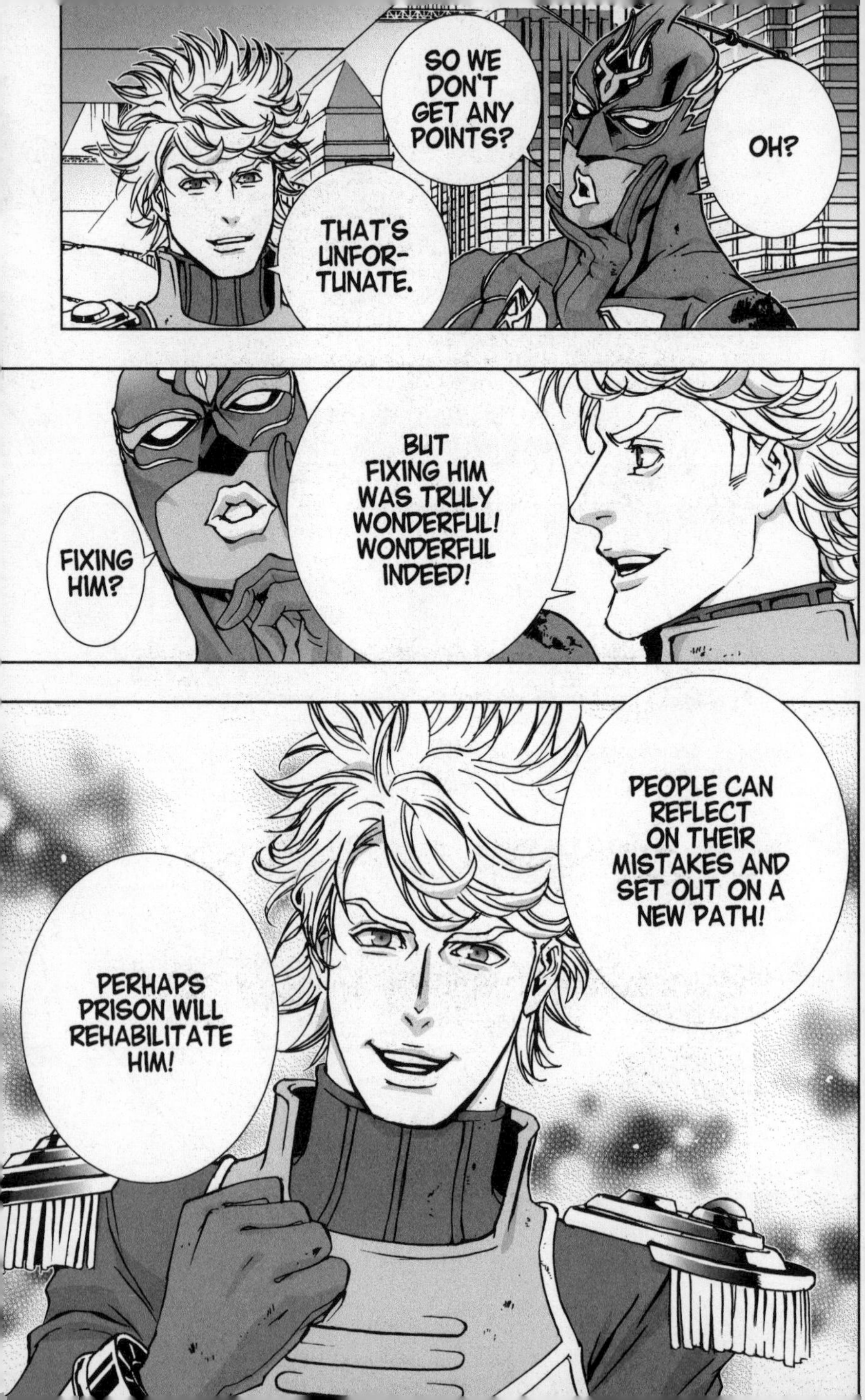
OH?
SO WE DON'T GET ANY POINTS?
THAT'S UNFOR-TUNATE.
BUT FIXING HIM WAS TRULY WONDERFUL! WONDERFUL INDEED!
FIXING HIM?
PEOPLE CAN REFLECT ON THEIR MISTAKES AND SET OUT ON A NEW PATH!
PERHAPS PRISON WILL REHABILITATE HIM!

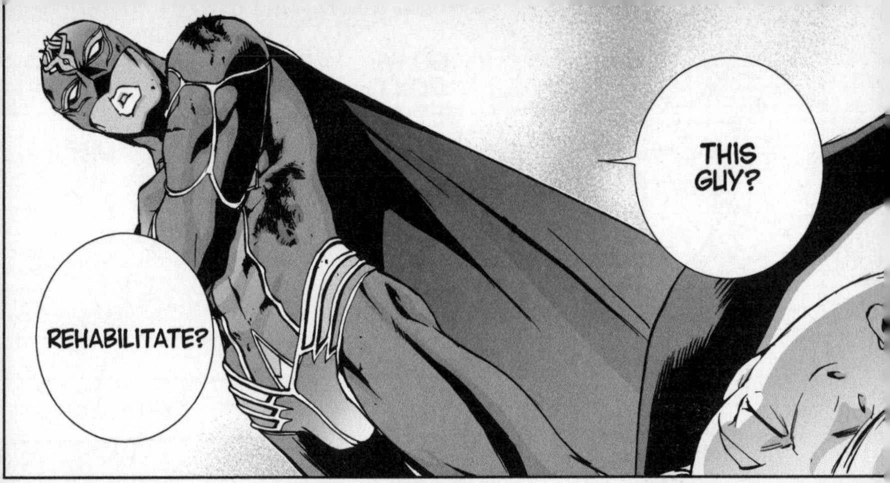
THIS GUY?
REHABILITATE?
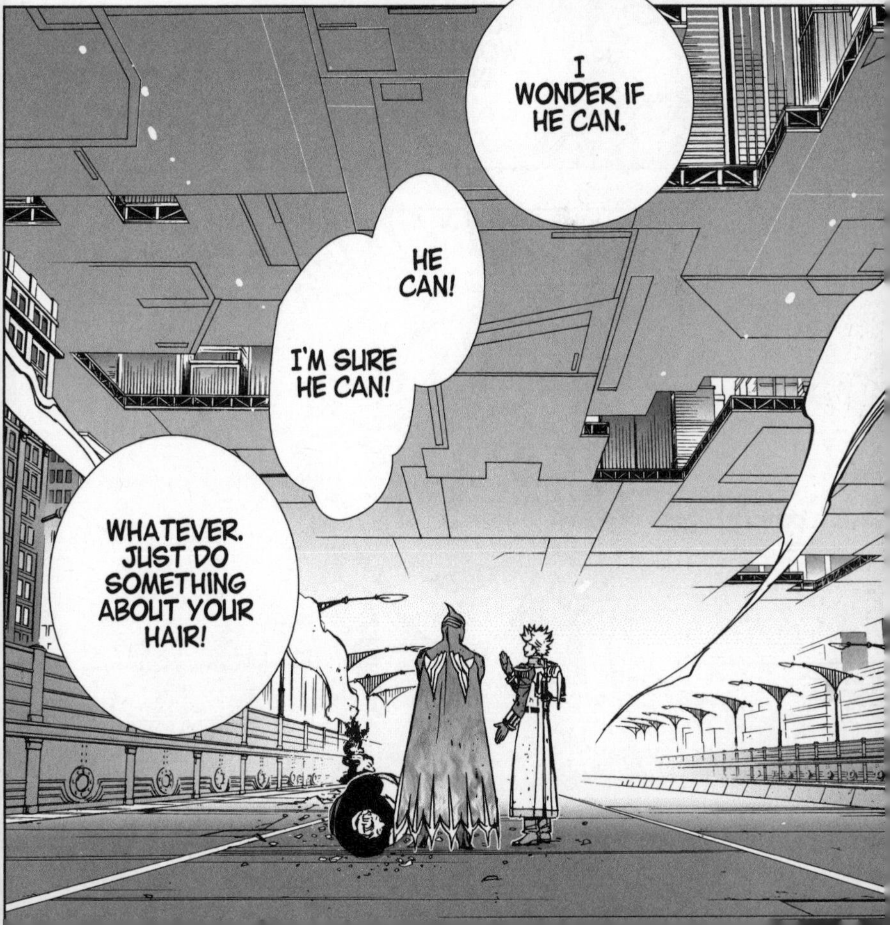
I WONDER IF HE CAN.
HE CAN! I'M SURE HE CAN!
WHATEVER. JUST DO SOMETHING ABOUT YOUR HAIR!

**TIGER&BUNNY**

**TIGER & BUNNY**

# #25 Confidence Is a Plant of Slow Growth, Part 2

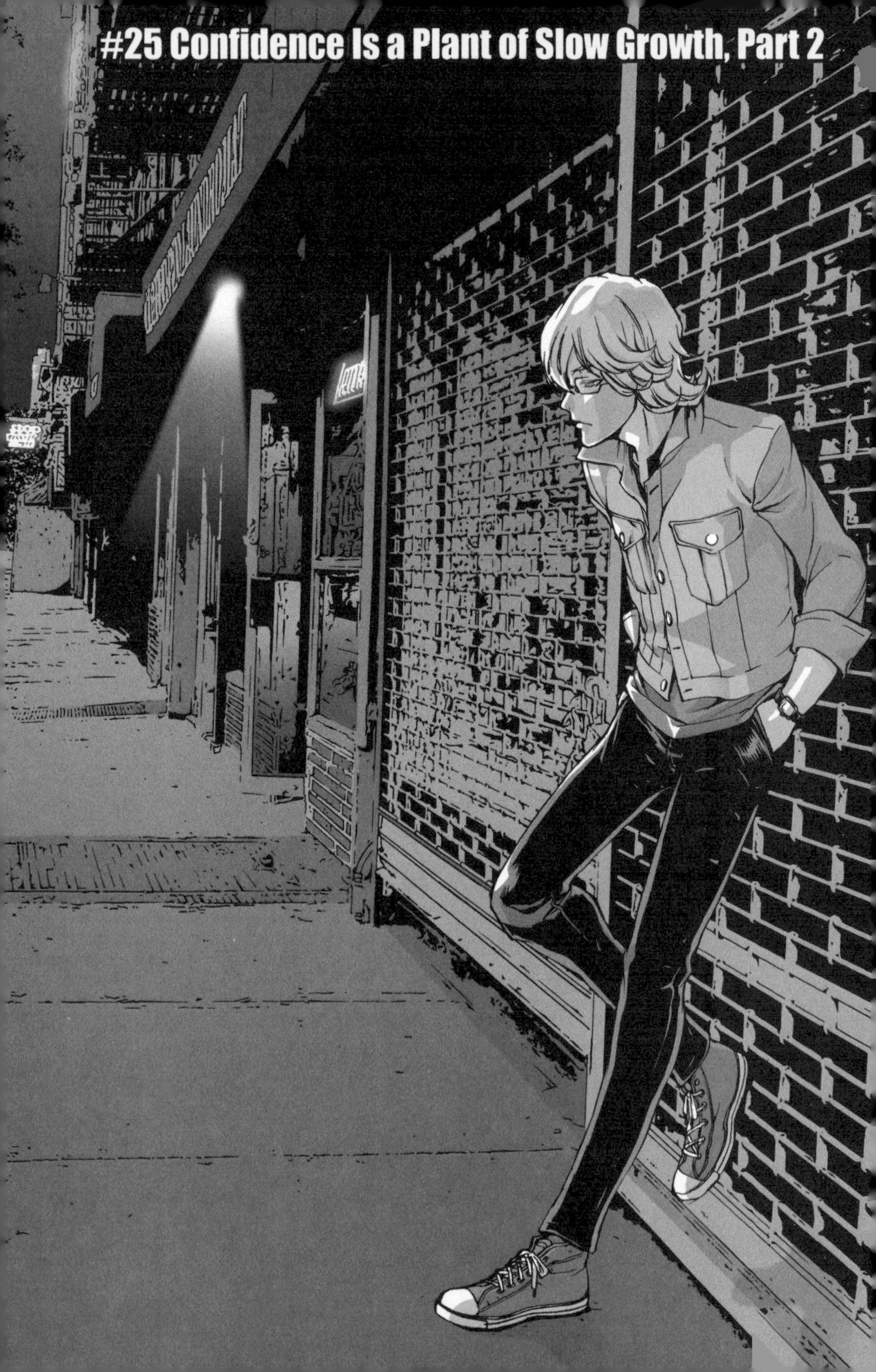

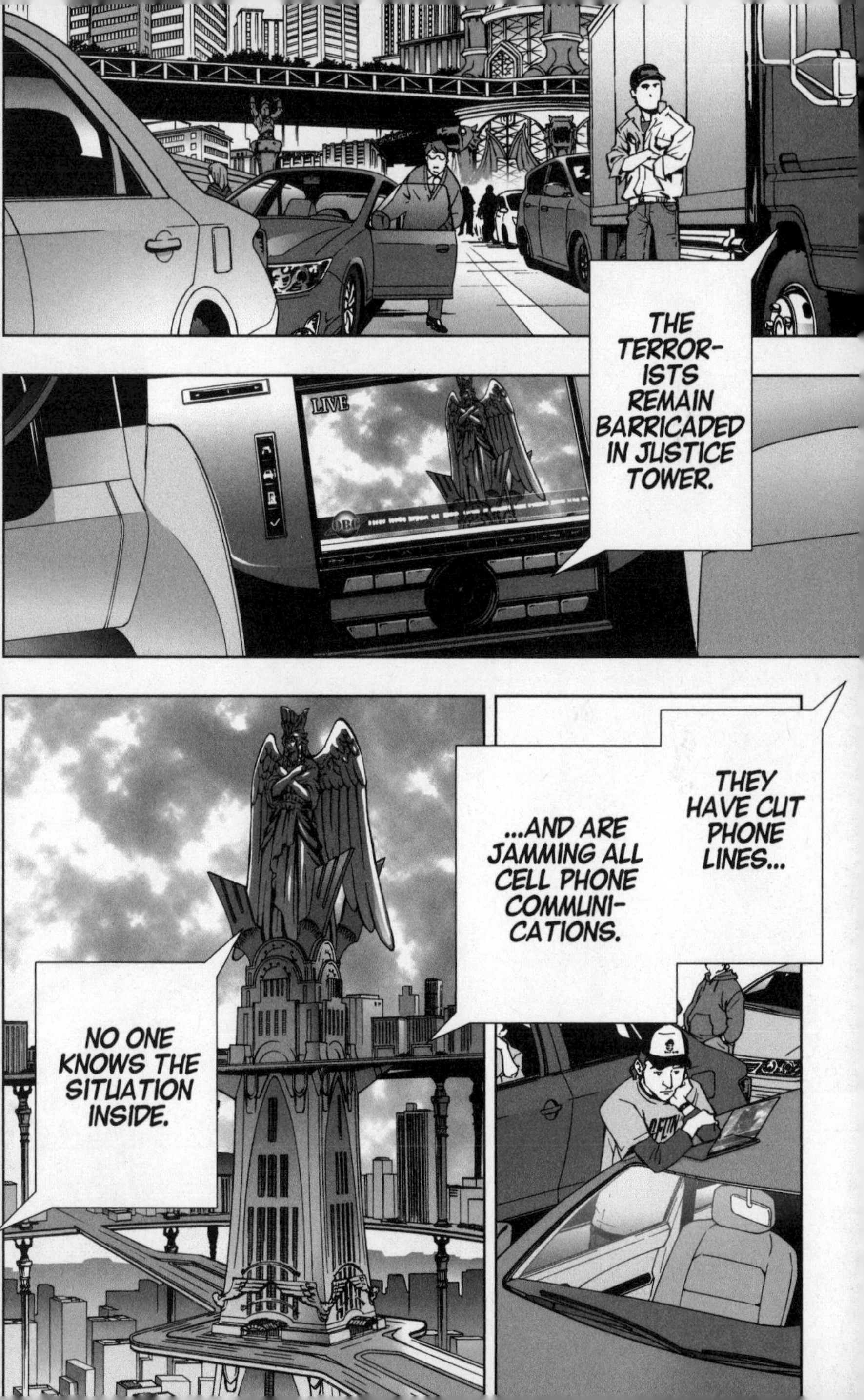
LIVE
OBC
THE TERRORISTS REMAIN BARRICADED IN JUSTICE TOWER.
THEY HAVE CUT PHONE LINES...
...AND ARE JAMMING ALL CELL PHONE COMMUNICATIONS.
NO ONE KNOWS THE SITUATION INSIDE.

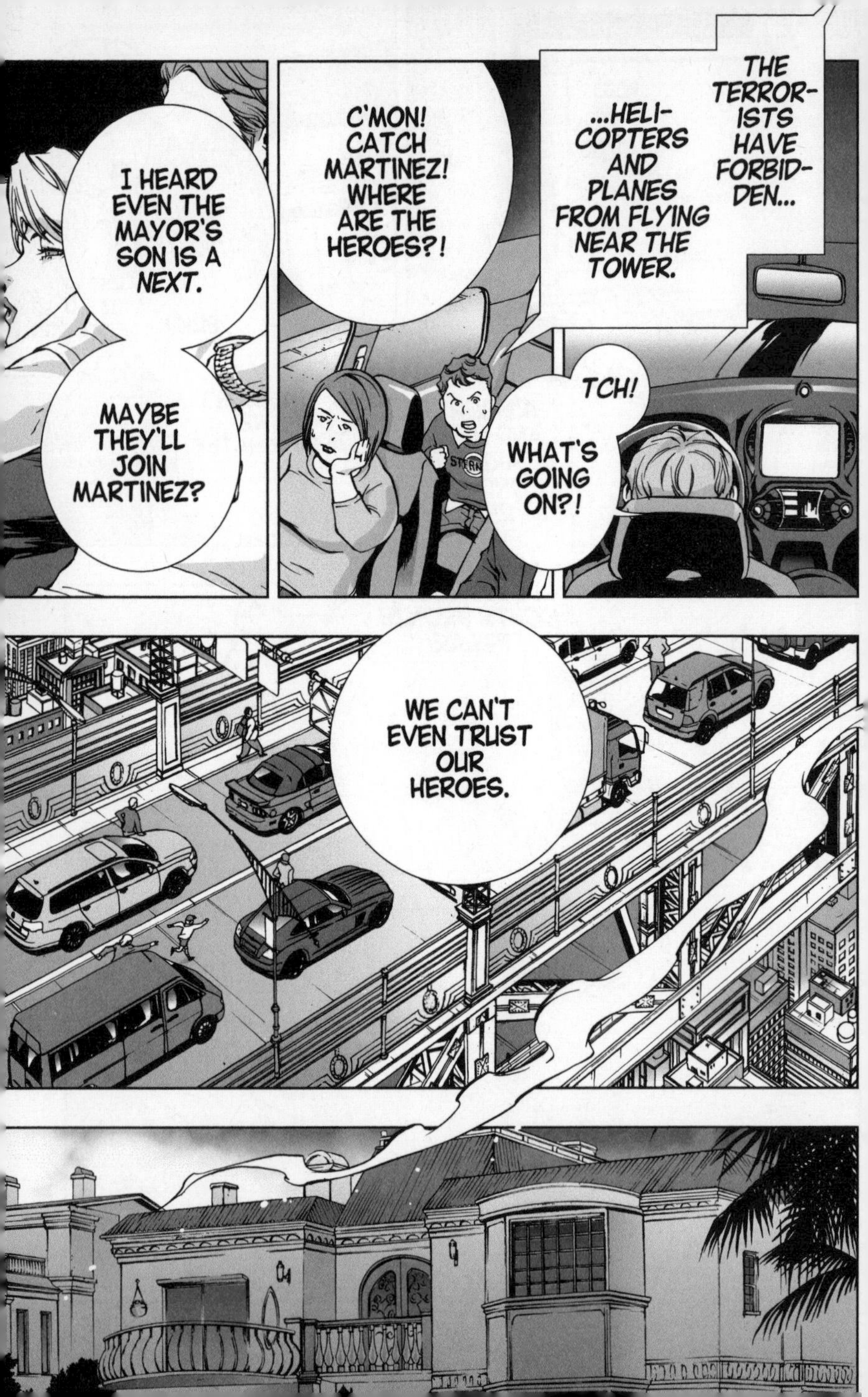
THE TERRORISTS HAVE FORBIDDEN...
...HELICOPTERS AND PLANES FROM FLYING NEAR THE TOWER.
TCH!
WHAT'S GOING ON?!
C'MON! CATCH MARTINEZ! WHERE ARE THE HEROES?!
I HEARD EVEN THE MAYOR'S SON IS A NEXT.
MAYBE THEY'LL JOIN MARTINEZ?
WE CAN'T EVEN TRUST OUR HEROES.

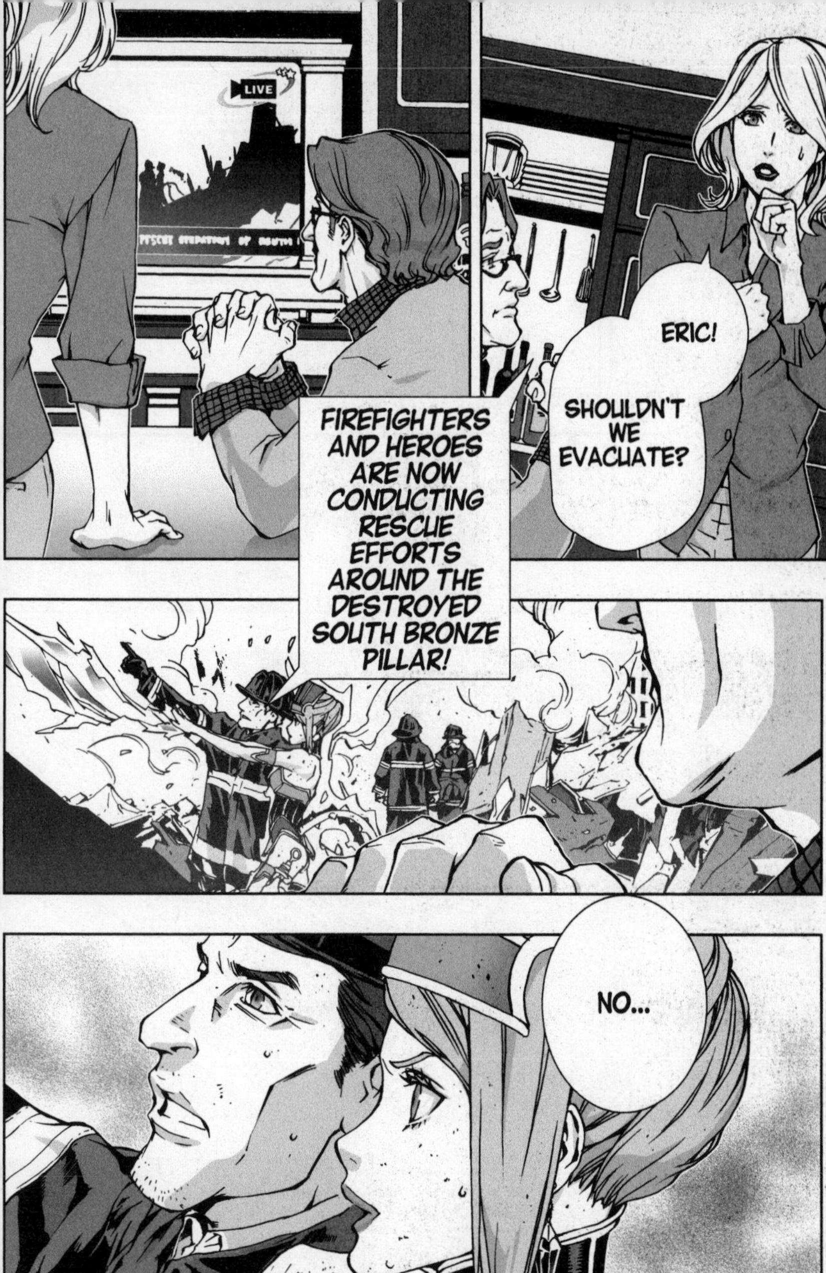
ERIC!
SHOULDN'T WE EVACUATE?
LIVE
FIREFIGHTERS AND HEROES ARE NOW CONDUCTING RESCUE EFFORTS AROUND THE DESTROYED SOUTH BRONZE PILLAR!
NO...

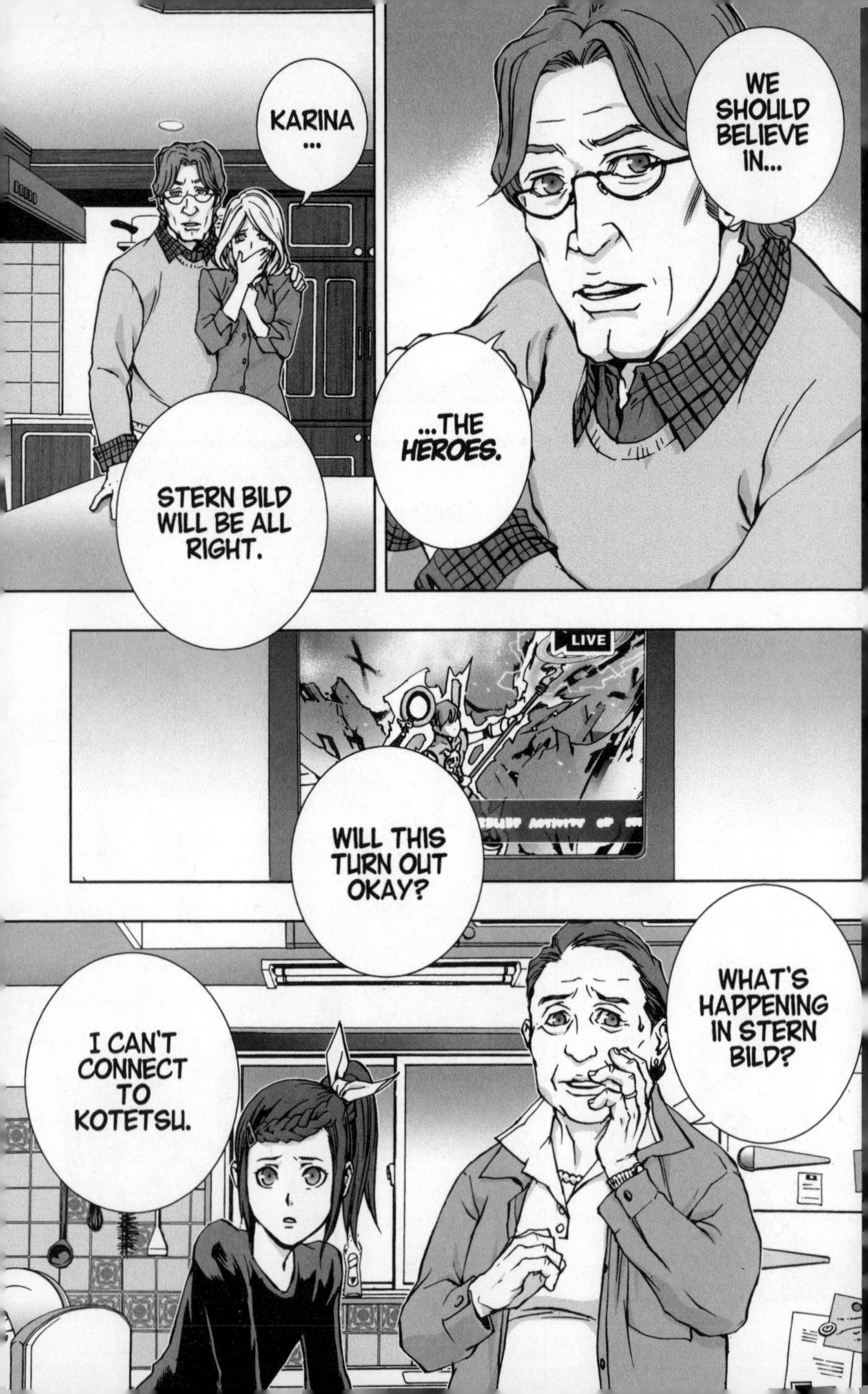
WE SHOULD BELIEVE IN...
...THE HEROES.
KARINA...
STERN BILD WILL BE ALL RIGHT.
LIVE
WILL THIS TURN OUT OKAY?
WHAT'S HAPPENING IN STERN BILD?
I CAN'T CONNECT TO KOTETSU.

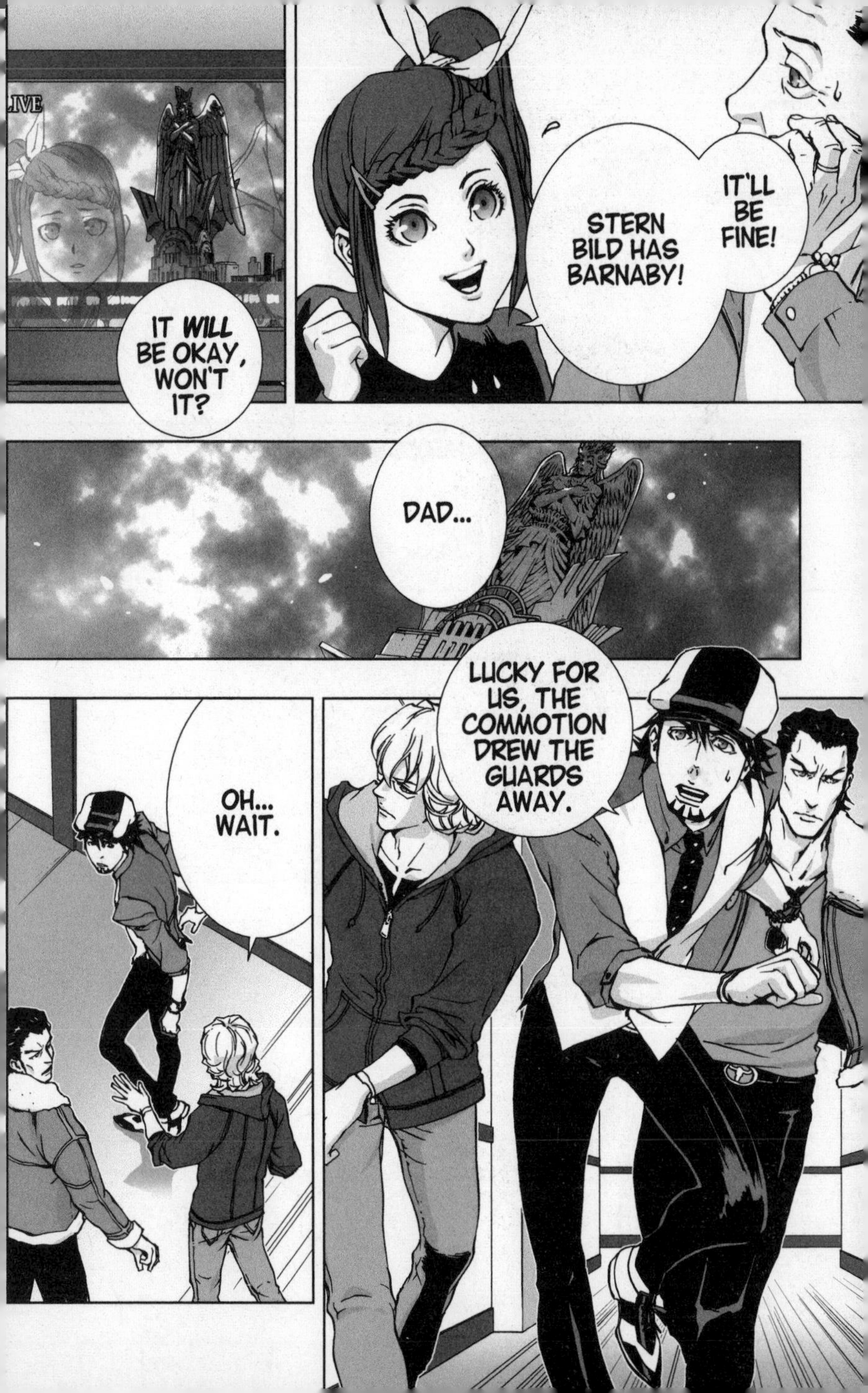
IT'LL BE FINE!
STERN BILD HAS BARNABY!
IT WILL BE OKAY, WON'T IT?
LIVE
DAD...
LUCKY FOR US, THE COMMOTION DREW THE GUARDS AWAY.
OH... WAIT.

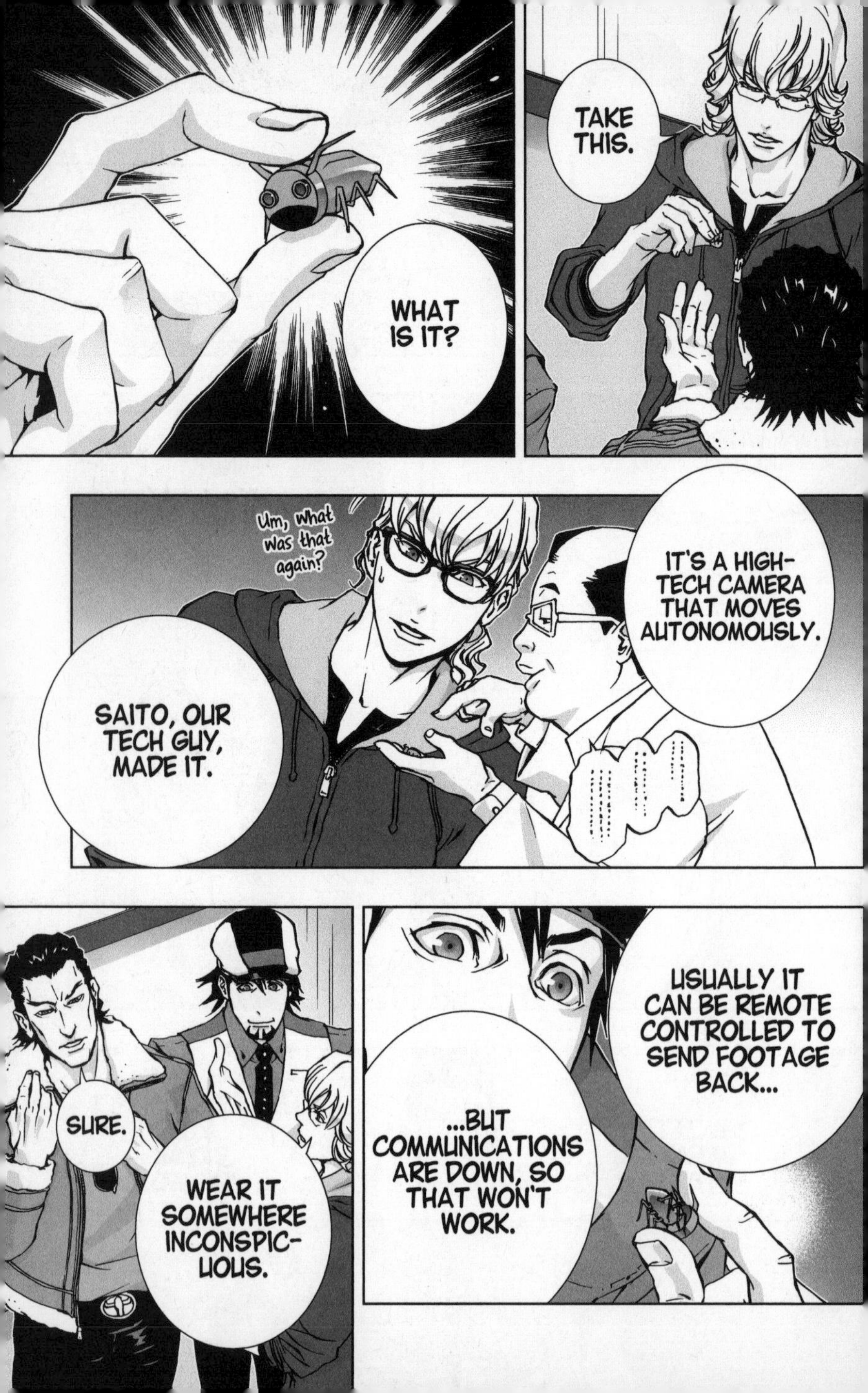
TAKE THIS.
WHAT IS IT?
IT'S A HIGH-TECH CAMERA THAT MOVES AUTONOMOUSLY.
Um, what was that again?
SAITO, OUR TECH GUY, MADE IT.
USUALLY IT CAN BE REMOTE CONTROLLED TO SEND FOOTAGE BACK...
...BUT COMMUNICATIONS ARE DOWN, SO THAT WON'T WORK.
SURE.
WEAR IT SOMEWHERE INCONSPIC-UOUS.

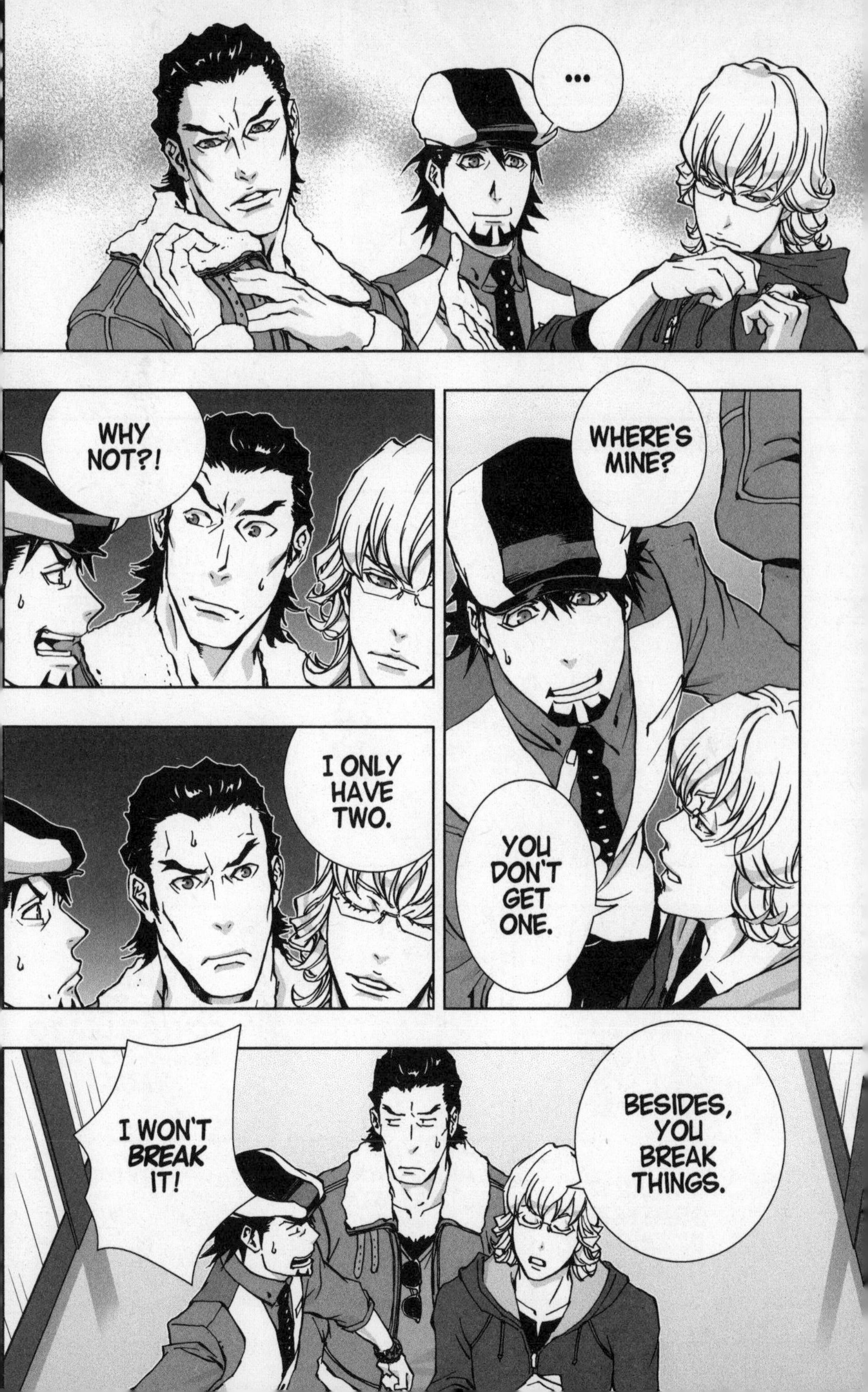
...
WHERE'S MINE?
YOU DON'T GET ONE.
WHY NOT?!
I ONLY HAVE TWO.
BESIDES, YOU BREAK THINGS.
I WON'T BREAK IT!

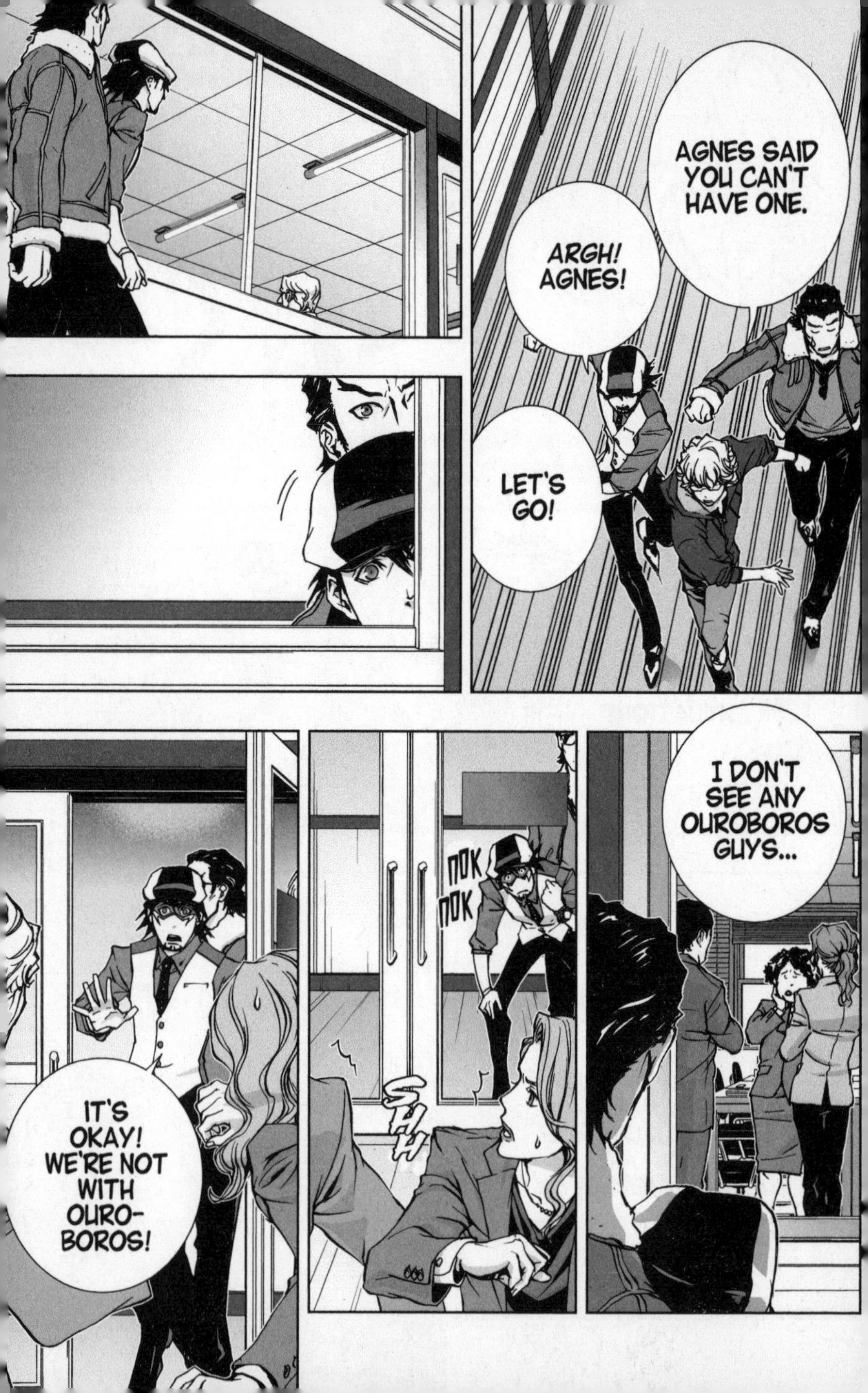
AGNES SAID YOU CAN'T HAVE ONE.
ARGH! AGNES!
LET'S GO!
I DON'T SEE ANY OUROBOROS GUYS...
NOK NOK
SHH
IT'S OKAY! WE'RE NOT WITH OURO-BOROS!

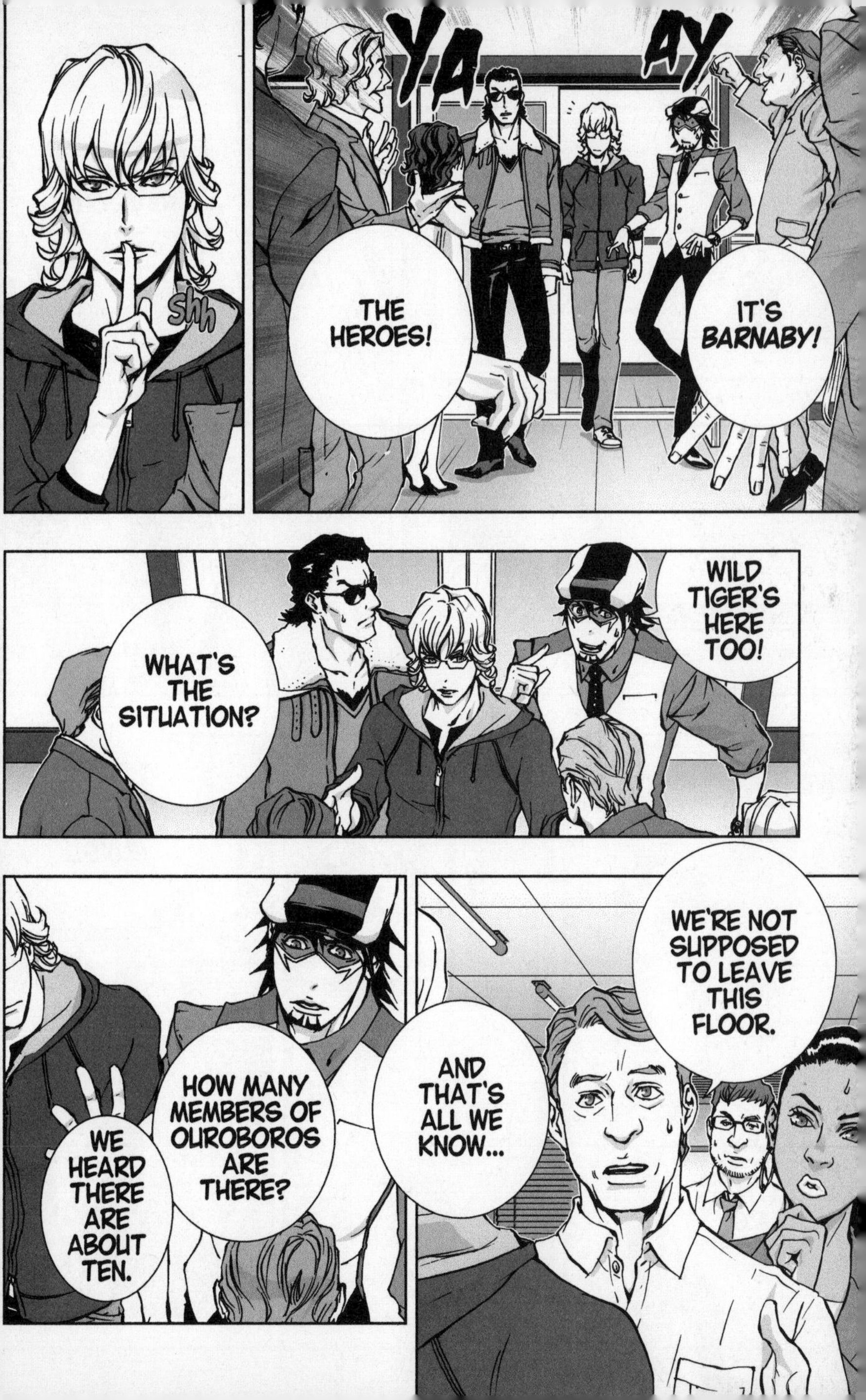
YAAY
IT'S BARNABY!
THE HEROES!
Shh
WILD TIGER'S HERE TOO!
WHAT'S THE SITUATION?
WE'RE NOT SUPPOSED TO LEAVE THIS FLOOR.
AND THAT'S ALL WE KNOW...
HOW MANY MEMBERS OF OUROBOROS ARE THERE?
WE HEARD THERE ARE ABOUT TEN.

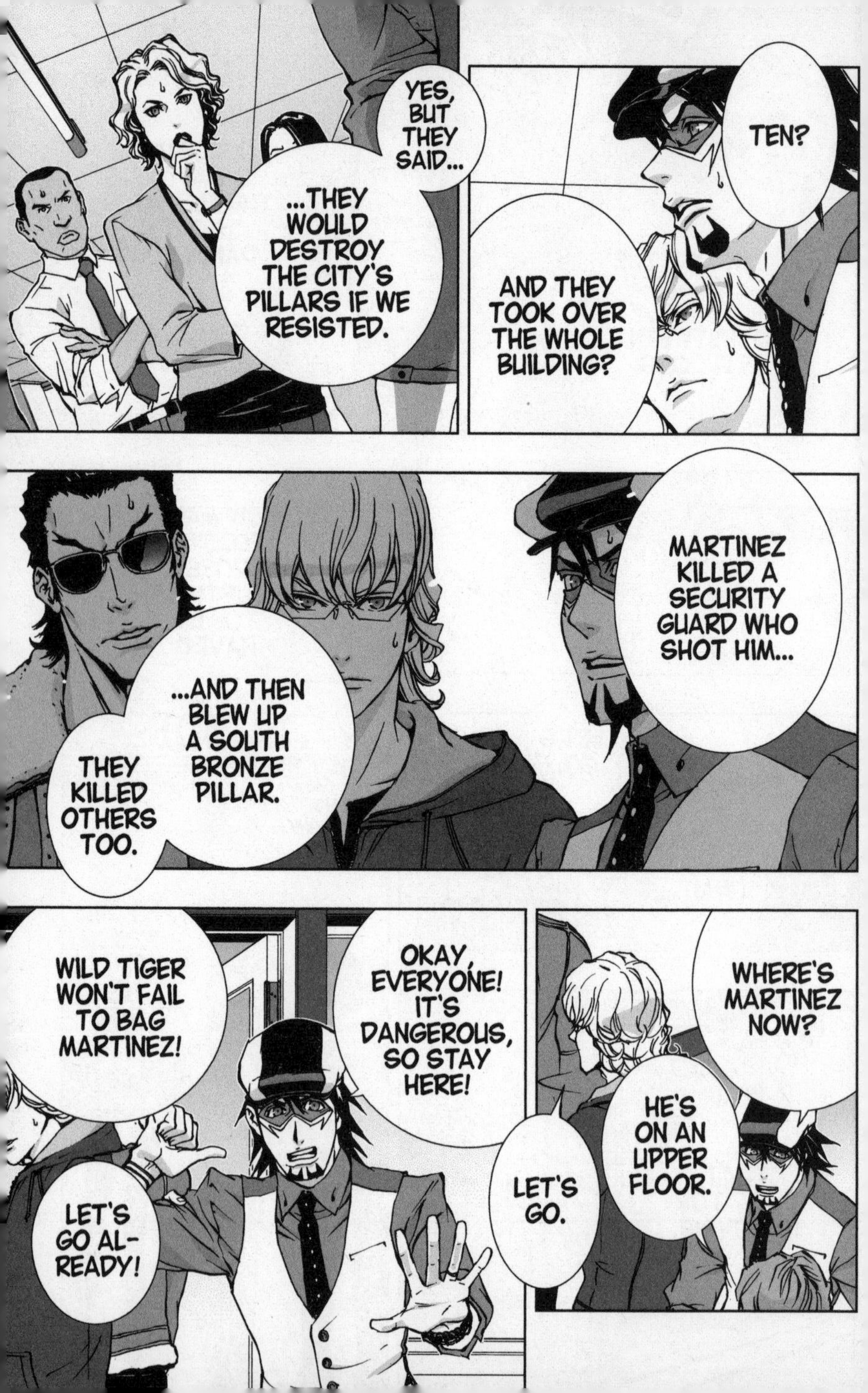
TEN?
AND THEY TOOK OVER THE WHOLE BUILDING?
YES, BUT THEY SAID...
...THEY WOULD DESTROY THE CITY'S PILLARS IF WE RESISTED.
MARTINEZ KILLED A SECURITY GUARD WHO SHOT HIM...
...AND THEN BLEW UP A SOUTH BRONZE PILLAR.
THEY KILLED OTHERS TOO.
WHERE'S MARTINEZ NOW?
HE'S ON AN UPPER FLOOR.
LET'S GO.
OKAY, EVERYONE! IT'S DANGEROUS, SO STAY HERE!
WILD TIGER WON'T FAIL TO BAG MARTINEZ!
LET'S GO AL-READY!

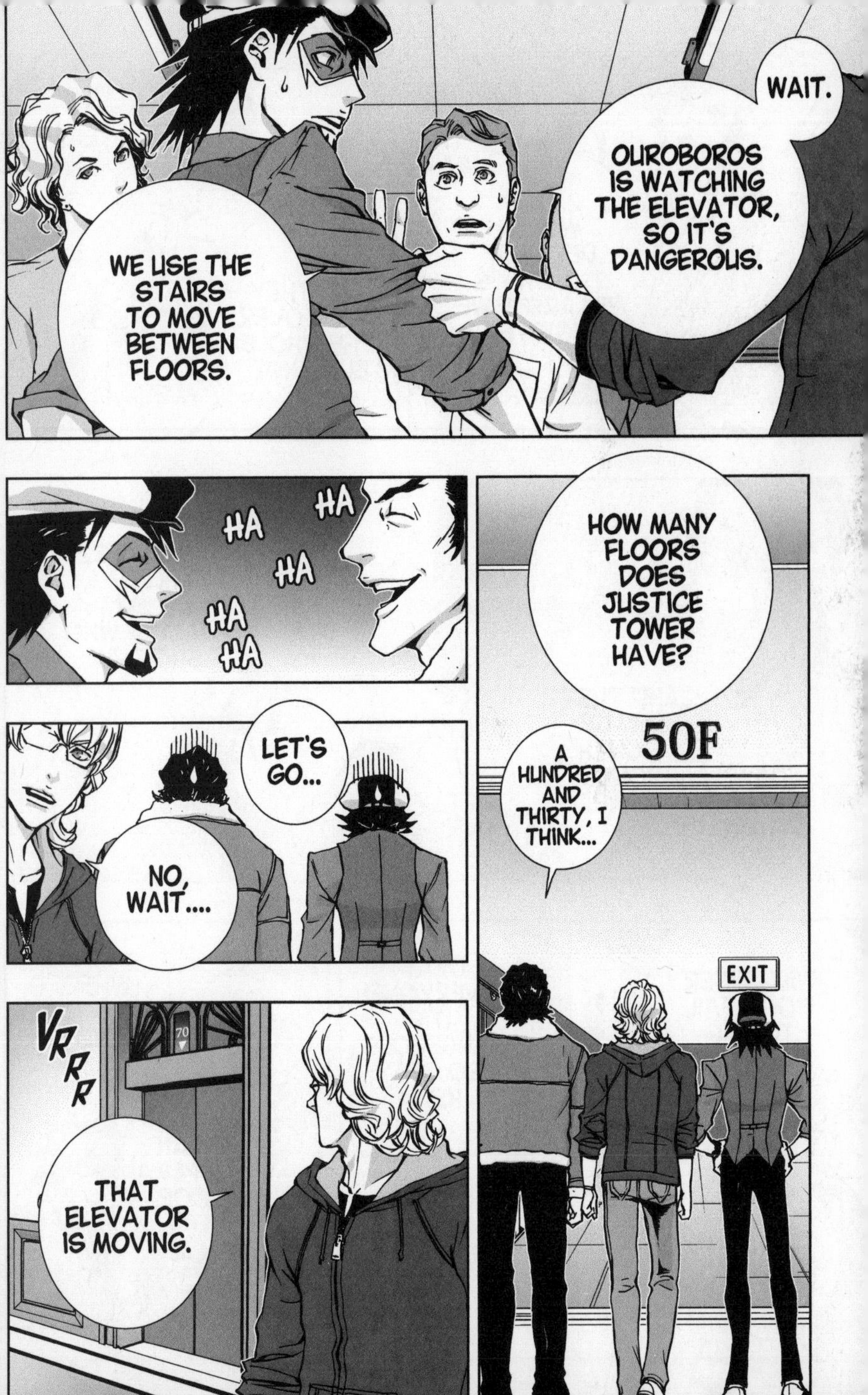
WAIT.
OUROBOROS IS WATCHING THE ELEVATOR, SO IT'S DANGEROUS.
WE USE THE STAIRS TO MOVE BETWEEN FLOORS.
HOW MANY FLOORS DOES JUSTICE TOWER HAVE?
50F
A HUNDRED AND THIRTY, I THINK...
EXIT
HA
HA
HA
HA
HA
LET'S GO...
NO, WAIT....
VRRR
70
THAT ELEVATOR IS MOVING.

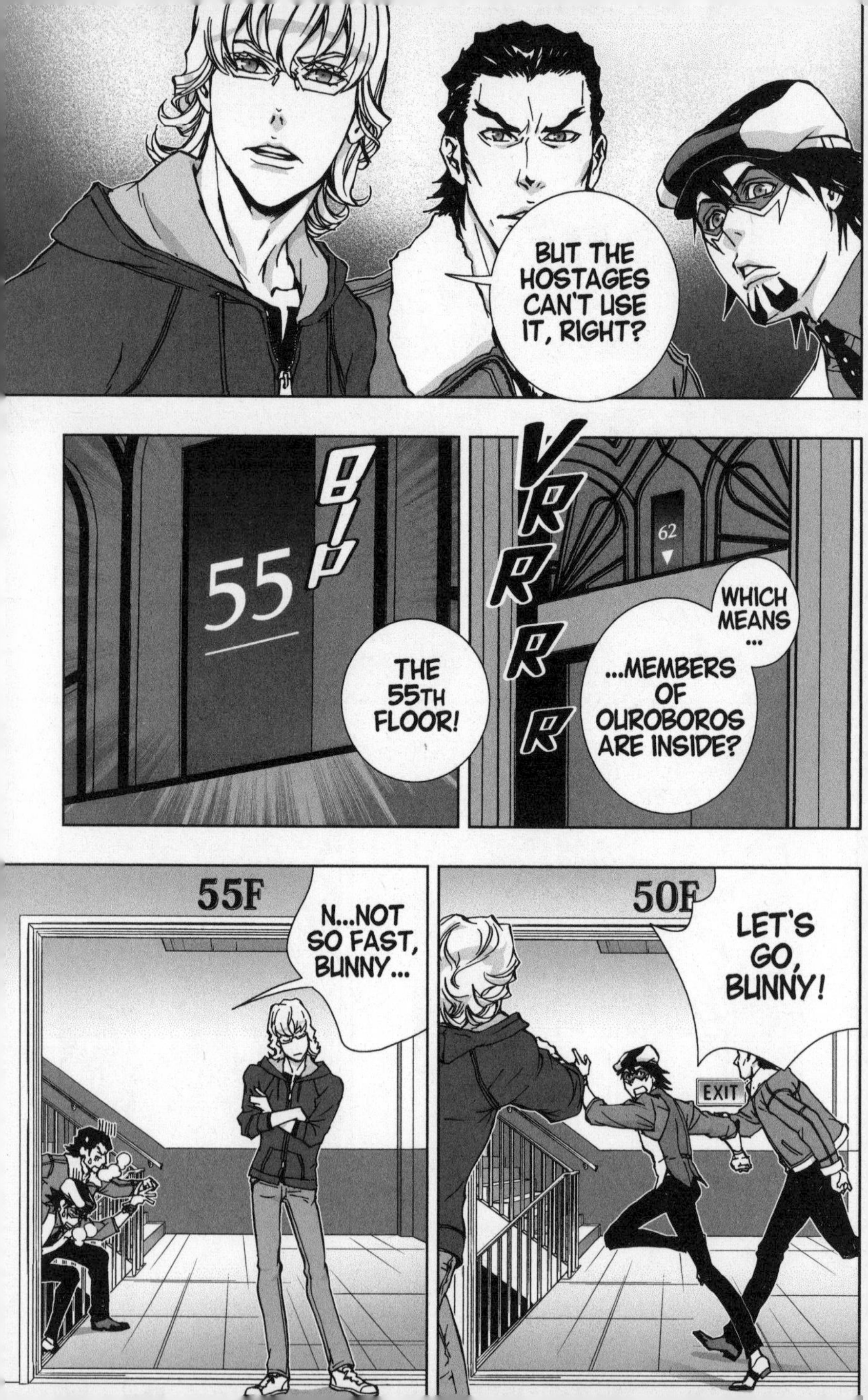
BUT THE HOSTAGES CAN'T USE IT, RIGHT?
VRRRR
62
WHICH MEANS...
...MEMBERS OF OUROBOROS ARE INSIDE?
BIP
55
THE 55TH FLOOR!
50F
LET'S GO, BUNNY!
EXIT
55F
N...NOT SO FAST, BUNNY...

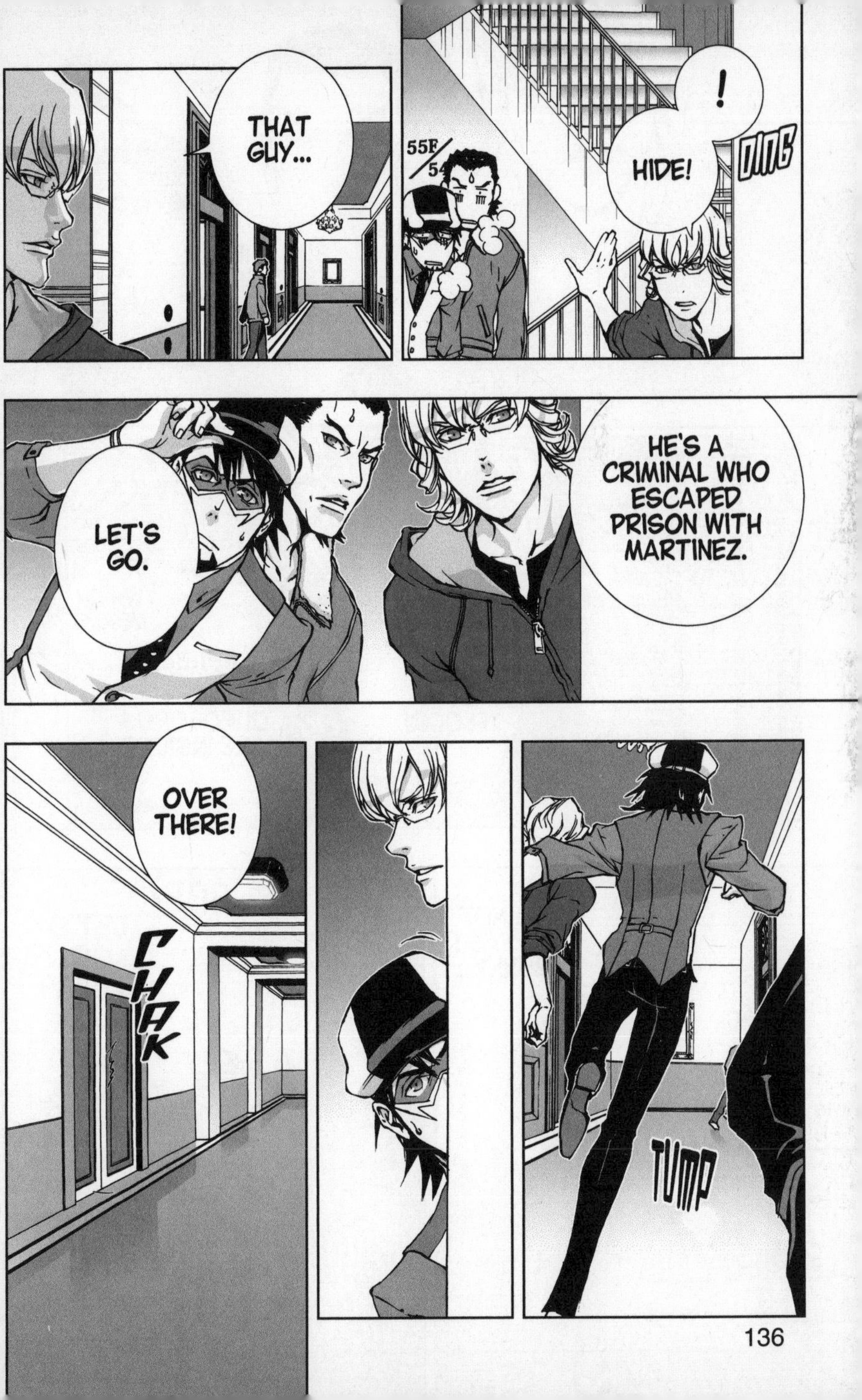
!
HIDE!
DING
THAT GUY...
HE'S A CRIMINAL WHO ESCAPED PRISON WITH MARTINEZ.
LET'S GO.
TUMP
OVER THERE!
CHAK

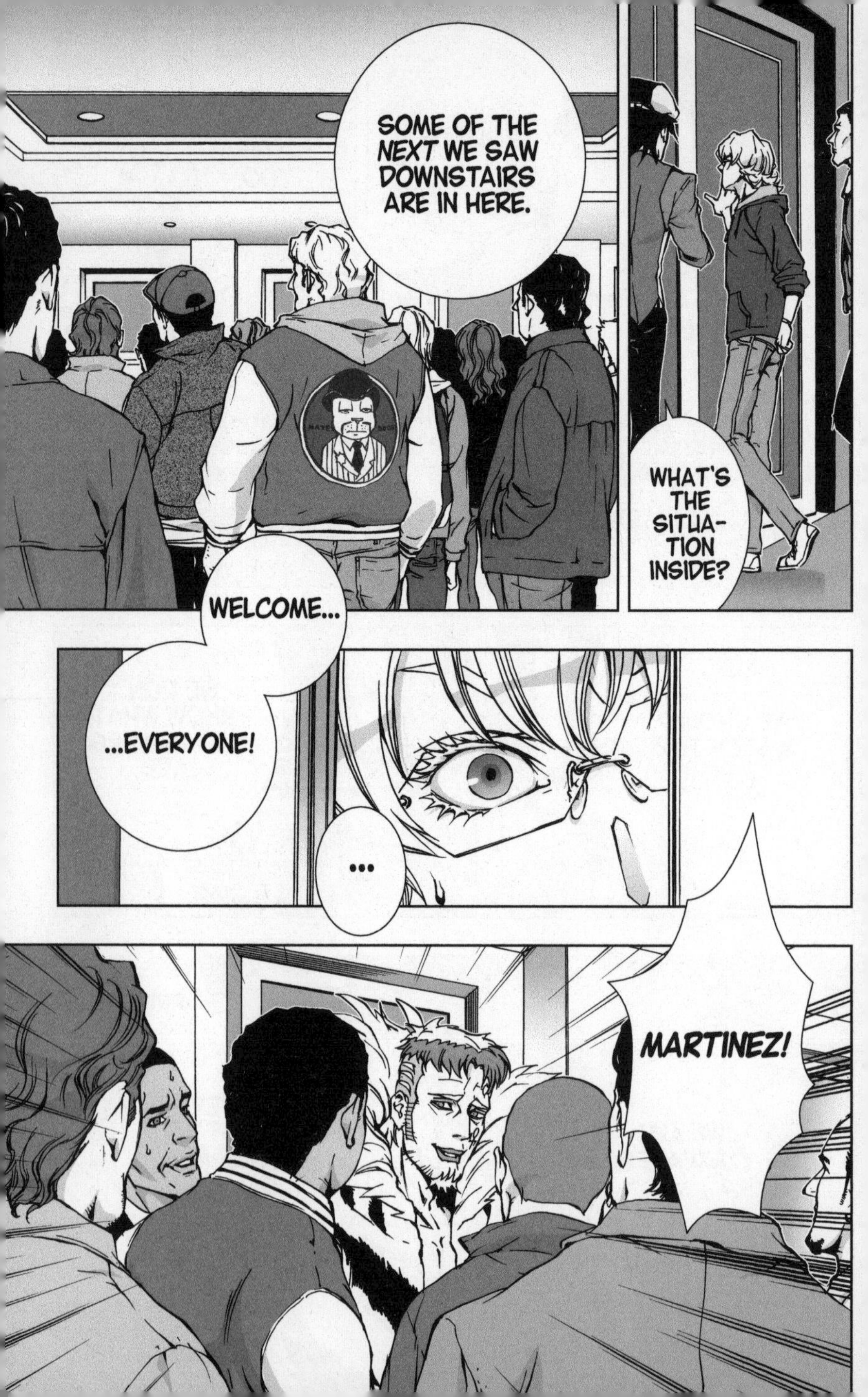
WHAT'S THE SITUATION INSIDE?
SOME OF THE NEXT WE SAW DOWNSTAIRS ARE IN HERE.
WELCOME...
...EVERYONE!
...
MARTINEZ!

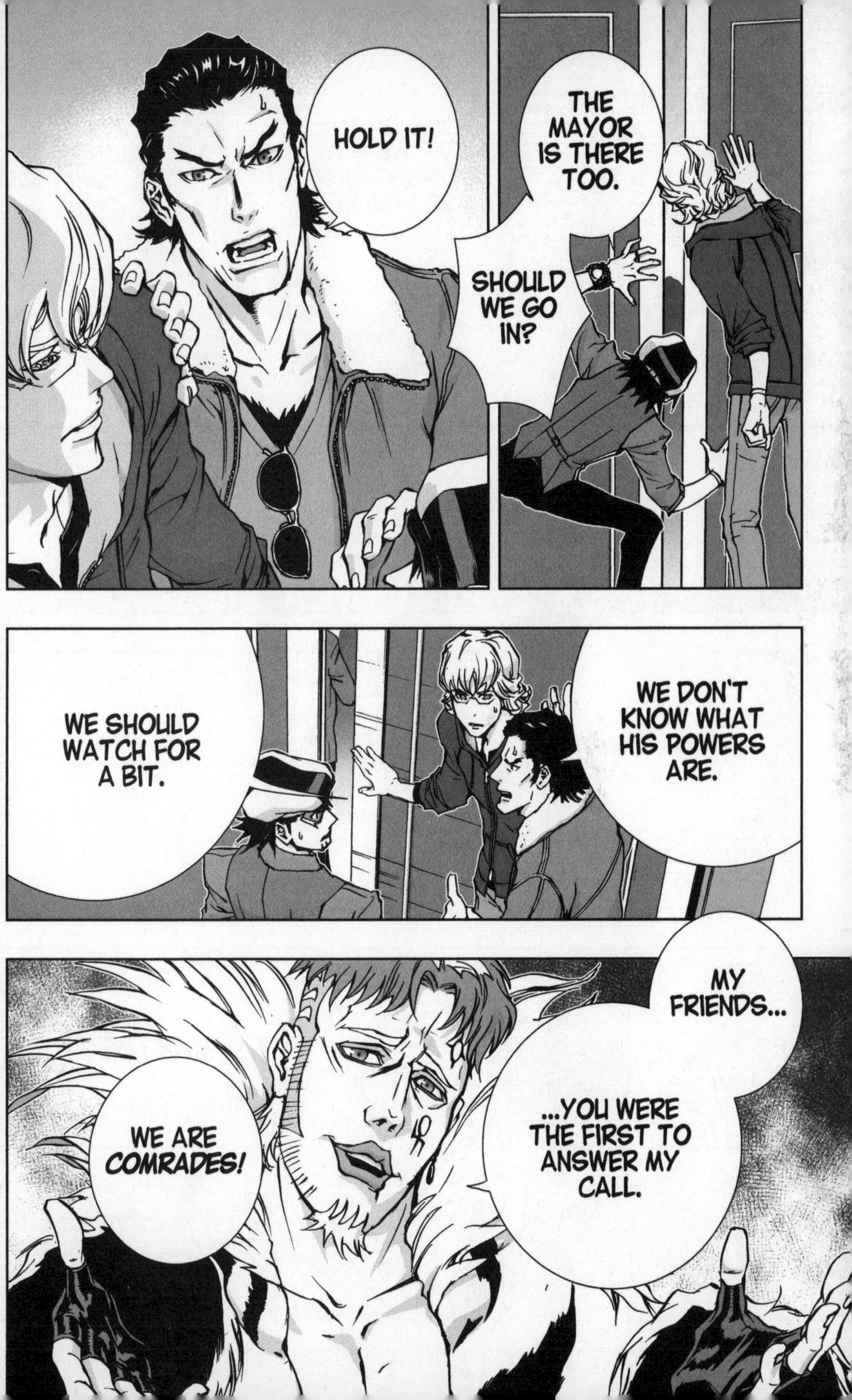
THE MAYOR IS THERE TOO.
SHOULD WE GO IN?
HOLD IT!
WE DON'T KNOW WHAT HIS POWERS ARE.
WE SHOULD WATCH FOR A BIT.
MY FRIENDS...
...YOU WERE THE FIRST TO ANSWER MY CALL.
WE ARE COMRADES!

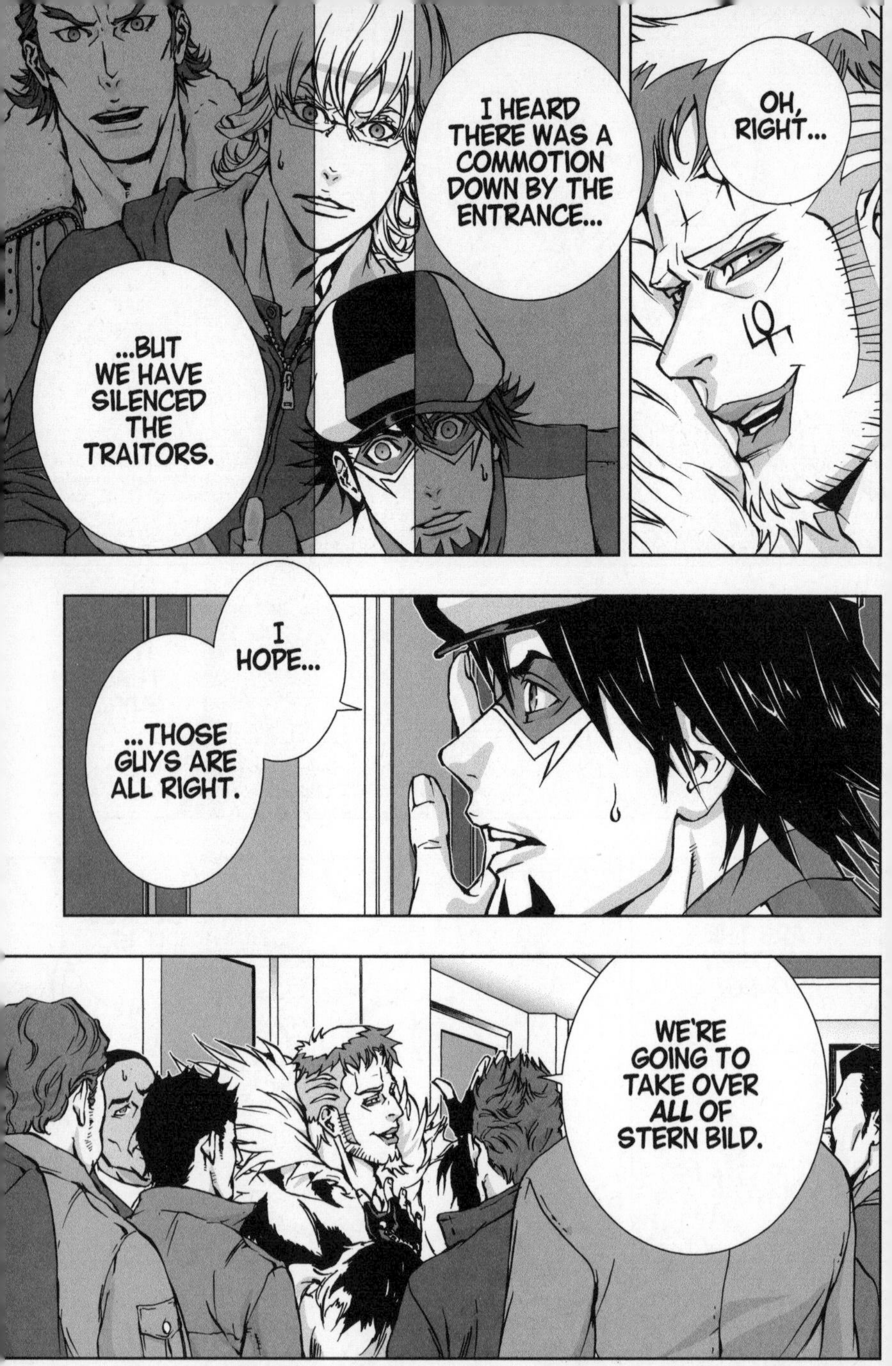
OH, RIGHT...
I HEARD THERE WAS A COMMOTION DOWN BY THE ENTRANCE...
...BUT WE HAVE SILENCED THE TRAITORS.
I HOPE...
...THOSE GUYS ARE ALL RIGHT.
WE'RE GOING TO TAKE OVER *ALL* OF STERN BILD.

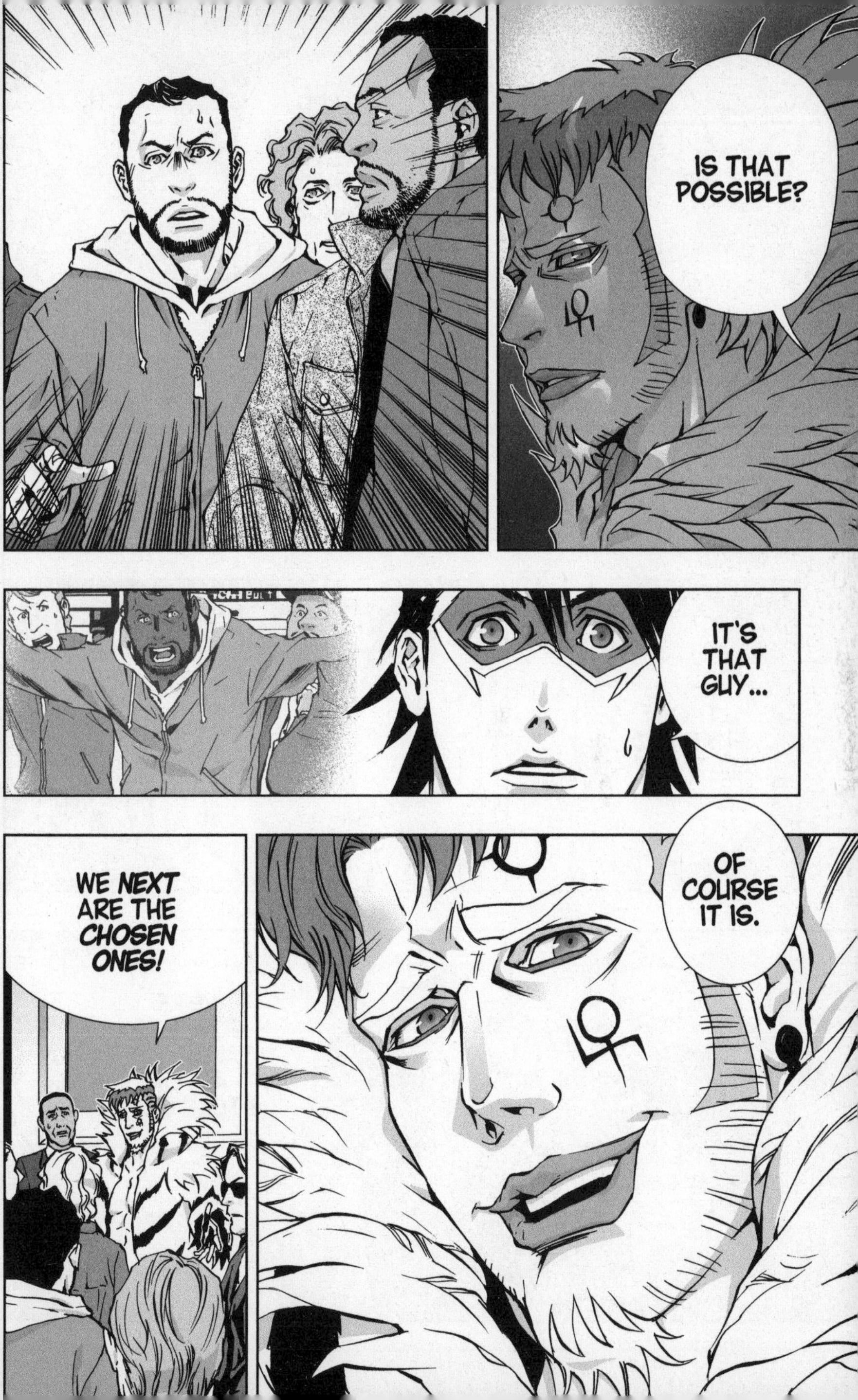
IS THAT POSSIBLE?
IT'S THAT GUY...
OF COURSE IT IS.
WE NEXT ARE THE CHOSEN ONES!

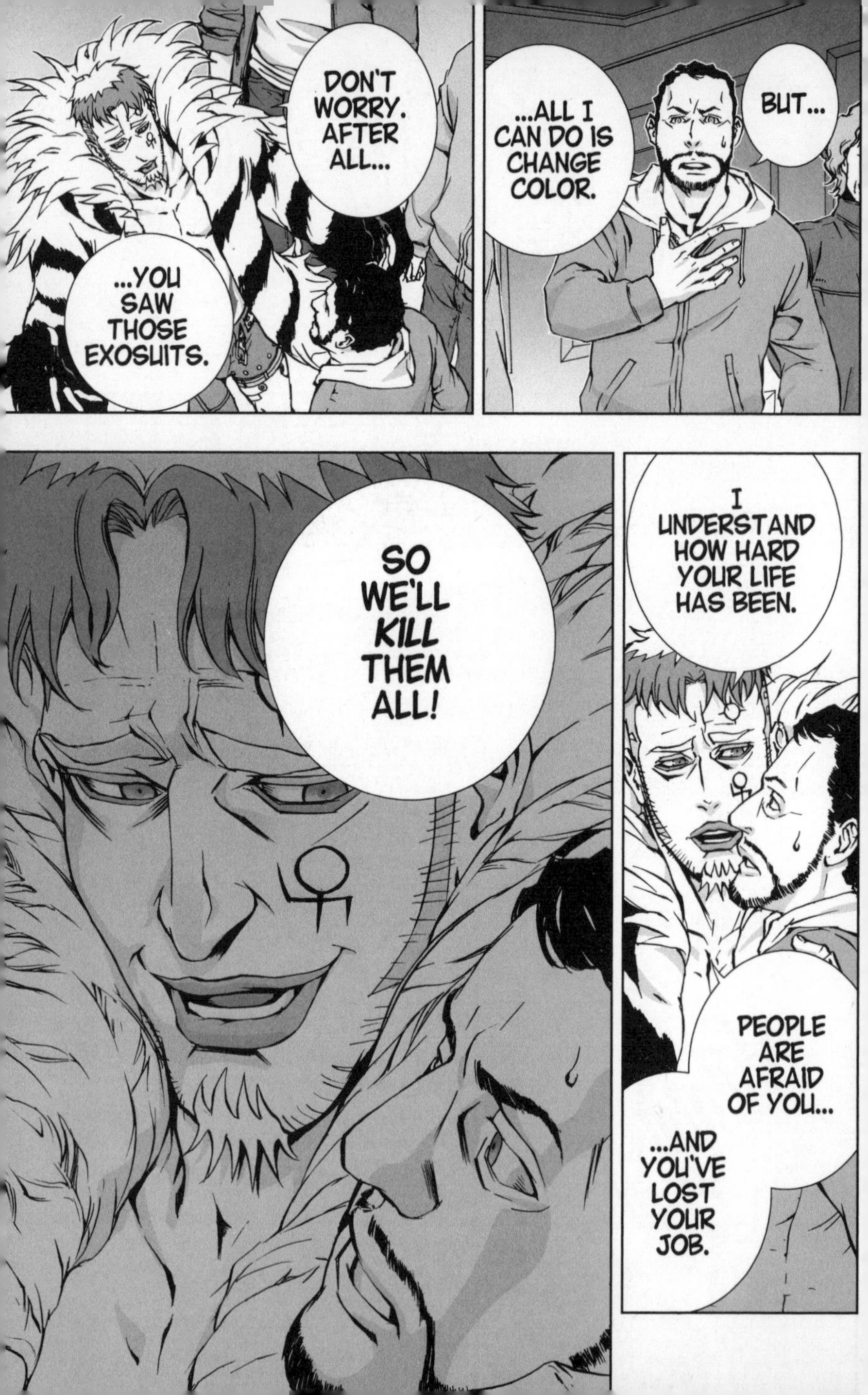
BUT...
...ALL I CAN DO IS CHANGE COLOR.
DON'T WORRY. AFTER ALL...
...YOU SAW THOSE EXOSUITS.
I UNDERSTAND HOW HARD YOUR LIFE HAS BEEN.
PEOPLE ARE AFRAID OF YOU...
...AND YOU'VE LOST YOUR JOB.
SO WE'LL *KILL* THEM ALL!

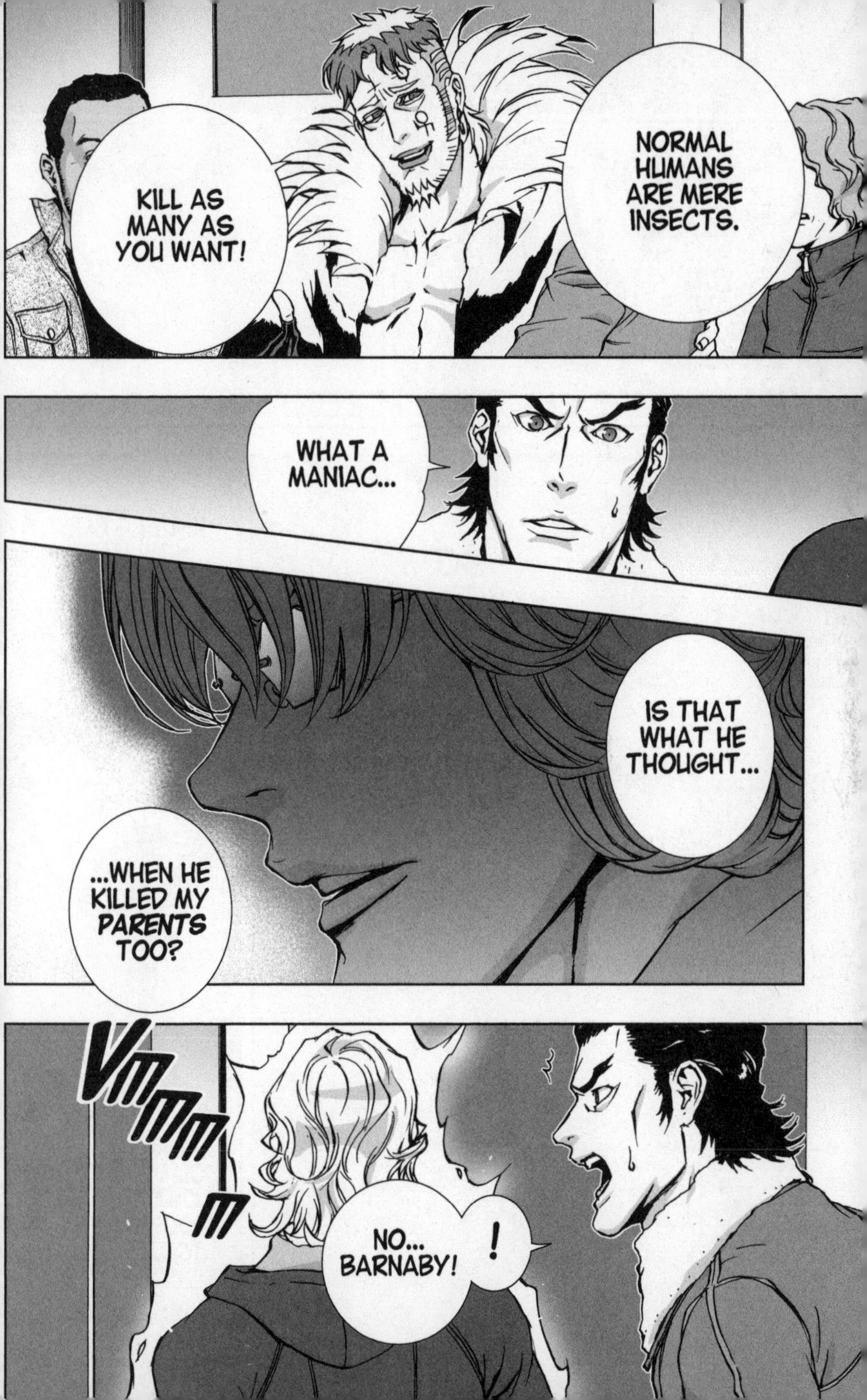
NORMAL HUMANS ARE MERE INSECTS.
KILL AS MANY AS YOU WANT!
WHAT A MANIAC...
IS THAT WHAT HE THOUGHT...
...WHEN HE KILLED MY PARENTS TOO?
VMMMM
!
NO... BARNABY!

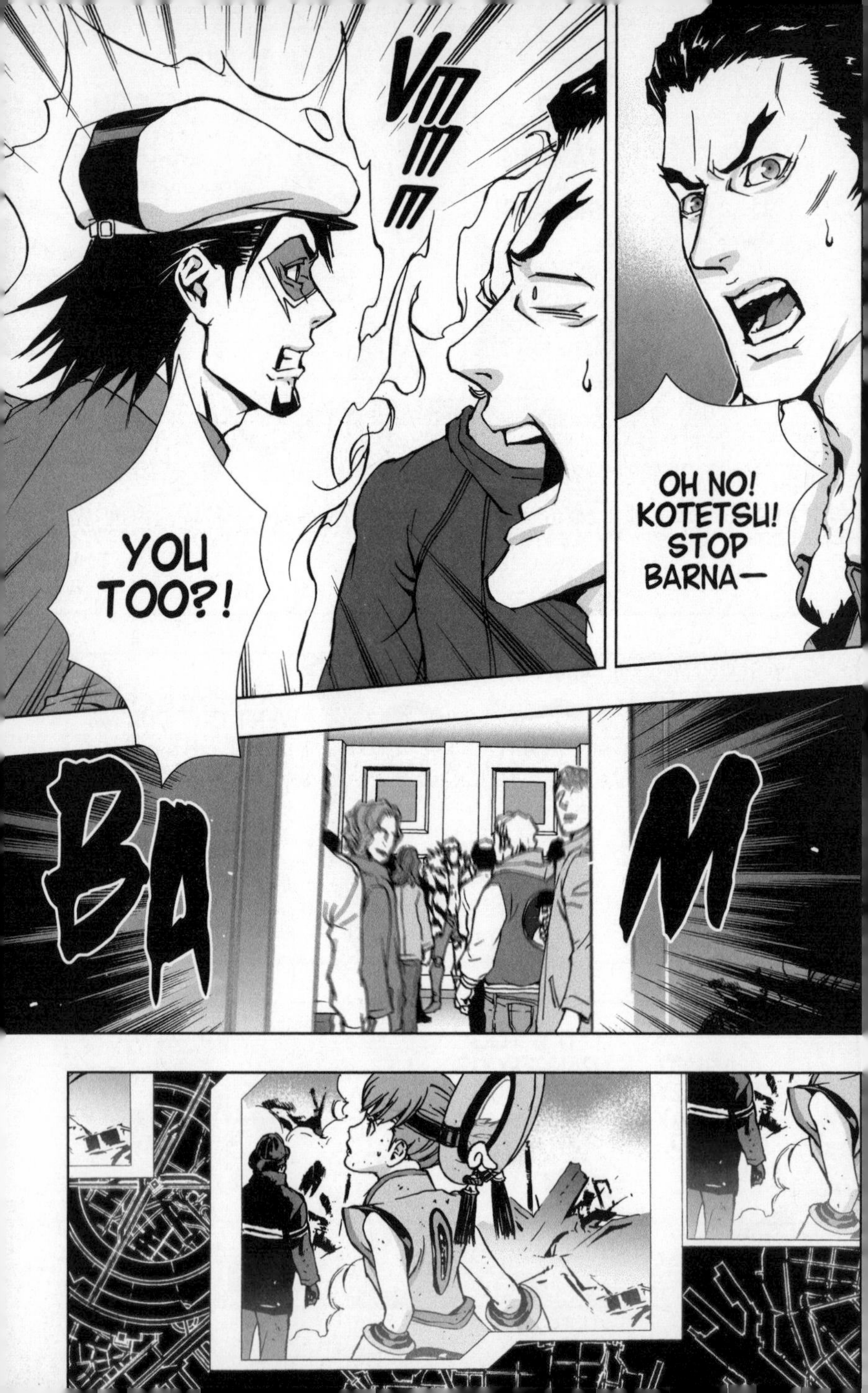
OH NO! KOTETSU! STOP BARNA—
VMMM
YOU TOO?!
BAM

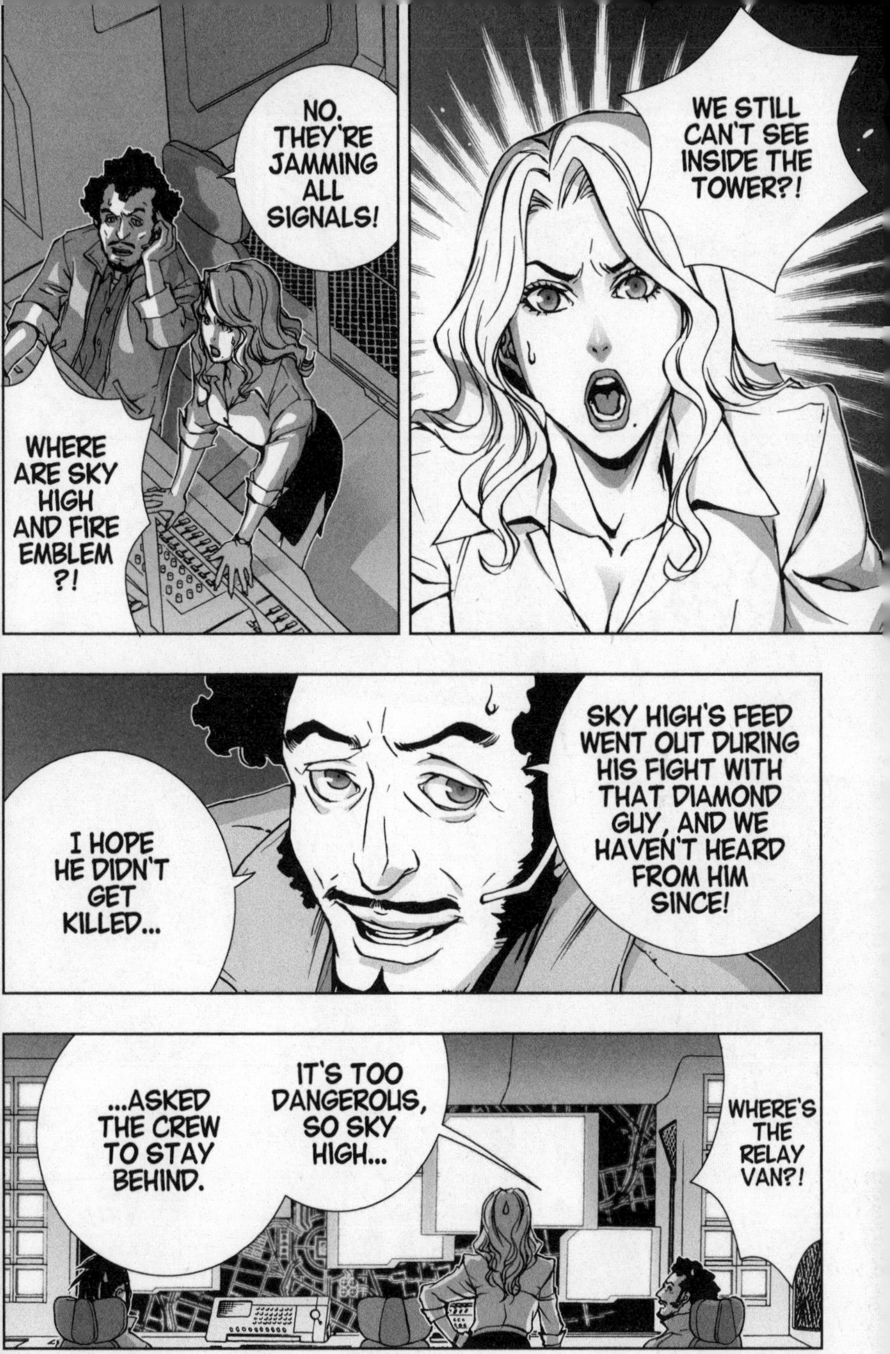
WE STILL CAN'T SEE INSIDE THE TOWER?!
NO. THEY'RE JAMMING ALL SIGNALS!
WHERE ARE SKY HIGH AND FIRE EMBLEM ?!
SKY HIGH'S FEED WENT OUT DURING HIS FIGHT WITH THAT DIAMOND GUY, AND WE HAVEN'T HEARD FROM HIM SINCE!
I HOPE HE DIDN'T GET KILLED...
WHERE'S THE RELAY VAN?!
IT'S TOO DANGEROUS, SO SKY HIGH...
...ASKED THE CREW TO STAY BEHIND.

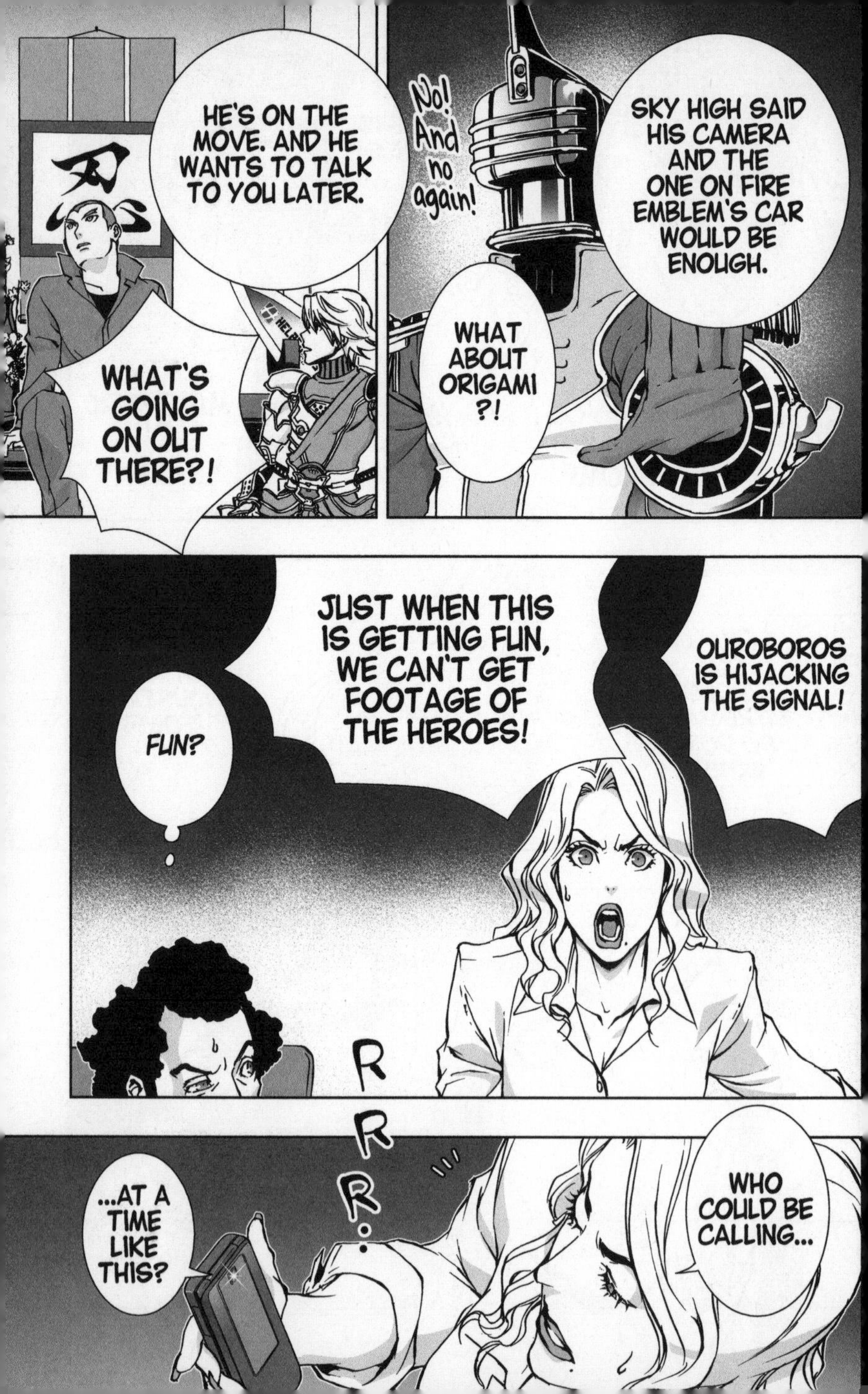
SKY HIGH SAID HIS CAMERA AND THE ONE ON FIRE EMBLEM'S CAR WOULD BE ENOUGH.
No! And no again!
WHAT ABOUT ORIGAMI?!
HE'S ON THE MOVE. AND HE WANTS TO TALK TO YOU LATER.
WHAT'S GOING ON OUT THERE?!
OUROBOROS IS HIJACKING THE SIGNAL!
JUST WHEN THIS IS GETTING FUN, WE CAN'T GET FOOTAGE OF THE HEROES!
FUN?
WHO COULD BE CALLING...
RRR
...AT A TIME LIKE THIS?

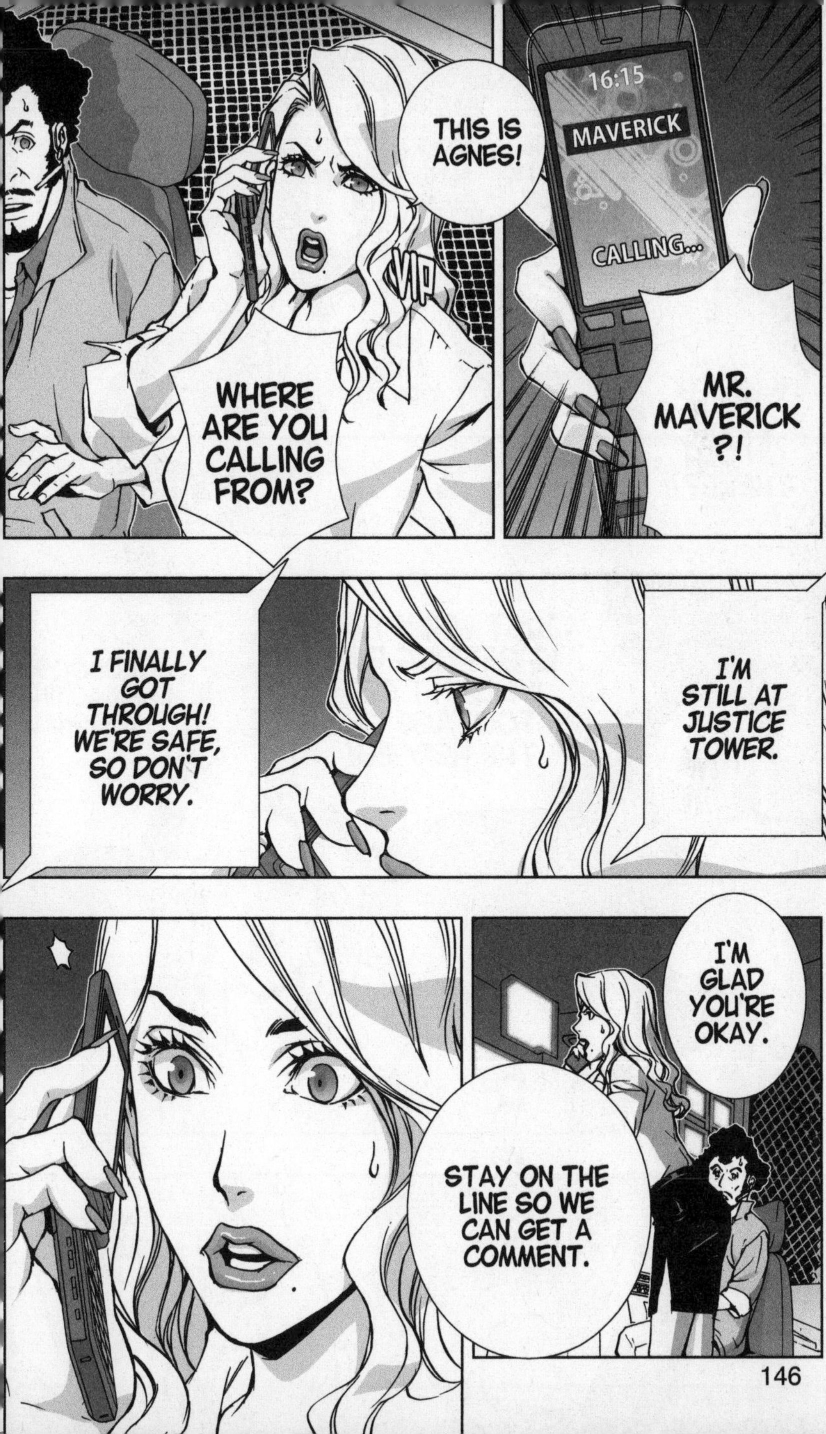
16:15
MAVERICK
CALLING...
MR. MAVERICK?!
THIS IS AGNES!
VIP
WHERE ARE YOU CALLING FROM?
I'M STILL AT JUSTICE TOWER.
I FINALLY GOT THROUGH! WE'RE SAFE, SO DON'T WORRY.
I'M GLAD YOU'RE OKAY.
STAY ON THE LINE SO WE CAN GET A COMMENT.

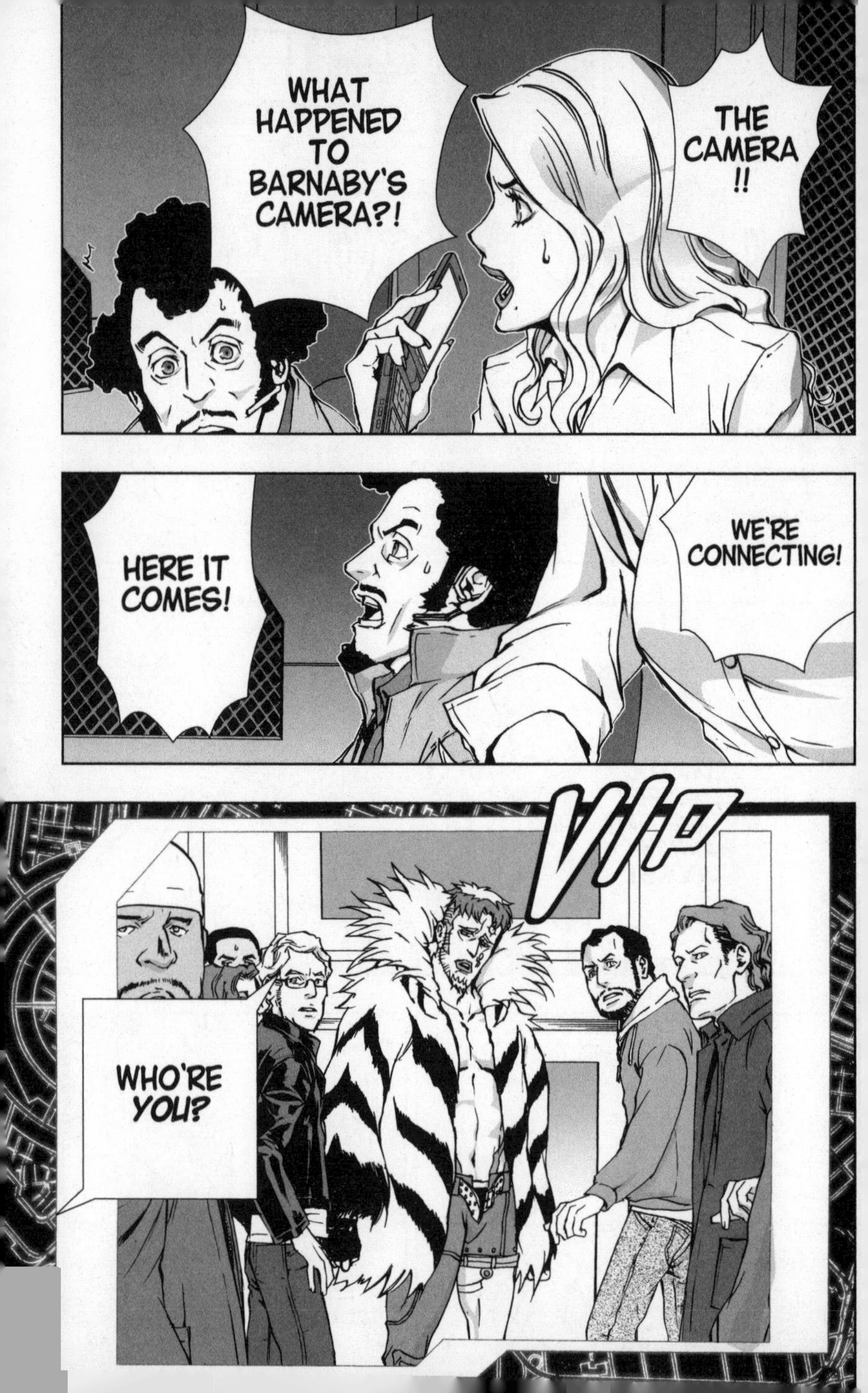
THE CAMERA !!
WHAT HAPPENED TO BARNABY'S CAMERA?!
WE'RE CONNECTING!
HERE IT COMES!
VIP
WHO'RE YOU?

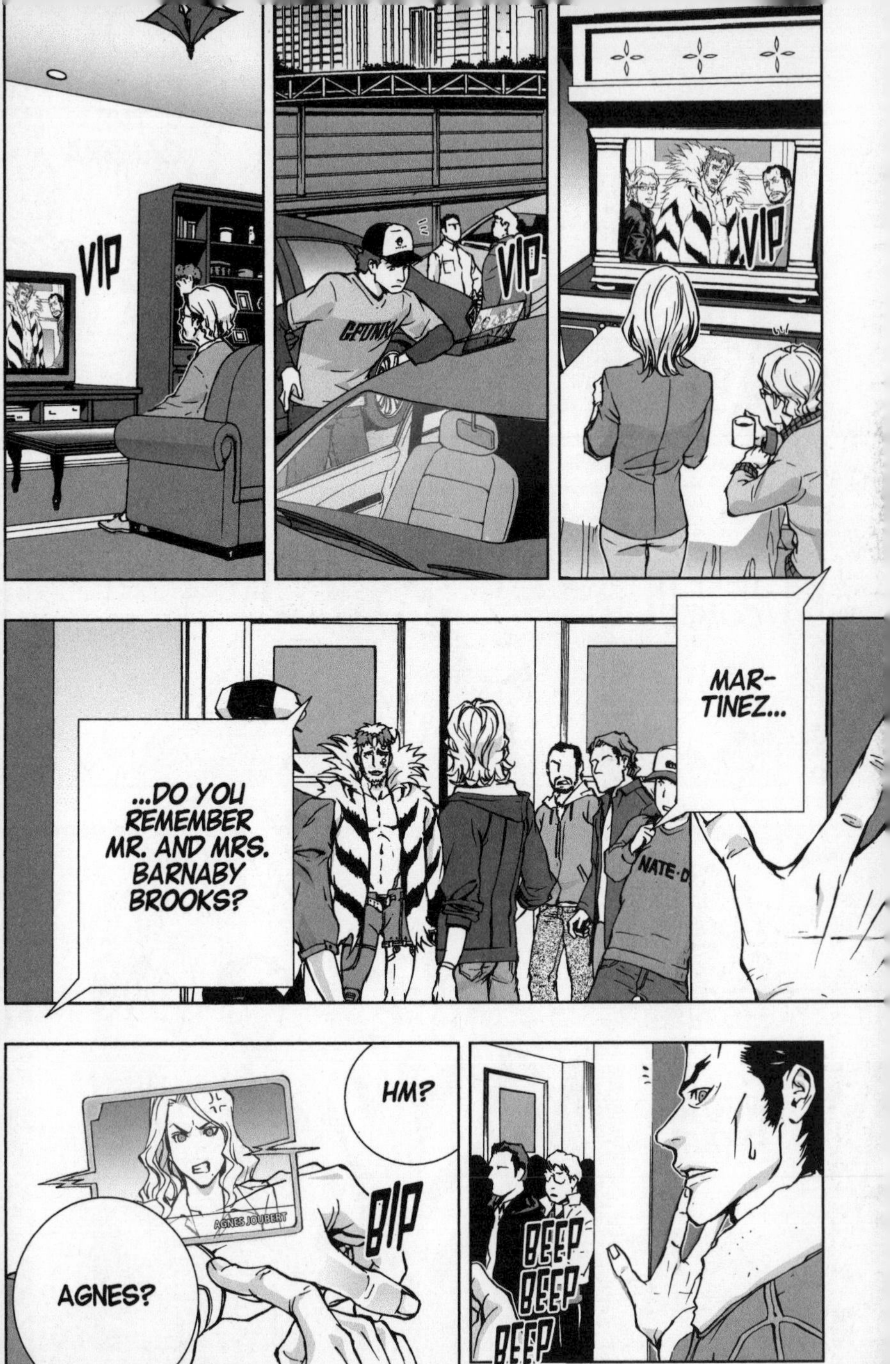
VIP
VIP
VIP
MAR-TINEZ...
...DO YOU REMEMBER MR. AND MRS. BARNABY BROOKS?
NATE-D
BEEP
BEEP
BEEP
HM?
BIP
AGNES JOUBERT
AGNES?

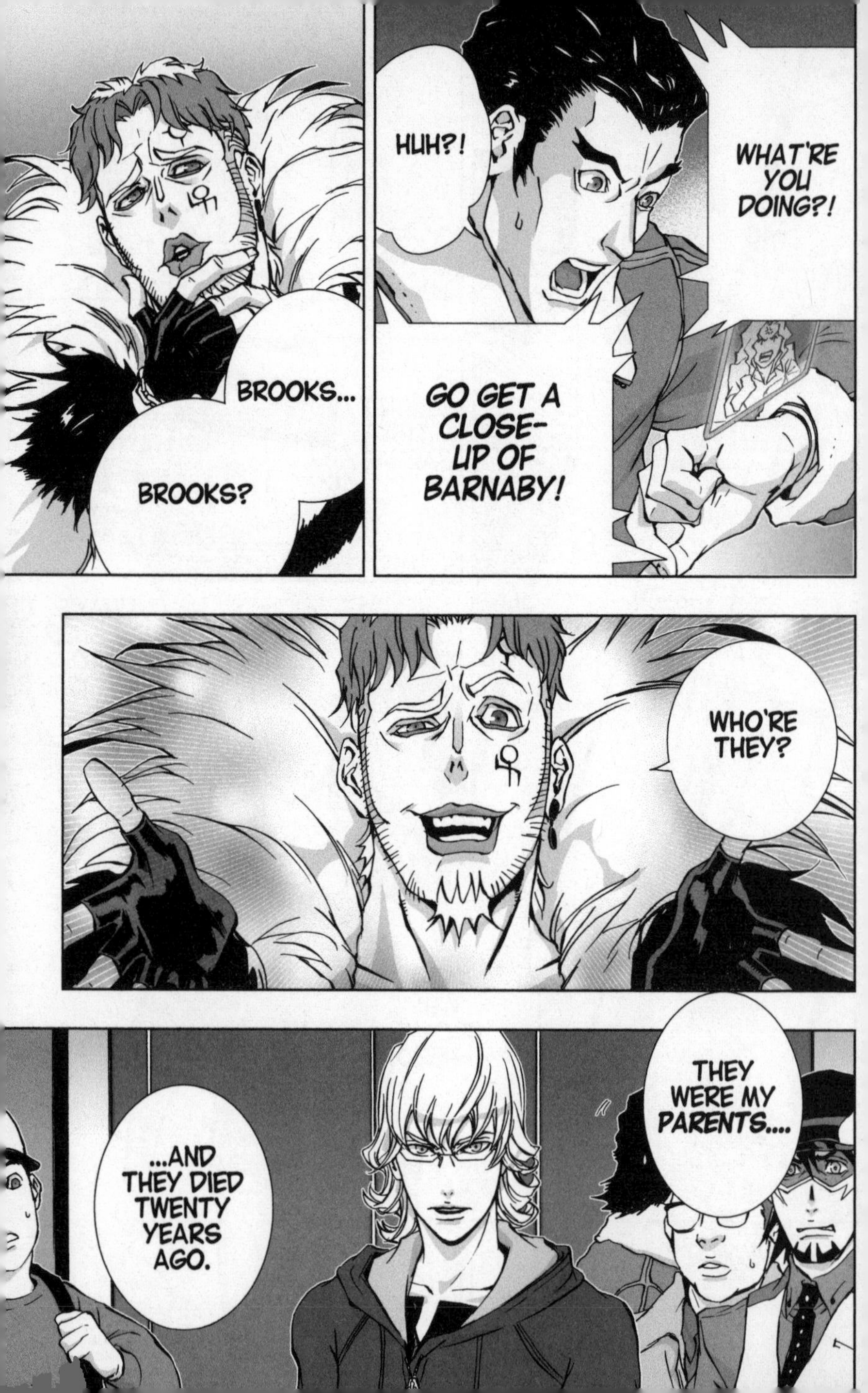
WHAT'RE YOU DOING?!
HUH?!
GO GET A CLOSE-UP OF BARNABY!
BROOKS...
BROOKS?
WHO'RE THEY?
THEY WERE MY PARENTS....
...AND THEY DIED TWENTY YEARS AGO.

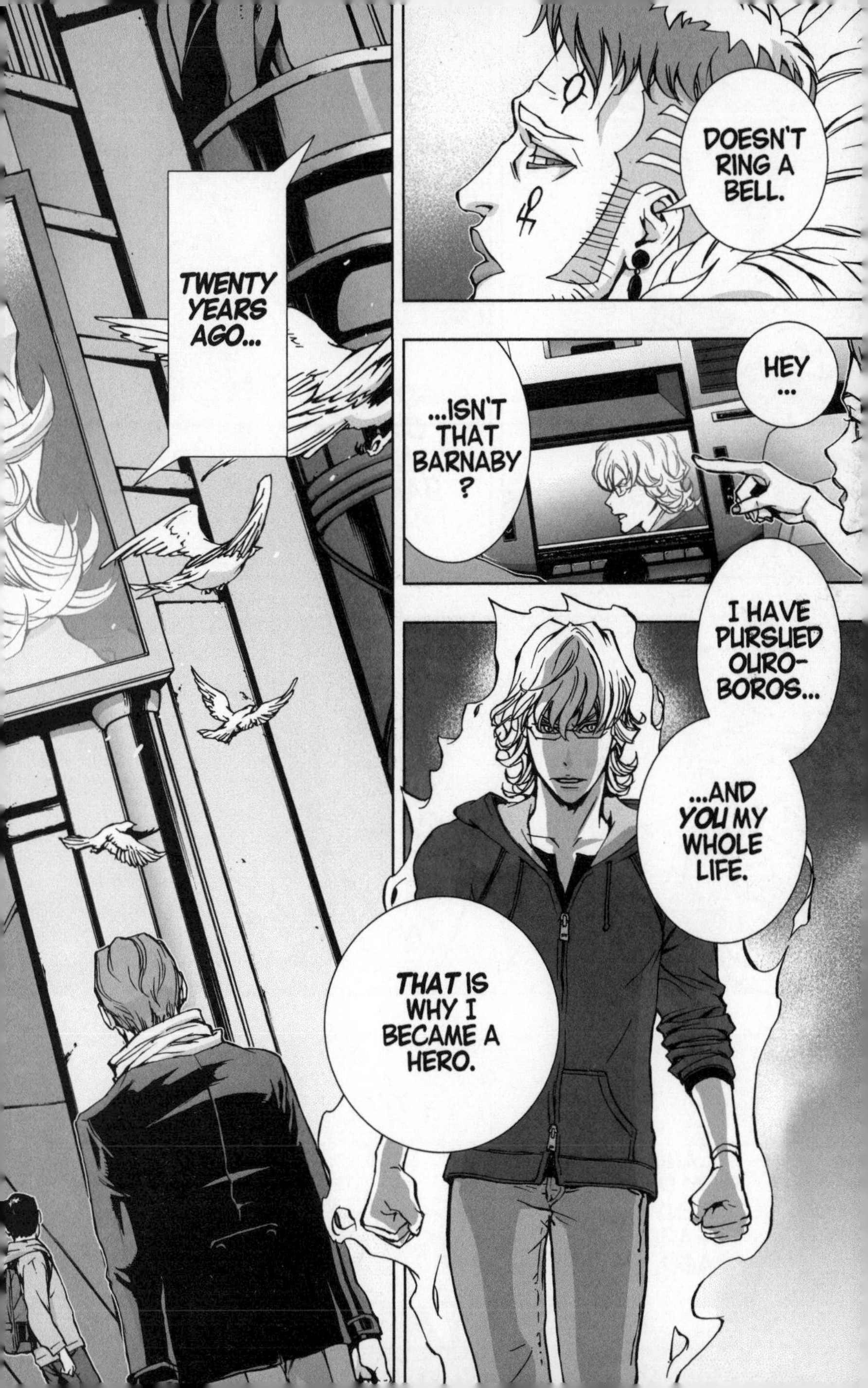
DOESN'T RING A BELL.
HEY ...
...ISN'T THAT BARNABY?
I HAVE PURSUED OURO-BOROS...
...AND *YOU* MY WHOLE LIFE.
*THAT* IS WHY I BECAME A HERO.
TWENTY YEARS AGO...

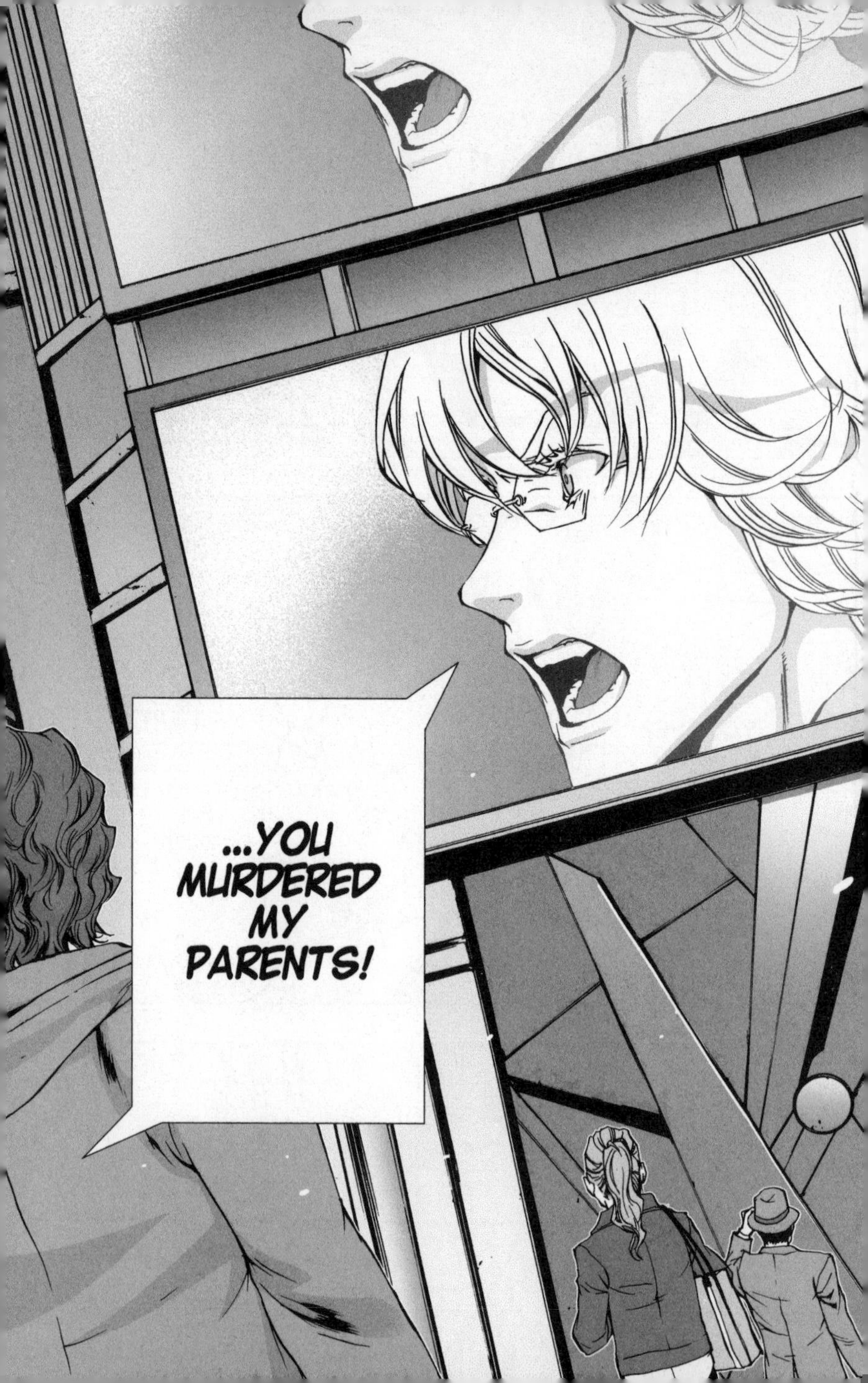
...YOU MURDERED MY PARENTS!

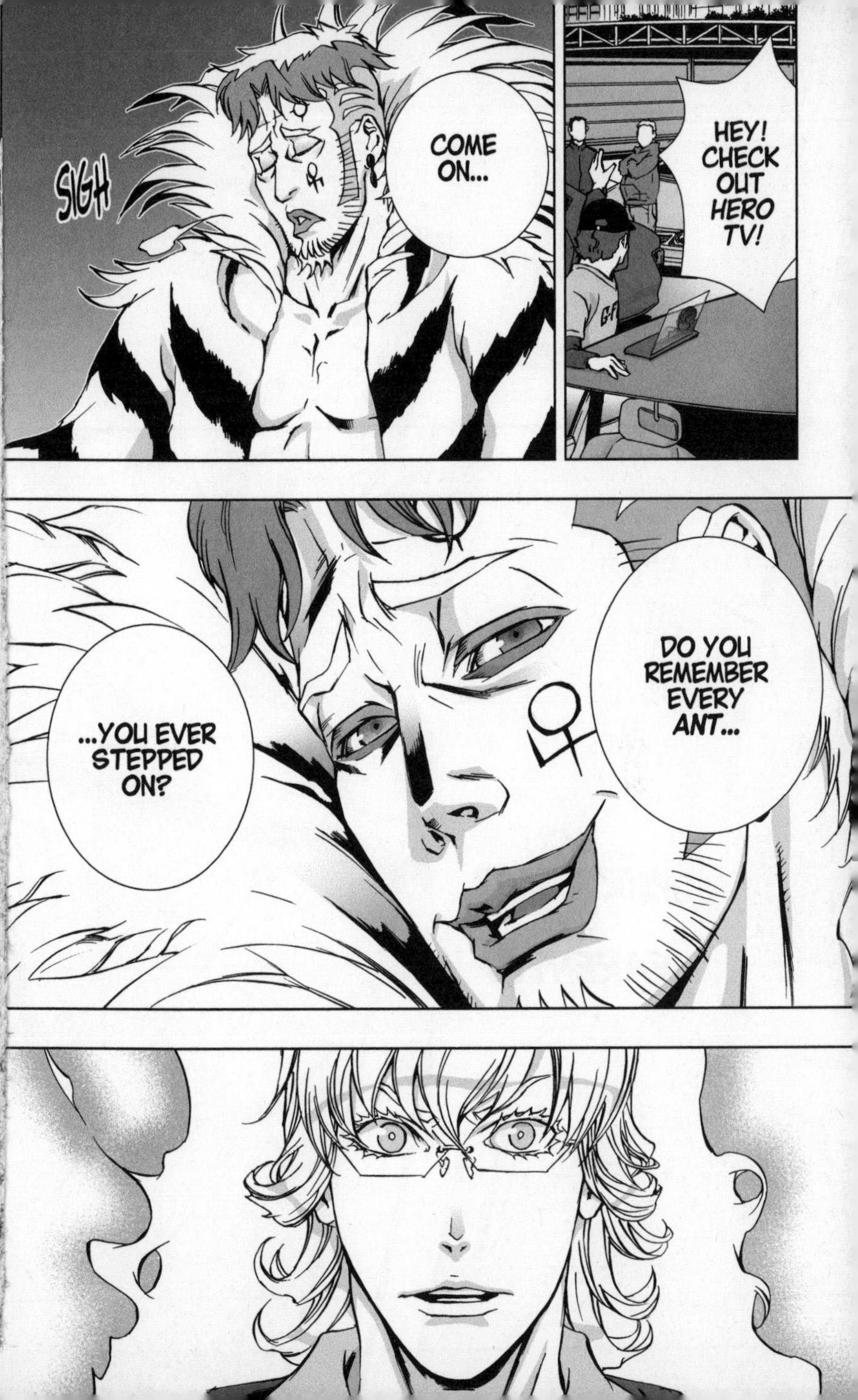
HEY! CHECK OUT HERO TV!
COME ON...
SIGH
DO YOU REMEMBER EVERY ANT...
...YOU EVER STEPPED ON?

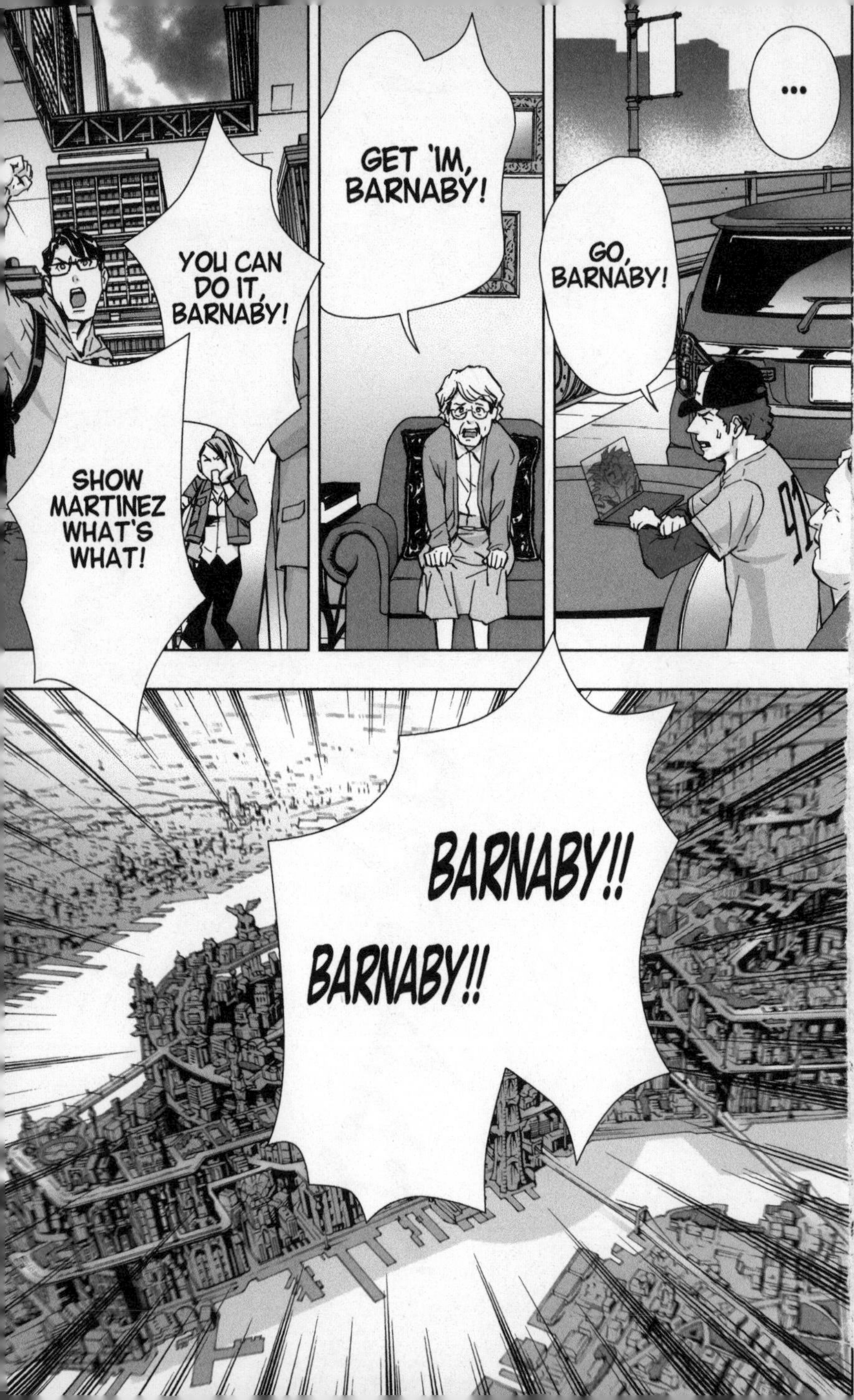
...
GO, BARNABY!
GET 'IM, BARNABY!
YOU CAN DO IT, BARNABY!
SHOW MARTINEZ WHAT'S WHAT!
BARNABY!!
BARNABY!!

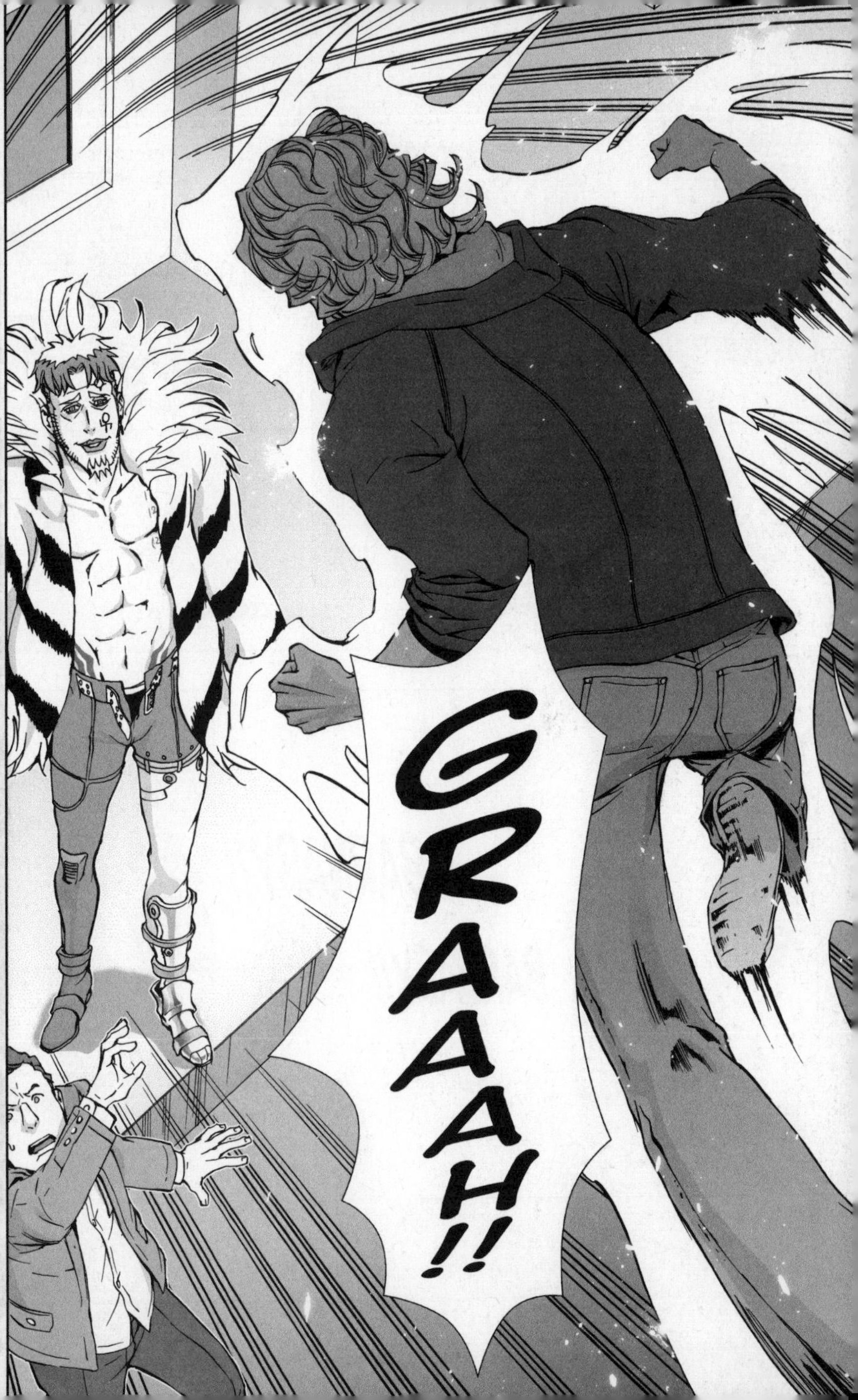
GRAAAH!!

# TIGER&BUNNY
## To Be Continued

**Mizuki Sakakibara**

**Assistants**
**Ayako Mayuzumi**
**Beth**
**Eri Saito**
**Sachiko Ito**
**Fuku**

## MIZUKI SAKAKIBARA

Mizuki Sakakibara's American comics debut was Marvel's *Exile* in 2002. Currently, *TIGER & BUNNY* is serialized in *Newtype Ace* magazine by Kadokawa Shoten.

## MASAFUMI NISHIDA

Story director. *TIGER & BUNNY* was his first work as a TV animation scriptwriter. He is well known for the movie *Gachi☆Boy* and the Japanese TV dramas *Maoh*, *Kaibutsu-kun*, and *Youkai Ningen Bem*.

## MASAKAZU KATSURA

Original character designer. Masakazu Katsura is well known for the manga series *WING MAN*, *Denei Shojo* (*Video Girl Ai*), *I"s*, and *ZETMAN*. Katsura's works have been translated into several languages, including Chinese and French, as well as English.

# TIGER&BUNNY 6

VIZ Media Edition

Art **MIZUKI SAKAKIBARA**
Planning / Original Story **SUNRISE**
Original Script **MASAFUMI NISHIDA**
Original Character and Hero Design **MASAKAZU KATSURA**

TIGER & BUNNY Volume 6
© Mizuki SAKAKIBARA 2014
© SUNRISE/T&B PARTNERS, MBS
Edited by KADOKAWA SHOTEN
First published in Japan in 2014 by KADOKAWA CORPORATION, Tokyo.
English translation rights arranged with KADOKAWA CORPORATION, Tokyo.

Translation & English Adaptation **LABAAMEN & JOHN WERRY, HC LANGUAGE SOLUTIONS**
Touch-up Art & Lettering **STEPHEN DUTRO**
Design **FAWN LAU**
Editor **MIKE MONTESA, JENNIFER LEBLANC**

Printed in the U.S.A.

Published by VIZ Media, LLC
P.O. Box 77010
San Francisco, CA 94107

10 9 8 7 6 5 4 3 2 1
First printing, February 2015

FIRE EMBLEM

www.viz.com

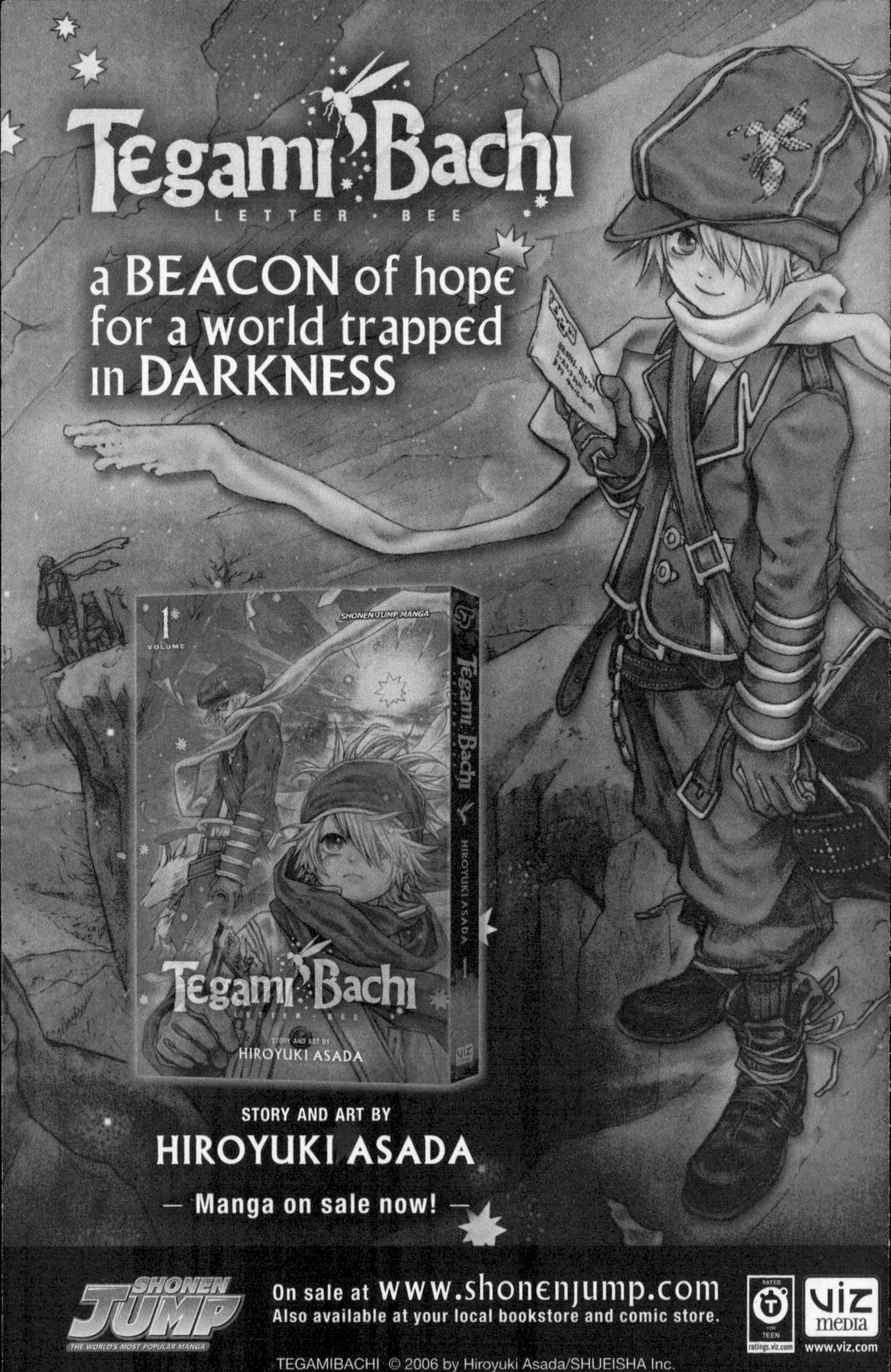
Tegami Bachi
LETTER BEE
a BEACON of hope for a world trapped in DARKNESS
SHONEN JUMP MANGA
1 VOLUME
Tegami Bachi
LETTER BEE
STORY AND ART BY
HIROYUKI ASADA
STORY AND ART BY
HIROYUKI ASADA
— Manga on sale now! —
SHONEN JUMP
THE WORLD'S MOST POPULAR MANGA
On sale at www.shonenjump.com
Also available at your local bookstore and comic store.
RATED T FOR TEEN
ratings.viz.com
VIZ media
www.viz.com
TEGAMIBACHI © 2006 by Hiroyuki Asada/SHUEISHA Inc.

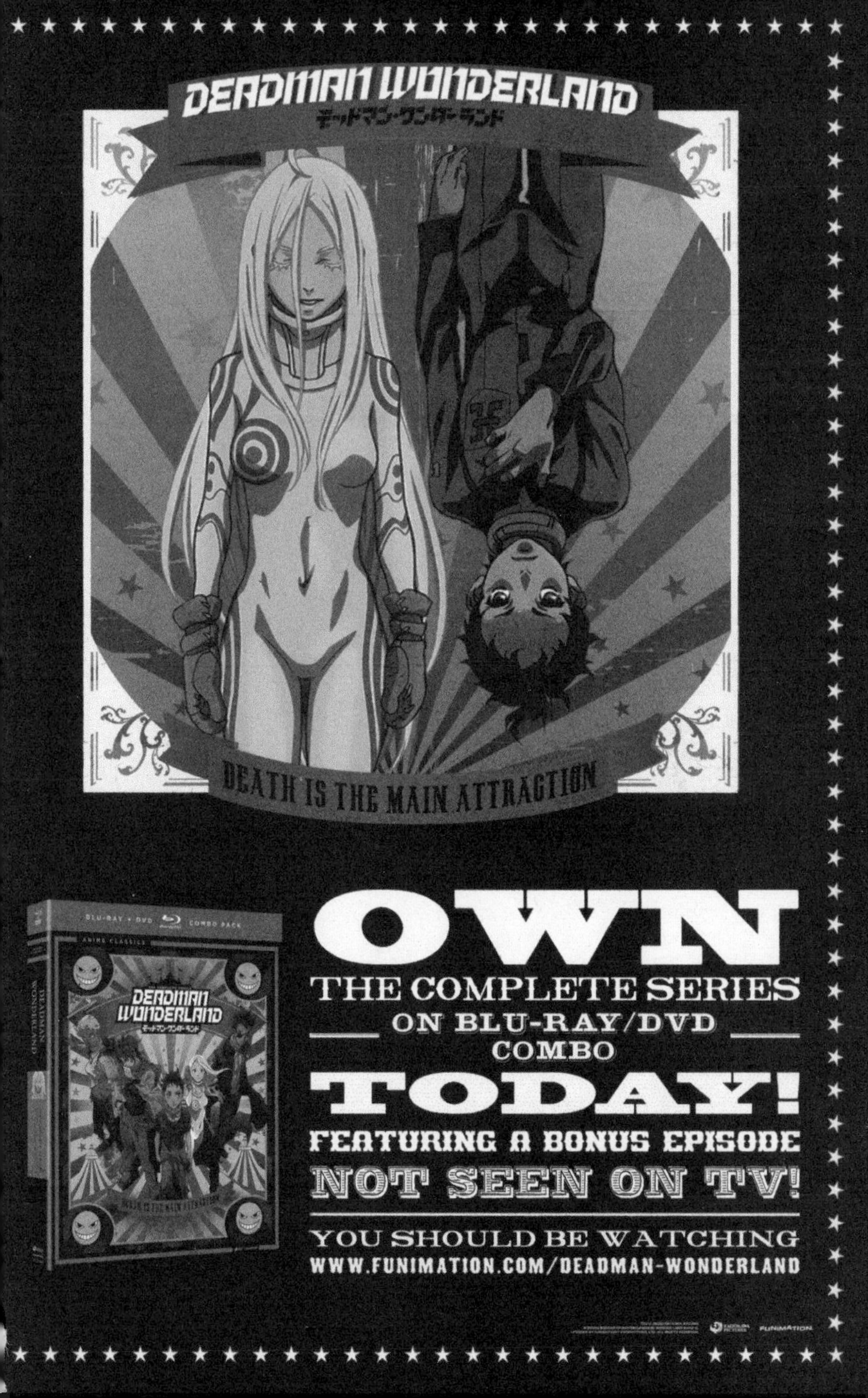
DEADMAN WONDERLAND
デッドマン・ワンダーランド
DEATH IS THE MAIN ATTRACTION
DEADMAN WONDERLAND
デッドマン・ワンダーランド
OWN
THE COMPLETE SERIES
ON BLU-RAY/DVD
COMBO
TODAY!
FEATURING A BONUS EPISODE
NOT SEEN ON TV!
YOU SHOULD BE WATCHING
WWW.FUNIMATION.COM/DEADMAN-WONDERLAND
FUNIMATION

# YOU'RE READING THE
## WRONG WAY!!

*Tiger & Bunny* reads from right to left, starting in the upper-right corner. Japanese is read from right to left, meaning that action, sound effects, and word-balloon order are completely reversed from English order.

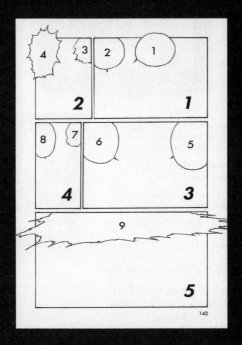